The Power of Writing

Published by :
Lotus Press Publishers & Distributors

The Power of Writing

B.D. Sharma

Lotus PRESS

4735/22, Prakash Deep Building
Ansari Road, Darya Ganj,
New Delhi - 110002

Lotus Press : Publishers & Distributors
Unit No. 220, 2nd Floor, 4735/22, Prakash Deep Building,
Ansari Road, Darya Ganj, New Delhi- 110002
Ph.: 41325510, 98118-38000
• E-mail : lotuspress1984@gmail.com
www.lotuspress.co.in

The Power of Writing

ISBN: 81-8382-139-1

Printed & Published by : **Lotus Press Publisher & Distributors,** New Delhi-02

PREFACE

The book 'The Power of Writing' has been designed with the aim of helping the students in various writing aspects which have became the integral part of English Syllabus at School and College level. This book consists of sufficient number of advertisements, notices, posters, resolutions, factual descriptions etc., ... These cover a wide range of subjects including those which have from time to time, been set for the higher and senior secondary examinations in different Indian books. The students are urged to make use of the book in the true sprit of acquiring the knowledge and skill of writing.

This book deals with the topics of—Advertisements, Notices, Resolutions and Minutes, Posters, Writing Invitations (Formal & Informal), Report Writing, Factual Description and Process Writing, Essay-Writing and Report-Writing, Messages, Writing of Telegrams, Note Making and Abstraction etc.

I hope that students and those in the educational field will find it useful for academic and competitive examinations. I owe a deep sense of gratitude to my publisher for materialising my present endeavour.

B.D. SHARMA

Contents

1

Advertisements

Advertisements are the public notices for asking or offering different services, buying or selling properties, goods, etc., or to provide information regarding missing persons or objects, etc. In the advertisements we try to use minimum words in the newspapers or magazines because charges are paid according to the words and space needed for writing an advertisement. So we should write all the main points in brief and try to maintain the sequence in a running way. All the contents should convey the main aim of the message. There should be clarity of information and try to avoid fulls sentences.

We can see the following categories of advertisements:

(a) Situations Vacant

(b) Situations Wanted

(c) Lost and Found

(d) Sale and Purchase

(e) Accommodation Wanted or To Let

(f) Matrimonials

SITUATIONS VACANT

Specimen Draft for Situations Vacant column.

Require/wanted Salesmen/Clerks/Stenographers/ Accountants/Receptionists, etc.... for our well reputed concern/School/Office...., candidate must be graduate/ post graduate (throughout Ist class), aged between 18-20 years, diploma/degree in electrical/computer/ stenography etc..., fluent in English/good command over English, must have two years experience in the same line/experienced hand will be given preference with attractive salary and other perks. Candidates possessing above qualifications. Apply within a week with complete bio-data to ABC Pvt. Ltd., New Delhi-110002.

Note:

While drafting an advertisement for Situations Vacant column the following points should be kept in mind:

(a) State the name of the post and company.

(b) Educational or Technical qualifications regarding the post.

(c) Age and sex required by the company.

(d) Experience and knowledge of English required.

(e) Mention salary and perks offered by the company.

(f) Mailing address or telephone contact number etc., if any of the firm.

(g) In case you are very specific about the interview, write date, time, venue and other requisite details.

Let us study the following example:

(A) SITUATIONS VACANT

1. Applications are invited from suitable candidates for the post of Stenographer in INFOCOM Pvt. Ltd. Yamuna Vihar, Delhi-110053. Draft a suitable advertisement to this account by giving necessary details in the newspaper.

SITUATIONA VACANT

Applications are invited on plain paper for the post of stenographer, candidates should be graduate, of either sex, between the age group of 18 to 25 years, diploma in computers with a speed of 100/50 w.p.m., fluent in English, must have two years experience in the same line, handsome salary and other perks. Candidates possessing above mentioned qualifications may apply with their complete bio-data within seven days to Manager, INFOCOM Pvt. Ltd. Yamuna Vihar, Delhi-53.

2. Allied Services, Yamuna Vihar, needs Computer Operators. Draft an advertisement for a local daily.

SITUATIONS VACANT

Allied Network Ltd. requires Computer Operators (Male), having 1-2 years experience, candidate must have sound knowledge of D-Base, Lotus and Wordstar and a good typing speed. Walkin for an interview tomorrow between 11.30 a.m. and 5 p.m. at C-3, 2nd floor, Main Shopping Centre, Yamuna Vihar, New Delhi-110057.

3. You are running a telephone booth in the Central Market, Vasant Vihar. Draft a suitable advertisement for Situations Vacant column of *New Delhi Times*.

SITUATIONS VACANT

We need the services of a well qualified and experienced telephone operator, possessing a charming personality between the age of 30 and 40, with pleasing manners for our telephone booth in the Central Market, Vasant Vihar. Candidate from either sex should be well versed in Hindi, English, Punjabi and knowledge of foreign language. Attractive salary. Interested candidates may contact Mr. Rajesh at 152/21 Gupta Colony, Central Market, Vasant Vihar, personally with details or ring 23910531.

4. You are the General Manager of Brakes & Brakes India Limited. You want to appoint two sales representatives for your company. Prepare an advertisement to be published in the classified columns of a local daily.

SITUATIONS VACANT

We urgently need the services of two sales representatives to promote the sale of automobile spare parts manufactured by our company. The job involves extensive travelling. The candidate must be graduate, with a charming personality and a minimum experience of three years in the sales line. Attractive remuneration with T.A. and D.A. Interested candidates may send their applications alongwith bio-data to the General Manager, Brakes & Brakes India Limited, Nitin Place, Rohini, Delhi-110052.

(B) SITUATIONS WANTED

1. Services of an accountant are available. Prepare an advertisement in about 50 words for the Situations Wanted column of your local daily.

SITUATIONS WANTED

AVAILABLE Accountant for Pending/Regular Accounts/ Audit, Tax, Excise, Co. Law, Share Accounts & Bank/ Project Financing. He is a commerce graduate, with experience of 5 years in a private organisation. He is available for interview at any time. Payment after job satisfaction. Please contact Dinesh-5812637, 5791518.

2. An aged person seeks part-time job in teaching. Prepare an advertisement in about 50 words.

SITUATIONS WANTED

An experienced qualified post graduate lecturer of English seeks part-time job of coaching in English. He has teaching experience of 30 years to his credit. Groups in full swing for XII and B.A. Students. Please contact N.K. Ahuja, 29 M.M. Road, New Delhi or ring 5925701.

3. A lady typist clerk seeks part-time work in typing. Write an advertisement for your local daily.

SITUATIONS WANTED

Lady typist clerk both in Hindi & English with experience of electronic typewriter/experienced office liasioning assistant, needs a part-time job. She is well conversant in office routine. She has an experience of job work for about 10 years. Please contact Radha, 301 Kanchan House, Commercial Complex, Delhi 110015.

4. A full time Mechanical Engineer seeks job. Write an advertisement for entry in the 'Situations Wanted' column of your local daily.

SITUATIONS WANTED

A young energetic result-oriented Mechanical Engineer from Australia with four years' experience in a reputed machine-tools factory seeks a suitable change. Any defect in every type of machinery can be checked in no time. Payment after job work and full satisfaction. Write Box No. 52, Times House, New Delhi-9 or ring 2759304.

5. A part-time Computer Engineer offers his services. Prepare a suitable advertisement for a local newspaper in about 50 words.

SITUATIONS WANTED

A well experienced Computer Engineer just returned from U.S.A., seeks part-time job for repairing computers. He has set up his own workshop and can train the students in computer work. Remuneration negotiable. Please give one chance and avail the best opportunity. Please contact R. Gupta, 4/501, Ashok Vihar, Phase-II, Delhi, or ring 7191231.

6. A full time Electrical Engineer seeks job. Write an advertisement for entry in the Situations Wanted column of your local daily.

SITUATIONS WANTED

Services of a well qualified young and experienced electrical engineer are available. He has graduated from Germany and has seven years experience in maintenance and upkeep of electrical machinery to his credit. For all types of electric services. Please contact Gupta, P-5, Guru Nank Road, Shekh Sarai, New Delhi-1 or ring 74219156.

7. A full-time experienced Naturopath offers his services for free consultation. Prepare an advertisement for your local paper.

SITUATIONS WANTED

Free advice is available for all types of cancerous diseases for those who believe in nature cure. Several have got permanent cures of their diseases. Visit for all your ailments. Working hours between 10.00 a.m. to 2.00 p.m. on all working days. Please contact Dr. S.K. Mittal 150/25 Panchsheel Colony, New Road, Delhi-9

8. Gaurav Sharma of N-15, Neel Kamal Apartments, Delhi, has a very sound knowledge of tourist places in Simla. He wants to work as a Tourist Guide during the winter break. Write out a suitable advertisement for publication in the Tours and Travel Section of a local newspaper.

SITUATIONS WANTED
(Tours and Travel Section)

A widely travelled well acquainted tourist guide, expert in hilly and historical places a round Simla seeks a part-time job during the winter break. He is a stout, experienced person perfect in mountain-climbing. He is well versed in English, Hindi, Punjabi and hill language. Desirous travellers may contact Gaurav Sharma N-15, Neel Kamal Apartments, Simla at any time or ring 22241880.

9. A part-time Computer Engineer offers his services for a suitable part-time job. Prepare a suitable advertisement for a local newspaper.

SITUATIONS WANTED

A well-experienced Computer Engineer just returned from U.S.A., seeks part-time job for repairing computers. He is well versed in Hardware and Software techniques. All defects of machine can be set correct in a few seconds. Give a chance and avail of the best opportunity. Please contact Verma 15/7, Ashok Vihar, Phase II, Delhi or ring 22940588.

FOR PRACTICE

1. You need two typists for your office. Write out an advertisement for the 'Situations Vacant' column of a local newspaper.

2. You need a tutor for Maths for a month. Write out an advertisement for a local daily.

3. You need some bearers for your hotel. Write out an advertisement for the 'Situations Vacant' column of a local newspapers.

4. You need two stenographers in your office (Export Branch). Write out an advertisement for the 'Situations Vacant' column of a local daily without disclosing the identity of your office.

5. As Principal, New Light Public School, New Delhi, draft an advertisement for a local newspaper, inviting applications for the post of a librarian in your school.

6. As Director of a public limited company, you need a personal secretary. Draft an advertisement for a local newspaper, inviting applications for this post.

7. You are Rajesh and want a dance teacher for your younger sister. Write an advertisement to be published in the classified columns of a local newspaper.

8. You have started a Centre for Personality Development for school children. Draft an advertisement to be published in a local daily about it, giving all relevant details.

9. You have started a Yoga Centre for school children. Draft an advertisement to be published in a local daily about it, giving all the relevant details.

10. You are Y.S. Sharma of Banaras. You want an English Tutor for your daughter. Write out an advertisement to be published in the classified columns of a local newspaper.

11. You are the Director of a Coaching Institute. Write out an advertisement for admission to various technical courses being provided in your institution.

(C) LOST AND FOUND

For the 'Lost and Found' columns of newspapers, we need the economy of the words and sentences keeping in view to give the complete detail of the item either lost or found. Before drafting this type of advertisement, let us pay attention to the following points:

1. Always keep in mind to write the name of the place, time and date where the item was lost or found.

2. Write down the relevant particulars of the article lost and give its description. You need not furnish full details of the item found lest there should be many claimants.

3. Mention the correspondence address or the person to be contacted for the delivery of the article.

4. If there is any specific incentive to be given that may be mentioned in the advertisement.

1. You have lost your wrist-watch in your school. Draft a notice about it for your school notice board. You are Vineeta of Class XII.

DURGA PUBLIC SCHOOL

LOST LOST LOST

Lost my golden Ricoh automatic wrist-watch, around 2.00 p.m. in the school playground while playing hockey on **14-7-07**. The watch is very beautiful containing day, date and centre second. It is round in shape with golden dial having a golden chain made in Japan. Running half an hour late. Finder may please restore it to the undersigned of class XII or to the Principal. He will be amply rewarded. Contact Vineeta, XII-Commerce

2. Your brother has been missing from home for the last two days. Draft an advertisement under the caption 'Missing' for a local newspaper. Provide necessary details and also offer an award.

MISSING

Raju, a 9-year old boy, 145 cm. fair complexion, round face, well-built physique, has been missing from Kamla Nagar, New Delhi, since 28th May. He has a scar on his forehead and curly hair wearing a white shirt, blue shorts and carrying a school bag when he was last seen. Speaks Hindi and English fluently. The person giving any clue or information shall be suitably rewarded. Contact M.K. Sharma, 24, Kamla Nagar, New Delhi, Phone: 9891150895.

3. You lost your spectacles somewhere in school. Write a notice for the 'Lost and Found' Notice Board of your school.

LOST

Lost my spectacles, golden rimmed with crookes glasses in the Science Lab. yesterday *i.e.* on 15.6.2007 between 10 a.m. and 12 noon. The spectacles are valuable and without them I am unable to perform my school and routine work. Finder kindly restore it to Amirta Arora, class XII-B or hand over the same to the librarian.

4. Mahender Singh, a student of class XII has lost his Chemistry Book titled 'Advance Chemistry' for class XII by K.P. Singh. He decides to put up notice on the Students Notice Board of the school.

ST. PATRICK SCHOOL, NEW DELHI

NOTICE May 15, 2007

LOST LOST LOST

Lost my chemistry text book titled 'Advanced Chemistry' for class XII (New Edition 2007). Written by K.P. Singh, paper back, in the front lawn of the school campus during the recess period between 3.40 p.m. and 4.00 p.m. while taking tea in the canteen. My name appears on the front and the last page of the book. Finder is requested to return it to the undersigned or deposit it to the Lost and Found Incharge of the school property. Finder will be given a treat.

Girish Singh, Class XII

5. You are Prabhat of 202, Nehru Nagar, New Delhi. You lost your brief-case while travelling by bus from Nehru Nagar to Connaught Place, New Delhi. Draft a notification to be published in the '*Indian Express*' under their column 'Lost and Found'. Include all necessary details about the lost brief-case to establish your claim.

LOST AND FOUND

Lost a new blue-coloured leather brief-case while travelling by a white line bus running between Nehru Nagar and Connaught Place on 5th March, Tuesday at about 2.30 p.m. somewhere near I.T.O. It is a V.I.P. brief-case with name plate fixed on the handle. The brief-case contains some important documents including my Board's Certificate of All India Secondary School Examination and my Identity Card issued by Ministry of Home Affairs. Handsome reward for restoring it to Prabhat of 202, Nehru Nagar, New Delhi, Phone No. 9110542311.

6. You are Mrs. Ruchi Sethi of Rajouri Garden, New Delhi. You lost your Tebby cat while you were away from home. Draft an advertisement suitable to be given in the local daily. Invent relevant details.

MISSING

Missing my cute Tabby cat Tessa white-brown fur, one and a half years old, robust in health since 12 December, 2006 from Rajouri Garden, New Delhi. Finder may please contact the undersigned. A suitable prize is promised.

Ruchi Sethi, Phone No. 26464919

7. You have found a purse containing some money and identity card while walking in the playground during the recess period. Write a suitable account in about 50 words in the Lost and Found column of your school notice-board.

GOVT. SCHOOL, HARI NAGAR, NEW DELHI
FOUND FOUND FOUND

10th March, 2007

Found a brand new shining leather purse while walking in the playground during the recess period today. The purse contains money and some other important documents of the owner. The owner is requested to contact the undersigned after telling the necessary details and identification marks. It will be a great pleasure for me to hand over the purse to the genuine owner.

Ramesh Jain, XII A

8. You have lost your wrist-watch in school. Give details of the watch and the probable time of the day you lost it. Your description should be fit for the 'Lost and Found' Notice Board of your school.

LOST AND FOUND

Lost a citizen wrist-watch, automatic with day and date, white and black dial, stainless steel frame, golden colour brass chain, on April 5, during school hours, at about 3 p.m. It was lost while playing a friendly match held in the University Ground. Suitable reward for restoring it to Ajay of Class XII, Section A of Principal Govt. School, Noida.

9. Write a short classified advertisement for the 'LOST AND FOUND' columns of newspapers stating the loss of your pet missing for more than a month.

LOST AND FOUND

Missing since April 5, my Alsatian pup, four months old, red and white in colour, brown whiskers, tail less, wearing a red collar-band round his neck. It has a black mark on his forehead. Finder please ring 27225653 or write to Anuj Gupta of 32, Vivek Vihar, Delhi. Suitable reward.

FOR PRACTICE

1. Write a short classified advertisement for the 'Lost and Found' column of a newspaper form where and how you can be contacted.

2. You have lost a library book of your school issued in your name. Write a description of your book alongwith the details of the place where you supposedly lost it. Your description should be fit for insertion in the 'Lost and Found' column of a local daily.

3. Your pet dog is missing. Write out a suitable notice of not more 25 words for the 'Lost and Found' column of a local newspaper.

4. Your brother aged 5, has been missing for a week. Write a suitable advertisement for the 'Lost Persons' column of a newspaper in about 40 words.

5. You have lost your pet dog. Draft a suitable advertisment to be published in the 'Lost and Found' coloumn of a newspaper.

6. You have found a geometry box in the school playground. Write a notice for the 'Lost and Found'; notice-board of your school.

7. Someone in your family has got lost. Give full details of this person to Doordarshan.

8. You lost your bus pass in the school. Give details of the pass and the probable time of the day you lost it. Your description should be fit for the 'Lost and Found' notice-board of your school.

9. You have lost your wrist-watch in a public park. Write a suitable advertisement for the 'Lost and Found' column of a newspaper.

10. You have lost your purse. Draft an advertisement suitable to be given in the local daily. Invent details.

11. You have dropped your purse somewhere in the school premises. Write a short notice for the school notice board requesting the finder to return it to you.

12. You have lost a library book issued in your name. Write an appropriate description of the book and give the particulars of the bus you travelled on the day you lost it for publishing in the local daily in the column 'Lost and Found'.

13. You have found a purse in the classroom of your school. Write a short notice for the school notice-board so that the real owners may collect it from you after giving all the related particulars.

14. You have lost your mobile phone No. 9868215143 while travelling in a bus. Write an advertisement to be published in a local daily giving your landline telephone number.

15. You have lost your wallet containing your valuable documents (ATM Card, and Driving Licence) while travelling by Himalayan Queen from Delhi to Kalka. Write an advertisement to be published in '*The Hindustan Times*' under the column 'Lost and Found'.

(D) SALE AND PURCHASE

Often we desire to sell or buy properties or articles in our day to day life. For this we generally send an advertisement in the newspaper. While writing such advertisement for publication we have to be very cautious leaving behind unnecessary and irrelevant details. The following facts should be taken into consideration while drafting such an advertisement.

1. Mention the particulars of the property giving its present condition and price range.

2. Clarify the terms and conditions for sale and purchase.

3. Do try to mention any other relevant fact to boost your sale.

4. Write down the mailing address or the contact phone number or both.

5. In case of accommodation give the location, rent and other facilities to be given. *e.g.* size, floor, no. of rooms etc., fixtures and fittings, location and surroundings.
6. In case of a vehicle, give the model/year of manufacturing, colour, accessories etc., mileage run, condition etc.
7. In case of household goods, give the brand, model, year of manufacturing, material used, condition and expected price.

1. You want to dispose your independent Bungalow at Active Apartments, Mysore. Draft an advertisement suitable to be published under the Classified advertisements column of *Deccan Herald*, Bangalore.

FOR SALE

A well-built air-conditioned and spacious bungalow is for sale at 12, Active Apartments, Mysore. It is in the posh area, exclusively designed, self-contained 4 bedrooms with ultra modern amenities, spacious lawn and two servant quarters. Price around 70 lakhs. Contact Mr. Y.K. Goel or dial 22437548.

2. You want to dispose off your land at Noida near Delhi. Draft an advertisement suitable to be published in *'The Hindustan Times'* New Delhi.

FOR SALE

Two hectare piece of land, at the main road, in the vicinity of Noida is available for sale. The land is suitable for a decent farm house as it is both easily approachable by road and train. There is no problem of electricity and the water is very sweet and cold. It is a free hold property with pollution free environment. Price Rs. 50 lakhs. Contact S.K. Verma of 17, Ekta Apartments, New Delhi.

3. You want to dispose off your independent house situated in the prime locality of Vaishali. Draft an advertisement suitable to be published in '*The Times of India*', New Delhi, under the Classified advertisement column.

FOR SALE

A spacious and fully furnished house in the prime locality of Vaishali, is available for immediate sale. It is specificially designed on western pattern and in accordance with 'Vaastu.' It has 4 bedrooms with a lawn and a servant-quarter. It is situated near the market and railway station. Price around 40 lakhs. Contact Mukesh, C-105 Shakti Nagar, Delhi or Ring 23543105391.

4. You want to dispose off your Maruti car, as you are going abroad. You are Dinesh of No. 10, Kailash Colony, Delhi. Draft an advertisement to be published in the daily, '*The Hindustan Times*', under classified columns.

FOR SALE

Available for sale a white coloured A.C. Maruti car, 2006 Model, used 1,5000 km. as the party is leaving for Japan immediately. Its tyres and tubes are in a very good condition. Its body has a shining get up with indicators, horns, back and front computerised lights. It was purchased only last month. Price negotiable upto 2,50 lakhs. Interested parties may contact Dinesh of No. 10, Kailash Colony, Delhi or ring 9896721621.

5. You want to purchase a flat. Draft an advertisement for a newspaper detailing about your requirements and your capacity to pay.

FOR PURCHASE

A four room flat, preferably situated on the ground floor is required near Patel Nagar, New Delhi. It should be well-equipped with electricity and sanitary fittings, having separate kitchen and two bathrooms. Preference will be given to a two side open flat with its situation near the main market. Suitable cash payment upto 10 lakhs in the court after sight seeing. Interested parties may contact Amit of 15/21 Panchsheel Garden, Delhi or ring 27331902.

6. You propose to sell your flat as you are going abroad. Draft an advertisement for it to be published in the '*The Times of India*', New Delhi, under classified columns.

FOR SALE

Available for sale an MIG flat on the ground floor in Rohini, Phase-II, A 18', 10' drawing-cum-dining room, two bedrooms with attached bathrooms, kitchen and a store. It is close to the main market. It has parking facility for car. Estimated price Rs. 20 lakhs. Must sell before 20th July, 2007, the owner going abroad. Interested parties please contact A-15, Rohini, Phase-II, New Delhi or ring 25329164.

7. You want to dispose off your car as you are going abroad Draft a suitable advertisement to be published in the classified column of '*The Hindu*', Delhi. You are Mahesh of Vijay Nagar, Delhi.

FOR SALE

Available for sale a navy blue-coloured computerized Maruti car 800 C.C. 2006 model hardly run 25000 kms. Its tyre and tubes are in good condition, complete papers, fully insured. Its body has a shining get up having indicators, horns, back and front lights of a new get up. Owner is going abroad. Price negotiable upto 2.50 lakh. Interested parties please contact Mahesh, Vijay Nagar, Delhi or ring : 2245354.

8. You want to sell your motor-bike. Draft an advertisement suitable to be published in the '*Indian Express*', Delhi under the classified advertisement column.

FOR SALE

A quite brand new black motor-bike, Hero Honda, Splendor 100 C.C. 6 months old, in excellent working condition is available for sale. The owner is leaving for abroad. It gives an average of 65 kms. a litre. Expected price about Rs. 35,000. Interested parties may contact Ajay, 82 Paschim Vihar, Delhi or ring 22435711.

9. You want to sell the first floor of your newly constructed house. Draft an advertisement for publication in the *Indian Express* under their classified column, marked, 'Property'.

ACCOMMODATION FOR SALE

The first floor of a newly constructed and well equipped house with 3 bedrooms, one drawing room, separate kitchen and bathroom with a store room is available for sale in the heart of Vasant Vihar. It is two side open with a main road of 25 feet in its front. There is separate arrangement for garage. Interested persons please contact Manoj of 75, Vasant Vihar, New Delhi or ring 2595991.

10. A suitable premise is available for embassies in Hauz Khas. Prepare an advertisement in the classified columns of newspaper.

FOR EMBASSIES
ONLY ADJACENT TO
K-BLOCK, HAUZ KHAS 418 sq. metres.

Basement, ground floor with drawing/dining with bath, guest room with bath, study, kitchen and store. First floor with 4 bedrooms, attached baths and store. Second floor with guest room with bath, store. Garage, servant quarters with bath and cooking area. Fax your proposals at 26863565, 26967823.

11. Department of Communications, Ashok Road, Delhi is in need of a suitable accommodation for office. Write an advertisement by giving details.

DEPARTMENT OF COMMUNICATIONS
SANCHAR BHAWAN,
20, ASHOKA ROAD, NEW DELHI-110 001
ACCOMMODATION WANTED

Offers are urgently invited for centrally located office accommodation measuring approximately 10,000 sq. ft. of carpet area. The accommodation offered should have all basic facilities such as proper lavatories/bathrooms, electricity, water supply, canteen space, etc., and sufficient parking space for cars/scooters/cycles.

Accommodation on first or second floor, with appropriate facilities for installing airconditioners/desert coolers, etc. would be preferred. Some additions/alterations/cabins may need to be provided by the owner of the building, depending upon the type of accommodation.

Offers, which should remain valid for at least three months, may be sent, by name to Shri D.K. Malhotra, Deputy Secretary, Department of Communications, Room No. 405, Sanchar Bhawan, 20, Ashoka Road, New Delhi, latest by 15-4-1997, alongwith detailed terms and conditions and plan of the building.

12. You want to hire accommodation for your newly started business in Delhi. Write an advertisement for the same to be published in the classified columns of *The Hindustan Times*.

ACCOMMODATION WANTED

Wanted a well furnished suitable accommodation with three rooms on the ground floor in the close vicinity of Delhi city to start the readymade garment business on whole sale basis. It should be near some nationalized bank for money transaction. Rent negotiable. Please contact 192959 or N.K. Sharma 125, Patparganj, Delhi.

13. You are looking for a house on reasonable rent. Write an advertisement for publication in a newspaper, giving essential details of your requirements.

ACCOMMODATION WANTED

Wanted for a doctor, an independent three bedroom with attached bathroom, drawing-cum-dining room, accommodation with modern amenities and facility for car parking in Greater Kailash on reasonable rent. Contact Ph. No. 9101521342 between 9 a.m. and 2 p.m. or meet Dr. P. Prashant 59-D Jawahar Nagar, Delhi-7.

14. You are in need of premises for a bank. Write a suitable advertisement, giving details in a local daily.

PREMISES REQUIRED

A leading private sector bank requires premises on rent for the opening of their branches at the following centres:

1. Greater Kailash Part-I, New Delhi.

2. Noida (Near Atta Market), (UP).

3. Janak Puri (Near District Centre), New Delhi.

4. Ghaziabad, (UP).

5. Gurgaon (DLF Qutab Enclave), (Haryana).

App. Area required

— 186 sq. mtr. preferably on ground floor/first floor.

— Premises should be in the conforming area.

Interested parties may write within 7 days alongwith following details:

Exact location of Bldg., parking space, available electric power load, water facility, sketch plan and expected rent to Box No. Det-5141 C, *The Times of India*, New Delhi-2.

15. You want to sell your furnance. Prepare an advertisement for a local daily.

FOR SALE

Channel Type induction Furnace 110 kw holding capacity 1000 kgs. of Copper with four furnace shells, two fully complete relined condition, including control panel, tilting arrangement with Hydraulic Power Pack with other accessories. In good running condition with balancing type brand new reactor input 360-440 capacity 95 KVA phase 1 continuous duty class A insulation temp. rise 50°C max, available for sale. Interested parties send their sealed offers to: Box No. BBG747K, *The Times of India*, New Delhi-2.

16. Your family is migrating to a new place and you want to dispose off some furniture. To this effect, prepare an advertisement to be published in a local newspaper.

FOR SALE

A newly purchased sofa set with dunlop seats, price expected Rs. 2500; dining table with six chairs, price expected Rs. 3000; a divan 3' × 6', price expected Rs. 500; a Godrej almirah, price expected Rs. 2700 are available for sale. All these items are sparingly used and look quite new. Interested parties please contact on Saturday and Sunday, D.K. Sharma 14, Civil Lines, Rajpur Road, Delhi.

(E) ACCOMMODATION WANTED OR TO LET

1. Rajesh of 54/7 Vasant Kunj, wishes to let out his house. He drafts an advertisement for publication in 'To Let' Section of a newspaper, giving the location, type of accommodation, rent expected and contact address.

TO LET

Available an independent, well-equipped house consisting of three bedrooms, drawing room, dining room with separate kitchen and bathroom having all the modern amenities. There is a separate car parking site. It is situated in the heart of the city with roads on both the sides amidst the pollution-free zone. Rent expected Rs. 5000/-. Please contact early, Rajesh of 54/7 Vasant Kunj. New Delhi-110052.

2. You want to hire accommodation for your newly-started business in Bombay. Write out an Advertisement for the same to be published in the classified column of the *Hindu*.

ACCOMMODATION WANTED

Wanted a well equipped large shop to start ready-made garments business with separate bathrooms in the vicinity of the central market of Bombay. It should be easily accessible by the customers. Rent and terms negotiable. Please contact immediately Mr. D. Gupta, 10 P. Road, Bombay or ring 22228922.

3. You have a set of three simple rooms exclusively suitable for single occupants and students. Draft an advertisement for 'To Let' column.

TO LET

A well-furnished set of three rooms on the first floor is available for rent exclusively suitable for single occupants and the students. It is adjacent to Maurice Nagar Delhi having separate bathroom and attached kitchen. It has a well-maintained spacious park meant for studies in the open. Rent payable in advance for six months. Interested persons can contact P. Rajender of 14-G, Kingsway Camp, Delhi or ring 22910540.

4. You are Anil Gupta of 15, Laxmi Nagar, New Delhi and wish to let out a portion of your newly built house. Draft an advertisement for publication in the 'To Let' column of *The Hindustan Times*, giving all necessary details like location, type of accommodation to be rented out, rent expected, contact address, including telephone number etc.

TO LET

A newly built accommodation of three rooms with attached bathrooms is available on rent basis. It is three side open. All the facilities are at hand. It is located in Laxmi Nagar behind Alok Cinema. Rent expected Rs. 5000 including electricity and water charges. Please contact Anil Gupta of 15, Laxmi Nagar, New Delhi or ring 5912910 between 1 a.m. to 2.00 p.m.

5. Draft a suitable advertisement about 'letting your newly constructed house'. Invent all the necessary details.

ACCOMMODATION TO RENT

A well equipped newly constructed house with separate bathroom, kitchen, three bedrooms and two stores with one spacious hall is available for rent. The house is situated in the vicinity of Raj Nagar, Delhi. It is two side open with parks on both the sides. Rent expected Rs. 5000/-. Interested parties may ring 2228921 or contact personally R.K between 10.00 to 2.00 p.m.

6. Ravi Menon of 45/3 Vasant Kunj, wishes to let out his house. He drafts an advertisement for publication in 'To Let' Section of a newspaper, giving the location, type of accommodation rent expected and contact address.

TO LET

A well equipped house having a separate set of 5 rooms including kitchen and bath is available on rent basis. It is very suitable for a small family. It is situated on the main road of Vasant Kunj having a Municipal Park before it. Expected rent Rs. 4500 including water and electricity charges. Interested parties may please contact, Rajesh of 45/3 Vasant Kunj, New Delhi-9 or ring 2523910.

7. You have a set of three simple rooms exclusively suitable for simple occupants and students. Draft an advertisement for the 'To Let' column.

TO LET

A set of three simple rooms well equipped in every way exclusively suitable for students are available for rent near the university campus. There is separate bathroom and kitchen with every room, Rent negotiable. Interested parties may contact Rajesh Sharma 22/5, Timar Pur Delhi on any working day between 8.00 to 12.00 p.m. or ring 7412912.

FOR PRACTICE

1. You want to let out a house. Prepare an advertisement to this effect, for publication in a newspaper giving location of the building, nature of accommodation, rent expected etc.

2. You want to let out your house suitable for a Diplomat, situated in a posh locality of New Delhi. Draft a suitable advertisement in about 50 words to be printed in the "Accommodation Wanted" column of a local newspaper.

3. A reputed multinational company requires on lease for two years a three bed-room independent flat/house in a posh locality, preferably around Defence Colony. Write out an advertisement suitable for publication in the column "Accommodation Wanted" of a local daily.

4. You are the Manager of ABC Sales Corporation Ltd. You want a suitable residential accommodation in a

good locality for two of your officers on rent or lease basis. Draft an advertisement suitable to be printed in the "Accommodation Wanted" column of a local daily.

5. You are a diplomat interested in an independent house in a very good locality in your city. Draft an advertisement to be published in a newspaper.

6. You want to hire accommodation for your newly started business in Delhi. Write out an advertisement for the same to be published in the classified column of 'The Hindu'.

7. You want to let out a portion of your house. Draft a suitable advertisement giving details to be published in the 'To Let' Column of a newspaper.

8. You want to hire accommodation for your newly-started business in readymade garments in Chennai. Write out an advertisement for the same, to be published in the classified column of 'The Hindu'.

9. You want to sell your scooter-Bajaj Super, Model 2000. Draft a suitable advertisement for 'Vehicles for Sale' column of a local newspaper.

10. You want to sell your car Premier Padmini 2000 (Air Conditioned) due to some personal reason. Write out an advertisement suitable for being printed in 'For Sale' column of a local daily in not more than 50 words.

11. A prestigious public sector company wants to buy a built up space (1850 sq. ft.) for its office in a centrally located market, preferably in NOIDA. Draft an advertisement suitable for 'Property for Sale' column of a local newspaper.

12. A Mumbai-based Exporter wants to buy around, 1,000 ft. space in old Dehi. Draft an advertisement suitable for 'Property For Sale' column of a local newspaper.

13. You are Roshan of 105, Kavi Nagar, Ghaziabad. You want to sell your house. Write a suitable advertisement to be published in the classified columns of a newspaper.

(F) MATRIMONIAL COLUMN

When we are writing any matrimonial, we should be clear whether the bride or the bridegroom is wanted. In addition to this, we should keep the following points in mind:

(i) Age, weight and height.

(ii) Caste, creed and religion.

(iii) Job, qualification and place of posting.

(iv) Contact address.

(v) Other particulars like decent or early marriage etc.

1. Write out a matrimonial column for publication in a newspaper for a suitable match for your daughter.

GROOMS WANTED

Proposals are invited for a very charming, pleasing personality Punjabi girl 165 cms., 25 years. MBA from Japan, daughter of a prosperous business family, owning his own house in Vivek Vihar, from sons of a reputed, cultured, business families. Kindly respond with full partculars to enable the parents to take an early decision. Send biodata with a photo to Box No. 2781-C.M., *Times of India*, New Delhi.

2. You are looking for a suitable match for your sister. Write the particulars of girl and ask for the particulars of the prospective bridegroom. Your written account should be suitable for entry in the 'Matrimonial Column' of a newspaper.

MATRIMONIAL

Engineer/Doctor/Executive match from a decent family for a beautiful, slim, charming and attractive featured girl belonging to Punjabi Malik and valued family 23, 158 cm. working as a Lecturer in Delhi University drawing a salary of Rs. 15,000/- Father in a Govt. job drawing salary in five figures. Owns his own house in Kamla Nagar, Delhi. Early decent marriage. Please contact Post Box No. 5185 C-A Hindustan.

3. Write out a matrimonial column for publication in a newspaper for a suitable match for your son.

BRIDES WANTED

A beautiful slim girl from respectable highly educated Gaur Brahmin family for a handsome graduate boy 23 years, 170 cms. dealing in wholesale business of garments. Father owning his farms worth crores in Narela. Girl only consideration and no dowry. Early marriage. Apply Box No. 2158-CD, Indian Express, New Delhi-1.

GROOMS

Draft a suitable matrimonial advertisement for your daughter for publication in a local newspaper.

Examples:

1. Punjabi Khatri NRI Family of Status. Invite Correspondence for their only daughter (Manglik), Slim, Smart, Aged 21 years, 5'4" tall with Indian values, professionally U.K. qualified accountant mixed blend for East and West. One brother studying in U.S.A. Boy should be professional either working or settled in own business. Apply with horoscope and photograph (returnable) to: B-208, Alok Appts. Rohini, Delhi. (Tel. : 27267937).

2. Suitable match for beautiful, sharp featured 25/170, convent educated, graduate, Punjabi Khatri girl. Family having well-established multi-crore business. Residing own bungalow posh South-Delhi. Only cultured leading Delhi based status families may send bio-data Box No. DES770C, Times of India, New Delhi-110002.

3. Suitable alliance is welcomed from parents with traditional business background having eligible, professionally qualified handsome, well settled boy for a good looking, homely graduate 23/160 girl, belonging to a well established traditional khatri business family of Delhi. Write in confidence with recent photograph/horoscope (Returnable) to: Box DET-826-C Times of India, New Delhi-110002.

4. Professionally qualified match willing to settle in Canada, recently granted Canadian immigration, beautiful, smart, slim, convent educated, Jat Sikh Girl, 25/5'2", B.A., LLB, DIP Computer, DIP tourism/travelling, Father class-I officer, Respectable Family. Early and decent marriage. Write Box No. DET 717C The Times of India, New Delhi-110002

5. Alliance invited from well settled educated boy with good family background, for smart good looking Gotra Bisa Aggarwal Garg girl 24, 5'3" (158 cms.), graduate in interior decoration, now working. Write with complete details to : Box No. DET 871C. The Times of India, New Delhi-110002.

6. Alliance invited from smart, well settled, independent, MBA/Architect/Computer Professional boy of status family preferably settled in metro cities or abroad for cultured 24/155 wheatish complexion Verma girl convent educated, Diploma Interior Design, 2 years work experience. Presently studying French language, belonging to a highly placed affluent family, cast no bar. Write to box No. CAC-2305-C The Economic Times 13/1 & 13/2 Govt. Place (E) Cal-69

8. Suitable Aggrawal Medico/Non-Medico match for 28/158, very fair, attractive Girl MBBS, DMRD, consultant Radiologist MRI (Mumbai) from cultured Bansal Business Family. Decent Marriage. Write Box. No. AHH093C Times of India, Ahmedabad-38000

9. Alliance invited, for a Mumbai based, charming, smart, well mannered, highly qualified, self-employed, age 29, height 170 cms, from a respectable Hindu family, the only daughter of a highly successful Doctor, owning a business establishment in Greater Mumbai. From a Doctor born of a respectable Hindu family, from Maharashtra, Karnataka, Goa, Tamil Nadu, possessing a Post Graduate qualification and preferably specialised in Cardiology or any other Medical or Surgical Superspeciality, who is willing to settle and practice in Mumbai. Please write with details of family background, personal information, qualifications, professional experience, a recent photograph and horoscope (or Date, time and place of birth) to Box No. BCG537C Times of India, Delhi-110001.

   All correspondence will be strictly confidential.

BRIDES

Draft a suitable advertisement for publication in the matrimonial columns of a local newspaper for your son.

Examples:

1. Affluent Cultured Millionaire Business Family, invite Alliance for a Hindu Khatri Boy, 34 years, 174 cms., very fair and goodlooking, well educated and well established in own business with income in six figures. Girl must be convent educated, smart, slim, fair, beautiful, warm caring, sweetnatured belonging to a status and cultured family. High caste North Indians and Punjabis will be preferred. Write with full particulars and photograph (Returnable) in strict confidence to Box No. BBX342R Times of India, Mumbai-400001.

2. Alliance invited from a sober Bengali family girl, fair, pretty, homely, convent educated, must be good in

cooking, for a very well established Bengali Baldya boy from a small family/167 cms./age 25yr./graduate/Builder and Developer having a car, office and own home at Nashik, early marriage, caste no bar, contact with recent photograph (Returnable) to Box No. BBA455K Times of India, Mumbai-400001.

3. Affluent business family based in Pune invite alliance for Punjabi Hindu handsome Engineer 29 year/163 cms. well settled in own industry. Girl must be convent educated smart fair slim exceptionally beautiful from good status affluent family. Apply with coloured photograph (Returnable) to Box No. PUG914K, TOI, East Street, Pune-411001.

4. Alliance for 28/172 Vaish (Porwal) handsome boy. B.E. (Hons), employed reputed multinational company posted at Ahmedabad. Wanted caring and charming preferably professionally qualified working girl from educated status family (.) Sub caste no bar, please correspond with details, coloured photograph (Returnable) and horoscope to Mr. Suresh Chandra Gupta, Company Secretary, U.P. State Cement Corporation Ltd., Churk 231-206, Distt., Sonebhadra U.P.)

5. Wanted an educated Girl for 25 years old, 5ft. 10 inch graduate from stephens, MBA. Director in multicrore family business with independent responsibility. Own houses in Delhi/Bombay. Fax Bio-Data with Details to 011-6967823, 6863565 Earliest.

6. Alliance invited for a Handsome Smart Aggrawal Boy 25 years 5'7" educated in USA belonging to industrialist family and running an industry in India. The Girl should be slim, fair, beautiful and professionally qualified from a respectable family. Write with detailed Bio-data and recent photograph (Returnable) to P. Aggarwal, G-4, Kavita Apartments, Vidyalaya Marg, Tri Nagar, Delhi.

8. Alliance invited for Hindu West Bangali boy, only son. Mumbai based 32-5.7" M.Sc Income 6000/- Central Govt. service. Hindu suitable bride slim fair-tall-good looking, good family background with similar educated girl. Age upto 29 yr. Cast no bar. Please write with full details bio-data, horoscope + photograph with family background Box No. BBG700C Times of India, Mumbai-400001.

9. Good looking Jat Doctor 27/175 doing export business in Russia. Parents Defence background, settled in Bombay. Seeks convent educated, beautiful, graduate, broad minded, homely girl, willing to settle abroad, from status family. Advt. given for better choice. Caste no bar. Write with returnable photograph to Box no BBG188C Times of India, Mumbai-400001.

❒

2

Notices

Notice is an invitation of an event or an advice to do or not to do a thing or certain things. The notices are circulated in schoos, colleges, offices, societies, etc. There are numerous occasions when the Secretary has to prepare a notice to be circulated among the members or it is sent to a member or to a few members or to the outsiders. Certain notices are to be published in newspapers. The nature of the notice, to whom the contents are to be communicated, how and when it is to be prepared and published or communicated, etc., points will have to be considered for this purpose.

The structure of the notice used in offices may be divided into following five heads or parts, *viz*:

1. Heading. The title or the name of the Company at the top of the notice alongwith 'NOTICE' word in the second line is necessary.

2. Purpose of the Notice. 'Notice is hereby given that...' in this way the purpose of the notice *i.e.*, the information or invitation or an event which the Secretary wish to communicate is narrated.

3. Place, Date and Time. Alongwith the infromation the place, date and time must be mentioned in the meeting, if any, where it is scheduled, on what day and time it is scheduled; or to deposit the call-amount with which Bank and its place, on or before such and such date alongwith such and such amount, etc., examples can give clear idea about this head.

4. Proper Authority to Sign with Designation, etc. The person who is going to sign, should sign it with his designation. Chairman, Managing Director, Secretary, Managing Agent, Secretaries and Treasurers etc, are the common authorities who sign the notices generally. When the notice is issued as per instructions of the Board then 'By Order of the Board' clause is used before signature. When it is as per instruction from the members 'For........ Co. Ltd.' clause is there before the signature of the authority.

5. Notes, Documents, Instructions, etc. According to the provisions of the Companies Act, 1956, every notice requires some notes, statements, documents, etc. Then proper notes, statements, documents, etc. should be stated and attached to the Notice. For example, Notice meant for meeting of the members should accompany Agenda, some statements, documents, proxies, explanatory notes, etc, if any.

The notices broadly can be divided into two major heads :

1. Notices about the meetings, 2. General notices excluding the notices about the meetings. Additional points for your guidance are as follows:

1. General Notices. To communicate the closure of Register of members and Transfer Book, call, the appointment or termination of or increase or decrease in the remuneration payable to or alteration or modification in terms of agreement with office bearers, dividend warrants, loss of share certificate, offer of additional issues, etc., are the subject matters of the notices which are grouped under this head. While preparing the draft of such notices the five heads or parts must be studied properly in the light of the details given against each of them.

If the notice is intended for one or two or few persons then preparation of it in the letter form is much more appropriate. On the other hand, if the notice is for more persons then Notice in the proper form is more desirable than the letter form.

2. Notices About the Meetings. While dealing with this group it must be stated at the first, that the group again can be divided into 3 sub-heads-Directors, Members and Others. Notice about the Board or Committee meeting is generally in a letter form. We have attempted to give, specimen letters on this subject earlier—'Correspondence with Directors'. Hence inclusion of the same here is not necessary. While preparing notices of the Members' meetings the nature about the meeting must, be considered and mentioned, *i.e.* the Statutory or Annual or Extraordinary or Class. The same may be considered in respect of the meeting of Others, *i.e.,* the creditors of the Company.

While preparing the draft of these meetings inclusion of agenda, or the business to be transacted, is not compulsory. But to save the time, trouble and money not only inclusion of agenda in the text of the meeting is common rule but to attach the necessary notes, documents explanatory statements, if any is the practice, Generally agenda is finalised, with due discussion, with the Chairman of the Company. While preparing the notice, notes, statements, explanatory statements, etc., as per provisions of the Companies Act, 1956, relevant sections must be quoted, wherever necessary and compulsory. But to avoid confusion only from the point of view of the students we have avoided this practice. But for the students who wish to know the same can go through the notes given at the bottom of the notice where we have quoted the relevant sections with brief description.

Some notices are to be filed with the Central Government and/or Registrar, some are to be published in the newspapers in addition to those for whom they are intended. Considering the duration or time limit the office of the Company must be very careful and particular for the same.

Generally, notices should be typewritten or got printed. Handwritten copy or copies are not, in majority cases, impressive, attractive, economical and neatly arranged.

The rules stated above are applicable for the notices of Co-operative Societies, non-profit organisations or associations. Except the rules and regulations of the Companies Act, 1956, shall not apply to them, as their activities are governed by other legislation and/or their own bye-laws.

Following are some specimen of notices usually used in offices companies etc.

1. Call Notice

AZAD OIL MILLS LIMITED, KOLHAPUR
NOTICE

Notice is hereby given to the shareholders of the Company that the Directors, by a resolution at the Board meeting dated 25th May, 1965. have made the first call of Rs. 25/- per share on 5,00,000 Equity shares of Rs. 100/each, payable on or before 31st July 1965, and to remit the required amount of the shares held by you to the Bankers of the Company, The Maharashtra Bank Ltd., Kolhapur. The Bank will accept the amount on and after 1st June, 1965. The amount if not paid by the 31st July, 1965, interest will be charged at the rate of 9% from the due date to the date of payment.

Notice of the call has been sent invidually to the shareholders whose name appeared in the Register of Members at their registered addresses.

69, Raviwar peth, By order of the Board of Directors,
Kolhapur. ABC
Dt. 28th May, 1965. Secretary.

2. Notice about the loss of Share Certificate(s)

VILAS TILES LIMITED, NAGPUR
NOTICE

Notice is hereby given that Share Certificate No. 932 for one hundred Equity Shares (from No. 2738 to No. 2837 both inclusive) in this Company, registered in the name of Shri S.B. Sachdev of Sangli, Maharashtra State, in the Register of the Company at Bombay, has been reported lost and an application has been received by the Company for the issue of a duplicate Share Certificate.

All persons having a claim or lien or interest in the said shares are requested to notify the same to the Company within one month from the date of this notice, and if no claim or protest is received within the said period a duplicate Share Certificate for the said shares will be issued by the Company.

Dated 18th July 2005.	XYZ
235, Deccan Gymkhana, Nagpur	Secretary, Vilas Tiles Ltd.

3. Specimen of Share Certificate.

Counterfoil	*Share Certificate*
Certificate No. 527	AJIT GLASS WORKS LIMITED.
Name: Shri. R. P. Gupta	27, Shukrawar peth, Poona
Address: 247, Budhwar, Sangli.	Certificate: No. 527 [Stamp]
Occupation: Agriculture	Capital, Rs. 50,00,000 divided into 50,000 shares of Rs. 100/- each.

For 500 Equity shares

Nos. 13433 to 13932 both inclusive	This is to certify that Shri. R. P. Gupta, 247, Budhawar, Sangli, is the registered holder of 500 Equity Shares numbered 13433-13932 inclusive of this Company, subject to in Memorandum and Articles of Association thereof and that the sum of Rs. 50/- (fifty) has been paid up on each share.
Date of Certificate 23-5-2004 Delivery : 27-6-2004	
Register Folio : 89	

Given under the Common seal of the Company, this 13th May of 1965.

Seal of the Co.	ABC Director DEF Director GHI Secretary

Back Side of the Certificate

Calls					*Transfers*			
Due Date	*Calls*	*Amt. per share*	*Date of payment*	*Signature of authorised officer*	*Date*	*To whom transferred-Name address & occupation*	*L.F.*	*Signature of authorised officer*

4. Notice to the public for receiving approval of the Central Government to the increase in the maximum number of Directors.

ATUL GLASS WORKS LIMITED, POONA

NOTICE

Notice is hereby given that the Company intends to apply, under provisions of the Companies Act, 1956, to the Central Government for its approval to the increase in the maximum number of its Directors from ten to fifteen.

27, Shukrawar peth,	GHI
Nagpur	Secretary,
Dt. 15th Sept., 2004.	Atul Glass Works Ltd.

(*Note:* Section No. 253-Govt's approval for increase in the number.)

5. Notice regarding the time limit extended for the receipt of application for consolidation of fractional certificates.

ATUL GLASS WORKS LIMITED, NAGPUR

NOTICE

Notice is hereby given to holders of Fractional Certificates issued in connection with the issue of Bonus Shares (2002) of the Gokak Mills Limited, that the time for presentation of Fractional Certificates for conversion into full Equity Share(s) which expires on 31st Dec. 2004, has been extended to 30th June, 2004. Please note that no further extension of time will be granted beyond that date. The holders of Fractional Certificates are, therefore, advised to make such presentation to the Company by the aforesaid date of 30th June, 2004.

27, Shukrawar peth,	By order of the Board,
Nagpur.	ABC
Dt. 12th Dec. 2004.	Secretary.

6. Notice regarding the reappointment of Secretaries and Treasurers.

ORGAN OIL MILLS LIMITED, KANPUR
NOTICE

Notice is hereby given that the Company is applying to the Central Government for its approval for the reappointment of M/S Chaitanya Brothers (Private) Limited, as Secretaries and Treasurers of the Organ Oil Mills Ltd., for a period of ten years from 1st January 2004 on the terms and conditions provided in the draft Agreement duly approved at the Annual General Meeting of the Company held on 26th March 2003. Dated at Kanpur this 9th April 2004.

By order of the Board,

271. Sholapur Bazar Road, ABC
Sholapur. Secretary.

Note: Section 326 - Government's approval
(As per Sec. 379).

7. Notice of adjournment of a meeting.

VISHAL TEXTILES LIMITED,
NOTICE

Notice is hereby given to the members of the Company that the Extraordinary General Meeting of the members of the Company on Thursday the July 21st, 2004 at 3.00 p.m. at the Registered Office of the Company, at 301, Gandhi Chowk, Gujrat, stands adjourned under the provisions of the Companies Act, 1956, to 28th July 2004 at the same time and place.

301, Gandhi Chowk, For Vishal Textiles Ltd.,
Gujrat, KBK
Dt. 21st July 2004. Managing Director.

8. Notice of postponement of a meeting.

VISHAL TEXTILES LIMITED
NOTICE

Notice is hereby given that the Extraordinary General Meeting of the Company called on Monday the 6th March 2005 at 3.00 p.m. at the Registered Office of the Company at 301, Gandhi Chowk, Gujrat, is NOW POSTPONED due to unavoidable cirscumstances and is now scheduled for Monday the 20th March 2005 (instead of 6th March 2005), at the same time and place. Members of the Company are requested to note the said change.

301, Gandhi Chowk,	By order of the Board,
Ichalkaranji	K B K
Dt. 11th Feb. 2005.	Managing Director.

9. Notice of Cancellation of a meeting.

ANIL TEXTILES LIMITED
NOTICE

In supersession ot the Notice published earlier (dated 1st March 1966), Notice is hereby given that an Extraordinary General Meeting of the Company, to be held at the Head Office of the Company at 301, Gandhi Chowk, Gujrat, on Thursday the 31st March 2005. as published earlier for the purpose of the approving the appointment of M/S. Vijay Agencies of Kolhapur, as Sole Selling Agents for the products of the Company BE CANCELLED.

301, Gandhi Chowk,	By order of the Board,
Gujrat,	KBK
Dt. 10th March 2005.	Managing Director.

10. Notice of the Statutory Meeting alongwith Agenda.

JAIN WATCH COMPANY LIMITED

NOTICE

Notice is hereby given that, according to the provisions of the Companies Act, 1956, the Statutory Meeting of the Company will be held at the Company's Registered Office at 37. Station Road, Kolhapur on Tuesday the 12th July, 2005, at 2.00 p. m. to transact the following business.

1. To read the notice of the meeting.
2. To consider the Statutory Report.
3. To discuss any matter arising out of the Statutory Report.
4. To transact any other business with due permission of the Chair.
5. Vote of thanks to the Chairman.

By Order of the Board,
XYZ
Secretary.

Note: A member entitled to attend and vote at the meeting is also entitled to appoint a proxy to attend and vote instead of himself and a proxy need not be a member of the Company.

37, Station Road, Kolhapur
Dt. 10th June 2005.

By Order of the Board,
XYZ
Secretary.

Note: Section 165-Statutory Meeting and Statutory Report of the Company.

11. Annual General Meeting along with agenda-Notice.

HINDUSTAN LIVER LIMITED
NOTICE

Notice is hereby given that the Annual General Meeting of the Company will be held at Hindustan Lever House, 165/166 Backbay Reclamation. Bombay-1 on Tuesday, 28th April 2005, at 4 p.m. to transact the following business.

1. To receive and consider the Accounts and Balance Sheet, and the Reports of the Directors and Auditors.
2. To declare a dividend.
3. To elect Directors.
4. To appoint Auditors and fix their remuneration for the year ending 31st Dec., 2006.

A member entiled to attend and vote is entitled to appoint a proxy to attend and vote instead of himself. A proxy need not be a member.

The Transfer Books of the Company will be closed from 21st April to 28th April 2005 (both days inclusive).

Hindustan Lever House,
165/166, Backbay Reclamation,
Bombay-1.

By Order of the Board,
S. H. Gursahani
Secretary.
24th March 2006.

GENERAL NOTICES USED IN SCHOOLS/OFFICES/SOCIETIES

1. The Students Council of your school has organised an excursion to Ajanta and Elora for the students of classes XI and XII during winter break. As President of the Council write a notice, telling the students about this excursion and. inviting their names for joining it.

ALLIED PUBLIC SCHOOL, BANGLA ROAD,
EXCURSION NOTICE

5th Dec., 2006

On the demand of the students of class XI and XII, the students Council has organised an excursion to Ajanta and Elora caves alongwith a trip to South India. The Trip will leave Delhi on 20th Dec. for 10 days. Interested students should give their names, permission letter from parents and deposit Rs. 1500 towards the travelling and other expenses by 15th of this month.

N.K. Pandey
President

2. Your school has just completed 25 years of its meritorious services to society. The Students Council of your school has decided to celebrate its Silver Jubilee. As 'President of the Council write a notice for the students of your school, informing them about the council's decision and seeking their co-peration for the success of the proposed Silver Jubilee Celebrations.

DELHI PUBLIC SCHOOL, R.K. PURAM
NOTICE

15th Nov. 2005

The school has completed a span of 25 years of meritorious service in the field of education. It has prepared high intellectuals and other genius to serve our motherland. In order to acclaim its service to the cause of the community, it has been decided to celebrate its Silver Jubilee on 1st Dec. 2005 Sh. D.K. Puri Chief Justice, the ex-students of this school will preside the function at 10.00 a.m. Your whole hearted cooperation will make the programme a grand success.

R. Jones
President

3. R.D. Gupta is the Secretary of the Sports Club of your school. He drafts a notice about a today trek to Rohtang Pass during the summer holidays. Write the notice board, giving all the necessary information.

ST. PETER PUBLIC SCHOOL, NEW DELHI
NOTICE
ENJOY TREKKING DURING HOLIDAYS

12th March, 2006

The Sports Club of the school is organising a trekking trip to Rohtang Pass during the summer holidays. The group will consist of 20 students under the careful guidance of our Scout Lecturer. It will leave Delhi on 1st May and return on 10th May. Interested students should contact the Scout Lecturer within 3 days of this notice.

R.D. Gupta
Secretary

4. You are the Head boy Arjun of Bal Bharti School. Write a notice to be circulated among all the students of your school, inviting the names of those who would like to go on an excursion to South India. Invent all necessary details.

BAL BHARTI PUBLIC SCHOOL, KAROL BAGH, NEW DELHI NOTICE

15th April, 2006

The History club of the school has organised a sight-seeing tour to South during the summer vacations. The tour will last for ten days *i.e.* from 1st May to 10th May. The touring party will visit Bombay, Madras, Goa, Kanya Kumari and Bangalore and other important places. Interested students may contact by 18th April with the History lecturer Mr. P.K. Joshi. A written request from their parents alongwith a cash amount of Rs. 1500 may be deposited by

19th of this month. The History and Geography lecturers will be with the touring party.

Arjun
Boy

5. You are R.K. Trivedi, Secretary, Science Forum, Modern School. Write a notice for the school notice board inviting students to attend a lecture to be delivered by an eminent scientist.

NEW MODERN PUBLIC SCHOOL, PALAM
SCIENCE FORUM
NOTICE

10th March, 2006

All the students of Senior as well as Secondary sections are hereby requested to attend to a lecture to be delivered by an eminent scientist Sh. C.B. Raman of Delhi University in Ashoka Hall of the institution at 2.00 p.m. sharp on 15th March. Your questions will be dealt with after the lecture is over. I hope you will cooperate the esteemed lecturer and maintain the required decorum. This lecture will be benefical to those who are appearing for their Board Examination.

R.K. Trivedi
Secretary

6. You are Secretary of the Ex. Students' Association of your school. The association proposes to celebrate its Silver Jubilee Foundation Day. Draft a notice to be published in the newspaper inviting suggestions about how to celebrate.

EX. STUDENTS ASSOCIATION N.P. SCHOOL,
GOAL MARKET NEW DELHI
NOTICE

18th March, 2006

The association of ex-students has decided to celebrate the Silver Jubilee Foundation Day in Auditorium of the school on the eve of Republic Day. So the association desires to celebrate this function with great pomp and show. It will be appropriate to call it an old students' meet. It is requested to all the ex-students of this school to send their suggestions in this regard by 25th Nov., 2006 so that necessary details can be chalked out. Your whole hearted cooperation will be appreciated.

Amit
Secretary

7. You have been elected the Head boy of your school. Write a note to be put up on the school Notice Board thanking the students for their support in getting you elected.

NATIONAL PUBLIC SCHOOL, NAGPUR
NOTICE

15th August, 2006

I send my thanks to all my colleagues for giving me their whole hearted support in getting me elected to the post of Head Boy of the school. I can assure you that I will fight for the students' welfare and come to their expectations. I once again send my heartiest thanks for this.

I also do expect that you will show the same feeling in discharging my lawful activities.

Shrey Bhardwaj
Head Boy.

8. In response to an appeal of the Prime Minister of India you have arranged a Charity Show in your school in aid of the cancer patients of the country. Write out, a Notice to be displaced on the School Notice Board informing the students about the show and seeking their co-operation for the success of the Charity Show.

LITTLE FLOWER PUBLIC SCHOOL, BIJNORE
NOTICE

15th July, 2006

The Prime Minister of India has made an earnest appeal to help the cancer stricken people of this country. In this connection, our school has organised a charity show on 28th July of this month at 2.00 p.m. in the school compound. The Education Minister has consented to inaugurate the function. Tickets worth Rs. 10/- and 15/- are available in school office. All are requested to contribute to this noble cause. They thus collected will be sent to the Prime Minister's Relief Fund. Your co-operation can set records for the future.

R.K. Ahuja
Head Boy

9. You are Anil working as the Students' Representative on the School Development Committee. The committee is going to meet next week to prepare a calendar of activities for the school for the year 2004-2005. To ensure that you play your role effectively at the proposed meeting you have decided to invite the students' suggestions on this subject. Write a notice in this regard to be put up on your school notice-board.

GOVERNMENT SR. SECONDARY SCHOOL, DELHI
NOTICE

5th March, 200...

The School Development Committee is going to meet on 12th March in the Committee Room at 11.00 p.m. to prepare a calendar of activities for the school for the current academic year 2006-2007. In this connection, all the students are requested to give their suggestions about different activities to be included in the calendar. Your proposals will be given due regard. Please send your suggestions by 10th March to the undersigned.

Anil
Students' Representative

10. You are Amit the school captain of A.P.J. International School. You wish to call a meeting of the students council to discuss the measures to be taken to check the explosion of crackers in the school premises during Diwali time. Draft the Notice in not more than 50 words.

**A.P.J. INTERNATIONAL SCHOOL,
PATNA STUDENTS FORUM
NOTICE**

5th October 2007

It has been decided to call the meeting of the students council to discuss the measures to be taken to check the explosion of crackers in the school premises during Diwali time. The meeting will be held on 7th October in the Arts Room at 10.00 a.m. so that the necessary awareness may be created among all and they can keep themselves hale and hearty.

Amit
School Captain

11. You are the Secretary of DIWAN Housing Welfare Society. Draft a notice to be circulated to its members stating that the second instalment of payment towards the cost of construction is due.

**DIWAN HOUSING WELFARE SOCIETY,
NOTICE**

5th January 2007

All the worthy members of the Housing Society are hereby informed that the second instalment of payment towards the cost of construction is due for the month of February. All the members are requested to deposit their dues by the last week of February with the cashier on any working day. The defaulters will not be entitled for the accommodated at any cost.

P.K. Mishra
Secretary

12. As the Chief Librarian of Bacon Public Library, draft a notice informing the members of the increase in membership fee with effect from 1st June 2005 and the change in the library timings.

BACON PUBLIC LIBRARY, DELHI
NOTICE

20th May 2007

All the members of the Library are hereby informed that the membership fee has been enhanced from Rs. 10 to 15/- with effect from 1st June 2007. The governing body has accepted of our precessing demand of time changes and consequently the new timings will be as under from 1st June:

Morning	:	8.00 a.m. to 2.00 p.m.
Lunch Break	:	2.00 p.m. to 3.00 p.m.
Evening	:	4.00 p.m. to 9.00 p.m.

Arun Kumar
Chief Librarian

13. Your school is organising a tour to Mumbai and Goa during the winter vacation. Write a notice giving detailed information to the students. You are Vivek, School Pupil Leader, St. Columbia's Senior Secondary School, Ameenabad, Lucknow.

ST. COLUMBIA'S SENIOR SECONDARY SCHOOL
AMEENABAD, LUCKNOW
NOTICE

10th October, 2006

The school is organising a tour to Mumbai and Goa during the winter vacation. The students who are interested in joining this tour are requested to give their names to the undersigned by 20th October alongwith a permission letter signed by their parents. They are to deposit Rs. 2,500/- also towards the expenses. The touring party will leave on 15th November and return on 26th November.

Vivek
Pupil Leader

14. You are Prashant as President of the Dramatic Club of your school you have organized an inter-school competition in one act plays on the occasion of the Silver Jubilee Celebrations of your school. Write a notice informing the students of your school about, this proposed event.

L.M. PUBLIC SCHOOL, SONEPAT
DRAMATIC CLUB
NOTICE

4th March, 2007

The Dramatic Club of your school is organizing an inter-school competition in One Act Play on the occasion of the Silver Jubilee Celebrations of the school to be held on 16th March, 2005 at 3.00 p.m. in the school hall. The participants may give their names to the undersigned by 6th March. The best group will be awarded by the Chairman of the school. Hoping for your best cooperation on this grand occasion.

Prashant
President

15. As the President of the Literary Club of your school you are organizing a programme for Public Speaking for XI & XII Standard students of your school. As a part of this programme, you will be inviting a few television anchors.

Write a notice giving all the details of it to be displayed on your school notice board.

N.P. BENGALI PUBLIC SCHOOL, NEW DELHI
(LITERARY CLUB)

10th Sept., 2006

In order to enhance the speaking skills of the students, the literary club has arranged a Public Speaking Programme for the students of class XI & XII on 15th Sept. at 10.00 a.m. in the school auditorium. The views and thoughts will be shared by the famous television anchors from Star News, Zee T.V. and India Today. The programme will last for two hours. Please make it imperative to attend it.

Rekesh
President

16. In response to an appeal to the P.M. of India, you are arranging a Musical Evening in your school to raise funds for earthquake victims. Write out a notice to be put up on the school notice board giving details about the programme.

ADARSH VIDYA MANDIR, PANIPAT
NOTICE

25th August, 2007

MUSICAL EVENING!

In response to an appeal made by the Hon'ble Prime Minister of India our Club has organised a spendid musical evening with you in Ashok Hall of the School on 25th

Sept., 2007 at 7.30 p.m. in aid of the earthquake victims of Gujrat. Artists of world repute like Pran, Dharmendra, Rekha, Madhuri Dixit and Lata Mangeshker will entertain the audience. The tickets worth Rs. 20/- and 50/- are available at the counter. This fund will be sent to the Prime Minister's Relief Fund to help the earthquake victims. Your cooperation will be highly appreciated.

B.K. Sharma
Secretary

17. You have planned a six-week course to help the children of your Housing Society Complex in developing their skills of oral communication. Prepare a notice for the society's Notice Board stating the objectives of the course and give all necessary details asking people to join your course.

MILAN GROUP HOUSING SOCIETY COMPLEX, DELHI
NOTICE

15th May, 2007

For the residents of this complex a six week course is being organised by Ministry of Communication, G.O.I. It will benefit the children in developing their skills in oral communication. Necessary details of the course are given for your perusal.

1. Objectives of the Course : Developing the skills of Oral Communication.

2. Eligibility : 5th pass.

3. Timings: 8.00 a.m. to 10.00 a.m. (on all working days).

4. Venue: Rajaji Hall, Hindu Group Housing Society.

5. Fees : Rs. 100/-.

6. Date of Commencement of the course: 25th May, 2007.

This course will help the children in communicating English language properly. The residents will avail of this golden opportunity and register their names before 20th May.

Y.K. Goel
Communicator

18. You are Avtar Singh, Secretary Students' Union, Govt. School, Jaipur. Write a notice for the school notice board requesting contributions from the students for the victims of an earthquake.

STUDENTS' UNION, GOVT. SCHOOL, JAIPUR
NOTICE

10th Nov., 2006

HELP! HELP! HELP!

It is knwon to all of us that the earthquake in Assam has caused a great havoc to the life and property of the public. Most of them have rendered homeless, destitude and helpless. So they need immediate help. The union has decided to contribute at least Rs. 15/- or more per student. This contribution will be sent to the Prime Minister's Relief Fund. Please donate generously and send your donations within three days to the Secretary of the Union.

Avtar Singh
Secretary

19. You have planned a six weeks course to help the children of your Housing Society Complex in improving their spoken English. Prepare a notice for the Society's Notice Board stating the objectives of the course and other necessary details like eligibility, timings; venue and whether. It is a part of social service or a paid course. Invite people to join the course in large numbers. You are

Y.K. Paul an effective communicator and a member of the society.

HINDU HOUSING SOCIETY COMPLEX SONEPAT
NOTICE

1st May, 2007

IMPROVE YOUR ENGLISH

A six weeks course in spoken English for our school going children in collaboration with the Ministry of Education is being organised by the members of the society. The necessary details are as under :

1. Objectives of the course	:	Fluency in Spoken English
2. Eligibility	:	4th Standard
3. Timings	:	10.00 a.m. to 12.00 noon (on all working days except Sunday)
4. Venue	:	Ashok Hall, Hindu Housing Complex, Sonepat
5. Fees	:	No charges. It is a part of social service
6. Date of commencement of the course.	:	16th May, 2007
7. Registration	:	5th May to 8th May (8.00 a.m. to 10.00 a.m.)
8. Written Test	:	11th May 10.00 a.m.
9. Declaration of Result	:	14th May 5.00 p.m.

I hope that the residents will avail this golden opportunity and get their wards trained in spoken English.

Yashpal Kapoor
Communicator

20. You want to start a Readers club in a centralised place in your colony called MERI BASTI. Draft a notice to be put upon the notice board of the Residents Welfare Association giving details of your requirements asking for terms and conditions. You are Seema Rao, Secretary.

RESIDENTS WELFARE ASSOCIATION, MERI BASTI, JAIPUR

NOTICE ***10th August, 2007***

ATTENTION! ATTENTION! ATTENTION!

It is matter of great zeal for all of us that our association is doing a yeoman's service in the field of education. It is running 2 separate schools (Boys and Girls). Now the association has decided to start a 'Readers club' in our colony 'Meri Basti' at the Community Hall. It is a centralised place and all can approach to read the newspapers, magazines and other library books. For this, money, members and your heartiest cooperation to needed on your behalf.

I hope you will like this programme and send your views in a week's time. Your whole hearted cooperation is needed to run the Readers Club.

Seema Rao
Secretary

21. You are Amrita Arora, Cultural Secretary of Golden Academy Indore. Write a notice for the school Notice Board informing the students that the Inter School Declamation contest to be held in your school has been postponed for a week. Give details of new programme.

GOLDEN ACADEMY,INDORE (CULTURAL SOCIETY)

NOTICE ***10th Sept., 2006***

Due to sudden outbreak of Dangu fever the Government has closed the schools for one week. So it is brought to the notice of all concerned that the Inter School Declamation

Contest which was scheduled to be held in our school on 17th Sept., 2006, has been postponed for a week. It will now be held on 24th Sept., 2006 as usual at the fixed time in Rangshala of the academy. Please make it convenient to attend and grace the occasion.

Amrita Arora
Secretary

22. You are B.K. Pathak, Sports coach of ABC School, Delhi. Write a notice for the school notice board informing the students that your school is playing against M.N. School, Delhi in the Zonal Football Finals. Invite them to come and watch the match and cheer the Team.

ABC SCHOOL DELHI SPORTS
NOTICE ***10th Sept., 2005***

It is brought to the notice of all the students of our school that our football team will play a very exciting friendly zonal match (finals) against the M.N. School, Delhi, on Saturday at 4:00 p.m. sharp on 14th September, 2005. The match will be played in Delhi University compound. All are requested to come, watch and encourage our players.

B.K. Pathak
Sports Coach

23. You are Rajesh of Apex Academy, Delhi. As an editor of your school magazine, write a notice for the school notice board inviting contributions for the magazine by a certain date.

APEX ACADEMY, DELHI
(PUBLICATION SECTION)
NOTICE ***21st Dec., 2005***

The school-magazine "SHIKSHA" will be brought out in the 2nd week of February. All the students and the worthy teachers are requested to send their articles upto 30th

December to the undersigned so that the school magazine should come out well in time. The articles should be entertain able with moral giving teachings. They must be written legibly on one side of the sheet.

Rajesh
Editor

24. Your school has decided to celebrate the Golden Jubilee of National Independence by arranging a day-long programme. As the Pupil Leader of your school, write a notice, giving details of the programme and calling for the participation and co-operation of your school students.

S.M. PUBLIC SCHOOL, RAJPURA
NOTICE ***5th August, 2006***

The school authorities have decided to celebrate the Golden Jubilee of National Independence by arranging a day-long programme in the school auditorium from 11.00 a.m. to 3 p.m. on 13th instant. The programme will consist of debates, songs, fancy dress competition, speeches, national songs, drama and an exhibition of National heroes and their works. Interested students for participation may submit their names along with their field of participation to the undersigned by 7th August positively. Your co-operation will be well-acknowiedged.

M.C. Gupta
Pupil Leader

25. You are Vivek the Editor of Gandhi Memorial Senior Secondary School Magazine. Draft a notice for your school notice-board inviting contributions for the Annual school magazine.

GANDHI MEMORIAL SR. SEC. SCHOOL, SONA
NOTICE ***2nd August, 2006***

The school is going to publish its magazine 'Joyti' in the month of February 200... For this, articles in the shape of essays, stories, songs, quiz and short speeches are invited from the interested students by 14th August. The articles should be neatly written on one side with stress on development of moral values. The selected items will be sent for publication. I hope your co-operation will help in bringing the magazine published well in time.

Vivek
Editor

26. You are Dinesh. As the Secretary of the Cultural Club of your school, you have organised a Cultural Evening on the last day of your school as a thanks-giving programme. Write a notice for your school notice-board, giving necessary information about the programme.

EDUCATION ACADEMY, SHIMLA
NOTICE

25th January 2007

The Cultural Club of our school has decided to organise an awe-striking cultural evening as a thanks-giving programme in the Ashoka Hall of the school on 31st January, 2007. The programme is scheduled to be organised and started at 10.00 a.m. sharp with the burning of 101 candles. The Director of the Academy will be there to grace the occasion. Participating students may please contact the undersigned before 25th instant. Your whole-hearted cooperation is earnestly needed.

Dinesh
Cultural Club

27. You are Pooja. As Secretary of the Social Service League of your school, you have organised a cultural benefit show in aid of mentally handicapped children of your town Vijayawada. Write a notice for your school notice-board, giving necessary information about the programme.

S. B. SR. SEC. SCHOOL VIJAYAWADA
(Social Service League)
NOTICE

20th Oct., 2006

In order to provide aid to the mentally handicapped children of this town, the Social Service League is organizing a cultural benefit show. The show will be organized on 5th September at 10.00 a.m. in the school auditorium. The students willing to participate should see the undersigned by 25th October. The State Social Minister will inaugurate the function.

Pooja
Secretary

28. You are Vishal, Sports Secretary of ABC School, Banglore. Write a notice for the school notice-board informing the students that your school is playing a match against Birla. Senior Secondary School in the T.N.C.A. Cricket Finals. Invite them to come and watch the match to cheer the team.

ABC SCHOOL, BANGLORE SPORTS
NOTICE

20th August, 2007

Our school is playing a match against Birla Senior Secondary School in the T.N.C.A. Cricket Finals on 26th August in Anna Ground. There will be no teaching work in the school on that day. All the students are requested to reach the ground to raise the morale of the team.

Vishal
Sports Secretary

29. On the demand of the students of X and XII. The Principal of your school has arranged special coaching classes in Maths and English during the winter-break. He

invites Pushpa, Head girl to draft a notice for the information of all the students.

AUCKLAND HOUSE SCHOOL, PATNA
NOTICE
Students of X and XII-Attention

12th Dec., 2006

The Principal has kindly acceded to our demand for starting special coaching classes in English and Maths both during the winter break as per programme given below :

Timings	:	10.00 a.m. to 12.00 a.m.
Days	:	Monday to Saturday
Venue	:	Room No. 10 for class X
		Room No. 12 for class XII

Your attendance is compulsory. Absentees will be dealt with severely and their names will be struck off the school rolls. Please be attentive and make best use of your time.

Pushpa
Head girl

30. Your school has just completed 25 years of its meritorious services to society. The Students' Council of your school has decided to celebrate its Silver Jubilee. As President of the Council write a notice for the students of your school, informing them about the Council's decision and seeking their co-operation for the success of the proposed Silver Jubilee celebrations.

ST. JOHN PUBLIC SCHOOL, DELHI
NOTICE ***10th October, 2007***

The Students' Council of the school has decided to celebrate the Silver Jubilee of the school having completed 25 years of its meritorious services to society. The function will be organised in the school auditorium on 22 October, 2007. The active cooperation of all the students is solicited to make the function a success. The State Minister of Education will inaugurate the function at 10.00 a.m. sharp and unveil the exhibition organised in the memory of freedom fighters.

Pramesh
President
Students' Council

31. You are the Secretary of Yamuna Vihar Welfare Association. Write a notice to be circulated to all the residents of the colony informing them that there will be no water supply in your colony on 24th and 25th of August, 2005 due to maintenance work.

YAMUNA VIHAR WELFARE ASSOCIATION, DELHI

NOTICE ***23rd August, 2007***

It is hereby informed to all the residents of the colony that there will be no water supply on 24th and 25th of August as the maintenance work is in progress. The inconvenience caused to all is hereby regretted. All are requested to arrange accordingly.

Shrey Bhardwaj
Secretary

32. You are Amitabh, head boy of your school (Zenith Public School). Write a notice for your school-notice board calling for entries from desirous students for Britannia Quiz Contest—Preliminary round to be held at your school.

ZENITH PUBLIC SCHOOL, KANPUR

NOTICE ***5th August, 2007***

An Enthusiastic Britannia Quiz contest of preliminary round is being arranged in the School Hall on 13th August at 2.00

p.m. Desirous students who want to participate in the Quiz may enlist themselves with the undersigned latest by 10th August during the recess. It will help us in finalising the requisite arrangements.

Amitabh
Head Boy

33. Write a notice for the school Notice Board inviting volunteers for the One Day Blood Donation Camp to be organised in your school. You are B.K. Paul, Head Boy, A.P.J. Public School.

A.P.J. PUBLIC SCHOOL, NEW DELHI
BLOOD DONATION CAMP

10th May, 2007

It has been decided to organise a one day Blood Donation Camp in the school campus on 15th May, 2007. All are invited to volunteer themselves for this noble cause. Honourable Education Minister Delhi Government will inaugurate the function at 10.00 a.m. Please cooperate and give your names by 13th to the Secretary, Cultural Association.

B.K. Paul
Head Boy

34. You are Ramesh the Secretary of L.M. Residents' Welfare Society, Green Park Extension, New Delhi. Write a notice requesting the members of the society to attend a meeting of the society to discuss the problem of security of the members of your society.

RESIDENTS' WELFARE SOCIETY, GREEN PARK EXTN. NEW DELHI

NOTICE ***5th August, 2007***

It is hereby informed to all the members that an emergent meeting of the society will be held on 10th August at

4.00 p.m. sharp in the Community Hall of the society in order to discuss the problems pertaining to security, safety and protection of all the residents. Please be in time and offer your suggestions.

Ramesh
Secretary

35. You are the Head boy/Head girl of your school. Prepare a notice for your school notice-board asking the students to contribute to the Kargil Relief Fund.

A.B.C. PUBLIC SCHOOL, DELHI
NOTICE ***5th August, 2007***

Due to evil designs of the Pak Intruders, our area of Kargil has come under invasion. Our brave and courageous soldiers are showing undaunting courage to protect their motherland at the cost of their lives. In this hour of need, it is our duty to contribute towards them. So all the students are requested to contribute at least Rs. 10/- towards the Kargil Relief Fund so that the same can be sent to the Prime Minister immediately.

Manoj
Cultural Secretary

36. You are Akash. You have planned a 2-week course to be arranged to help the children in Yoga and medication to help the residents of your Group Housing Society at Delhi. Prepare a notice for the Society's Notice-Board, stating the objectives of the course, giving necessary details of the course and requesting the people of the society to join the course.

NIDHI GROUP HOUSING SOCIETY, DELHI
NOTICE ***5th August, 2007***

All the members of the society are hereby informed that a 2-week course in Yoga and Medication has been planned for the residents at the society's community centre in collaboration with Nature Cure Society, Meerut. It will commence on 10th August and last on 24th August in between 5.00 p.m. and 6.00 p.m. This will help you to make them free from tension, stress, blood pressure, migrane and such major or minor ailments. There will be no change in the training programme. Registration starts from today at 4.00 p.m. All are requested to make use of the programme. Your cooperation is highly solicited.

Akash
Secretary

37. Your school (Amar Vidyalaya) is organising a cultural evening to collect funds for the slum children. The Education Minister has consented to be the Chief Guest on the occasion. Draft a notice about it to be displayed on your school notice-board. Imagine you are the Cultural Secretary of your school.

AMAR VIDYALAYA, NEW DELHI
NOTICE

5th August, 2007

The Cultural Association of the school is organising a cultural evening in order to collect funds for the slum children. T.V. singers, film artists and dancers of fame will exhibit their feats on 15th March at 8.00 p.m. in the Ashoka Auditorium of the school. The entry will be by obtaining ticket worth Rs. 10/- and the same can be purchased from school office on all working days. The Education Minister has consented to be the Chief Guest on this occasion. Please cooperate, help and enjoy the evening.

Sunita
Cultural Secretary

38. Your school is holding a summer camp for training students in Hockey and Basketball. Write a notice for the

School Notice Board of Anand Prakash Vidyalaya, Delhi. You are the Sports Secretary of the school.

ANAND PRAKASH VIDYALAYA, DELHI
NOTICE

25th March, 2007

Our school is holding a summer camp for training students in Hockey and Basketball. The camp will be held from 10th May to 20th May at the college playground. The participants will undergo rigorous training and will be selected for the Hockey team and the Basketball team on the basis of their performance. Those who are interested in participation should give their names to the undersigned by 15th April, 2007.

Roshan
Sports Secretary

39. Write a notice for the school notice board for an N.S.S. Camp.

GOVT. GIRLS SR. SEC. SCHOOL, DELHI
NATIONAL SOCIAL SERVICE CAMP

11th May, 2007

Our school is organising a week's N.S.S. Camp at village Bakner to help the Panchayat in repairing of the roads, drains and streets. It will give due attention to the cleanliness of the village. The Camp will function on Sunday the 25th May; 2005. The Education Minister of Delhi Govt. will preside over the function at 10.00 a.m. sharp. Interested students should submit their written permission duly signed from their parents by 22nd May to facilitate the function properly.

Your cooperation will make the programme a grand success.

P.K. Sen
Commander, N.S.S. Camp.

CIRCULAR

40. You are Secrearty, Residents Welfare Society, Gulmohar Park, Delhi. Write a circular to be sent to the members of a meeting to discuss the problem of thefts in your colony. Sign yourself as Lovely.

RESIDENTS WELFARE SOCIETY, GULMOHAR PARK, DELHI CIRCULAR

15th Sept., 2007

It has come to the notice of the society that cases of thefts are on increase in the area. The robbers break into the houses late at night and loot at dagger's point. They do not hesitate to murder or insult the residents. It is high time to make collective efforts to save all of us from these undesirable happenings. Keeping in view, all the members are requested to attend to an emergent meeting to be held in the Community Hall of the colony on 17th Sept. at 4.30 p.m. Please come prepared with your valuable suggestions.

Lokesh
Secretary

APPEAL

41. Write an appeal, inviting suitabled Donors to offer one kidney of theirs to save the life of a youngman both of whose kidneys of are damaged beyond repairs.

AN APPEAL

14th Sept., 2007

A promising young man both of whose kidneys are damaged beyond repair in a train accident is counting his time in a hospital. Donors are invited to offer one of their kidneys. Their help can save the precious life of a person who has to support a family of ten members. Please contact immediately to the Medical Superintendent, E.S.I. Hospital Ring Road, New Delhi.

42. A notice on the Students Notice Board is to be prepared regarding an ensuing tree plantation ceremony to be held on 7th July, 2007 in the school premises inviting students to participate in it by contributing at least five plants from each class. Draft a notice.

..... SCHOOL, ... CITY
TREE PLANTATION CEREMONY
NOTICE

3rd July, 2007

A tree plantation ceremony will be held in the school premises on 7th July 2007. Students are invited to participate this ceremony with whole-hearted cooperation to make it a grand success. A minimum of five plants should be contributed by each class. We intend to give a green and clean environment to the school.

Dinesh
Cultural Secretary

43. Write a notice for the school notice board informing students about school inspection to be held on 15 April 2007 by the District Education Officer. The notice should be of 50 words asking for punctuality, cleanliness and discipline.

ABC PUBLIC SCHOOL, DELHI
INSPECTION NOTICE

22 April, 2007

School inspection will be held on 15 April 2005 by the District Education Officer. Students are requested to maintain punctuality and proper discipline. Cleanliness must be observed strictly not to allow the spoiling of the fair reputation of the school. All must come up to the expectations of our school.

Seema
Head Girl

44. The school has decided to hold a fete in the school playground. The Principal has asked you to write, as the Headboy of the school, a notice about this fete, inviting the students and the teachers to participate in it. The notice should include all necessary details.

ABC PUBLIC SCHOOL, DELHI
A GRAND FETE

25 April, 2007

School is organising a Fete in the school campus on 2 May 3 May, 2005. Students and teachers are requested to give their names for booking various stalls by 28 April, 2007. Whole-Hearted Cooperation from all of them is expected to make the fete a grand and memorable success. The undersigned will be pleased to give all kinds of information concerning the Fete.

Amit
Head Boy

45. Shyam of Class X-A lost his Hall Ticket for the Board Examination in the school playground. He puts up a notice on the School Notice Board. Draft that notice and write it in your answer sheet.

ABC PUBLIC SCHOOL, DELHI
NOTICE

25 March, 2007

I lost my Hall Ticket for the Board Examination in the school playground near the P.T. Room. It has may photograph along with my Roll No. 1520360. Anybody who finds it, is requested to give it to me in my class X A or to the Administrative Officer. The person finding it and handing it over to me will be handsomely rewarded.

Shyam
Class X A

46. You are the Secretary of the Literary Association of your school. Write a notice for the School Notice Board informing students about the English debate on "Men are more Intelligent than Women" to be held on 10-3-2007 in the school hall.

XYZ PUBLIC SCHOOL, DELHI
LITERARY ASSOCIATION
NOTICE

1st March, 2007

Students are invited to give in their names for an audition to be held to select students for English debate, that will be held on 10 March, 2007 in the School Auditorium. The topic for the debate is "Men are more Intelligent than Women". The names of the willing participants may be given to Anil Rohilla by 1 March, 2007 during the Recess in the Literary Association Room.

Secretary
Literary Association

ACTIVITY

1. Write out a notice for a play your school is putting up, as a ticketed public show.
2. You are the Secretary of your school Volley-ball Club. Write out a notice inviting names of those who would like to participate in the proposed Volley-ball Tournament.

3. You are the Students Union Advisor of a college. Write out an election notice, inviting nominations for the posts of President, Secretary and Treasurer of the Students' Union.

4. The Science Forum of your School is holding an exhibition of various electronic or electrical gadgets. Write a notice inviting interested students to participate in the said exhibition with all the necessary details. You are Manoj/Mimansha, the Secretary of the Science Forum of your school.

5. Your School is arranging for a Show of a popular film to collect money in aid of Earthquake victims of the sea in Port Blair. Write a suitable notice in about 50 words for the School Notice-Board informing the students about this show and asking them to make it a grand success. You are Arun/Priyanka, Cultural Secretary of the School.

6. Write an appeal inviting suitable donors to offer one kidney of theirs to save the life of a young man, both of whose kidneys are damaged beyond repair.

7. You are the Editor of your school magazine. Write out a notice for your school notice-board inviting contributions for the magazine.

8. You are the Secretary of the Residents Welfare Association of your locality. Write a notice to be sent to the members of the Association to discuss the problems like bad street lights, insanitation, theft etc. Sign yourself as Meenu.

9. Your School is holding a Magic Show of a popular magician in aid of the blind. Write a notice for the School Notice-Board informing the students of this Show and asking them to make it a success. Add all the necessary details. Sign yourself as Ajit.

10. Write a notice to be circulated among all the students of your school inviting the names of those who would like to go on an excursion to South India. Invent all the necessary details.

11. You are Rohit/Rashi. As the Secretary of the Cultural Club of your school, you have organised a Cultural Evening as a thanks-giving programme on the last day of your school. Write a notice for your school notice-board, giving necessary information about this event (the programme) in not more than 50 words.

12. Write a notice for your school notice-board regarding your calculator which was lost in your school.

13. Write out a notice for your school notice-board inviting students to give their names for a Fancy Dress Competition.

14. You are President of the Cultural Society of your school. You are planning to organize a cultural programme. Write a notice for the school notice-board inviting names of students willing to participate (Sign yourself as Amar Singh of ABC School, Mumbai)

15. You are the Sports Secretary of your school. Write a notice in 50 words for the school notice-board asking the students interested in Hockey to give their names for selection for our School Hockey Team (Eligibility - Class VI to VIII Students)

16. You are Rahul/Rashmi. As President of the Literary Club of your school, you have organized an inter-school debate competition on the occasion of the Silver Jubilee celebrations of your school. Write a notice in about 50 words, informing the students of your school about the competition.

17. You are Ravi/Reena. As President of the Cultural Forum of your school you have organized an inter-school orchestra competition on the occasion of the Silver Jubilee celebrations of your school. Write a notice in about 50 words, informing the students of your school about this competition.

18. You are Secretary, Residents Welfare Society, Gulmohar Park, Delhi. Write a circular to be sent to the members for a meeting to discuss the problem of thefts in your colony. Sign yourself as Lokesh.

19. You are Sanjay/Sangeeta. As a President of the Excursion Club you have organized an excursion to Kathmandu (Nepal) during the summer vacation for the senior students of your school. Write a notice in about 50 words, informing the students about the proposed excursion.

20. Write a notice for the school notice-board inviting contributions for the earthquake victims. Sign yourself as Secretary, Students Union, ABC School, Dehradun.

21. You are the Director, Physical Education of your school. Your school is playing against CPM School, Meerut, in the Zonal Volley-Ball Finals. Write a notice in about 50 words for your School Notice-Board inviting your school students to come and watch the tournament and cheer the team.

22. You are Secretary of ABC, Navkranti Colony Welfare Association. Write a notice to be circulated to all the residents of the colony informing them that there will be no water supply in your colony on 24th and 25th of August, 1999 due to maintenance work.

23. In response to an appeal of the P.M. of India, you are arranging a Musical Evening in your school to raise

funds for earthquake victims. Write out a notice to be put up on the school notice-board giving details about the programme like the names of artists, rates of the tickets etc. Also seek their cooperation to make the programme a success. You are Secretary of the 'Brother-hood' Club of your School (about 50-60 words).

24. Write a notice for your school notice-board in 50 words inviting articles for your school magazine. You are Ramesh, Student Editor of your school magazine.

25. You are Avinash Rao, Cultural Secretary of Golden Academy, Indore. Write a notice for the school notice-board informing the students that the Inter School Declamation Contest to be held in your school has been postponed for a week. Give details of the new programme.

26. You are the Secretary of your School Library Association. Write a notice for your School Notice Board, giving details of the inauguration of the Literary Association activities. You are ABC of Queen Victoria Senior Secondary School, Nagpur. (Word Limited: 50)

27. As the Head Boy/Head Girl of your school, you are organizing a Career Counselling Session for XI & XII standard students of your school. Write a notice giving details of it to be displayed on your school notice-board (Word Limit: 50)

28. You are Seema/Navin, the Cultural Secretary of Ramjas Public School, Jhansi. Write a suitable notice for your school Notice-Board requesting the students to contribute towards the Earthquake victims due to Tsunami waves in the sea. (World Limit 50)

29. You are Narain/Namrata, the Cultural Secretary in Kings Senior Secondary School, Nainital. Write a notice suitable

for your school Notice-Board giving the details for participation of students in a cultural programme to be organized by your school.

30. You are Kumar, Sports Secretary of ABC School, Chennai. Write a notice for the school notice-board, informing the students that your school is playing a match against M.A.K. Senior Secondary School in the T.N.C.A. Cricket Finals. Invite them to come and watch the match to, cheer the team. (Word Limit: 50)

❐

3

Resolutions and Minutes

A resolution is nothing but the decision of a meeting. While issuing the invitation or notices of the meeting an Agenda or a list of items, to be transacted during a meeting is prepared by the Company Secretary or other officer in consultation with the Chairman or Board. The agenda includes either captions or concrete proposals. If only captions or titles are given in the agenda proposals, will be put before the meeting in writing. Then on the proposal discussion will begin. Some might try to amend the original or try to include or exclude some part(s) of the original proposal or motion. There will be exchange of views on the amendments, alterations and if they are carried on then are included or executed in the original text of the proposal or motion. When the discussion on the proposal is sufficient, then there will be ascertainment of the sense of the meeting. If it is passed it is, then, known as the decision of the meeting-Resolution-on the concern item of business.

While drafting the proposals the Secretary, must be very careful about the informatiom to be included therein and its language. There should be less amendments or alterations suggested by the persons attending a meeting. The proposals should affirmative and generally not negative in sense and wording; clear and exact and not ambiguous or complicated; and containing only one item or subject and not a mixture of different subjects into one Proposals begin with "That...." and when they at carried on " RESOLVED" word is added to the text before the word "That".

Generally resolutions are of two types—*(1)* Ordinary for which bare majority is necesary, and *(2)* Special for which, on the other hand, three-fourth majority is necessary. Due notice, explanatory statements or documents etc. Are the common conditions which must be practised properly, as per provisions of Companies Act, 1956. There is another group called as Resolutions which require 'Special Notice.' There is no deviation in respect of the points stated earlier for their preparation; only they differ in one respect and, *i.e.*, the period of notice. Some resolutions necessitate their publication in the press; and/or filing with the Registrar. The Secretary should consider the concerning provisions of the Companies Act, 1956. Some alterations in certain documents, communication of information to members or parties; might be the next duties expected from Secretary or Officer of the Company. While preparing draft resolutions even small matters should be observed. While doing this, you should keep brevity and clarity in mind, as "the minutes of the last Board meeting held on 24th December 1955." In the case of a meeting of the directors of a company where shares are allotted, the minutes should state the description of such shares, as "Ordinary or Equity Shares Nos. 25000 to 40,000 (inclusive)", "Cumulative Preference Shares Nos. 30,000 to 45,000 (inclusive)".

In the same way, sums of money, dates of letters deeds or other documents, rates of interest, statements of measurements, qualities etc. should be inserted in the minutes.

While keeping the points in mind, he should try to form a resolution in which, only appropriate or proper facts are inserted. Sometimes Secretary will begin the minutes in this form "The Chairman reported that prospectus had been issued and advertisement had been made, as he had been directed and that all the shares offered for subscription, had been applied for as per the list that was made for allotment." In this resolution, some words are unnecessary, such words should be dropped, and it could be written as "The Chairman reported that prospectus had been issued and advertised as directed, and all the shares offered for subscription had been applied for as per allottment lists produced."

We can take an another example in which lengthy sentences can be put aside. Sometimes you will write as, "Then all the directors came to an agreement that 10,000 5%. Cumulative Preference Shares of Rs. 10/- each from Nos. 1 to 10,000 inclusive, and 20,000 Ordinary Shares of Rs. 10/- each Nos. 1 to 20,000, the last 20,000 is inclusive. These will be allotted to the applicants in mannar set forth by all, in the allotment list and it was initiated by the Chairman." The better way is that it can be simplified so as to say everything that is necessary by employing the following as:—

"Resolved that 10,000 5% Cumulative Preference Shares of Rs. 10/- each Nos. 1 to 10,000 inclusive, and 20,000 Ordinary Shares of Rs. 10/- each Nos. 1 to 20,000 inclusive, be allotted to the applicants in manner set forth in the allotment lists initiated by the Chairman."

Minutes mean a record of the decisions of meeting. During any meeting some persons speak in favour of a proposal, some try to oppose it with reasons; or some try to suggest, some modification, alteration, deletion or addition. If all these are taken into account and narrated, it will be known as proceedings. Therefore under proceedings summary of the flow of discussion is accounted. In minutes, on, the other hand, such account is not necessary. After discussion on a particular proposal or motion finally majority of the members will agree, and it will then be known as the decision of the members on the proposal of motion. The decision on a proposal is always in the form of resolutions If such decisions or resolutions are narrated or collected or arranged in writing systematically, they are known as minutes.

The minutes of a meeting are recorded in Minute-Book maintained by the Secretary of every Company. The decisions taken during a meeting are reduced in writing. It will be for permanent record and such record can be used as a proof at any time. A person is generally unable to remember what was decided during a meeting held a few years ago, or even a few months ago; and if proper record of the decisions in writing is maintained, then there will be lesser chances of omission or forgetting in respect of decisions already taken. Hence preparation of minutes and maintenance of them, as a permanant record is most important from point of view of every Company.

While preparing the minutes the following four points should be considered properly by the Secretary:

1. Type of the meeting—Heading—The nature, date, place and time of the meeting should be narrated at the beginning.

2. The persons present—The persons who attended a meeting, their names generally are mentioned. In respect of the Board or Managing Committee meeting, the names are included but in respect of General meeting to include a lengthy list of present members will be a trouhlesome job. Therefore, the names of office-bearers are included and then a note is given about the total number of persons present; or a list of present members along with their signatures is annexed to the concerning minutes, and the total is mentioned in the text of the minutes. To annex the list of present persons is much more commended method.

   In addition to the office-bears and/or members, some other persons or parties attend a meeting. Their details also should be included in it *i.e.* the Secretary, Auditor, Solicitor, General Manager. Chief Engineer, Accountant, etc.

3. Business transacted—The decisions or resolutions carried on generally are included serially. Some use to mention

only the text of resolution, but others use to give brief narration wherein the text of resolution is included. Resolutions are sometimes carried on unanimously or by majority, Accordingly, a note is included by some Secretaries. In addition, some try to mention the total number of votes casted in favour of and against a resolution, but others do not. The proposals which are lost, are generally, not included in the minutes. But if some press or insist on its inclusion in the minutes, accordingly a note should he made. To mention the names of proposer and seconder is not a rule, but considering the value and importance as a permanent record of minutes to include these names is advisable. In respect of the Board or Committee records, on the other hand, the names of those, who opposed a resolution are to be mentioned.

The motions or proposals generally in the form of draft resolutions which are, generally circulated along with the notice of the meeting; hence there is no necessity of framing the resolutions while discussion on motion is going on. Only minor alterations or modifications will be there, provided these are carried during a meeting.

4. Date, place and signature—The Chairman and the Secretary both take their separate notes while discussion is going on. When the meeting is over the Secretary should tally his own notes with those of the Chairman and should finalise the minutes in consultation with the Chairman. While including them in the Minute—Book some Secretaries; try to sign and date the minutes, though not necessary.

The minutes of the Board meeting are read during the next Board meeting and are confirmed, *i.e.*, if nobody objects, then the Chairman will sign and put the date. If necêssary corrections are made with initials by the

Chairman, provided some suggest accordingly and genuinely. In resfpect of recording the minutes of the meetings of members there are two methods in practice. Under the first method, after the finalisation of the; minutes they are confirmed by the person who was in Chair during the meeting. On the other hand, under the second method, the minutes are confirmed during the next Board meeting. The method, to confirm the minutes of a members, meeting during the subsequent meeting of members is not satisfactory, though it is used in Co-operative Society meetings.

There are various methods or styles of writing minutes though no fixed form is prescribed, for example: Columner register, serial numbering or separate numbering, allotting heading to each item or not, etc. Whatever might be the method selected or used but it must be used forever. To keep and maintain Minute-Book is compulsory. To maintain separate Minute-Books for the Board meetings and meetings of shareholders is necessary.

SPECIMEN RESOLUTION

1. To Appoint a Company Secretary

"Resolved that Shri Ramji Sohrab Metha of Poona be and is hereby, appointed Secretary of the Company in terms of the draft agreement which is hereby approved and that the said agreement will receive the Seal of Company in the presence of the Directors: *(1)* Shri Ramesh Chandra Shah and *(2)* Shri B. C. Kothari who will sign the same on behalf of the Company."

2. To Amend the Articles

"Resolved that Articles of the Company be and is hereby altered by deleting Article 71 therefore and by substituting, in the place of the said Article, the following Article:

"71. The numbers of Directors shall not be less than five and more than twelve."

3. To Change the Name of the Company

" Resolved that the name of the Company be and is hereby changed from" The Western Steel Safe Company Ltd." to "The Western Steel Furniture Manufacturers Ltd." and that the Secretary be and he is hereby authorised to communicate the change to the Central Government to have of their consent to the alteration and that on receipt to such consent, the Secretary should take necessary steps to bring out changes in Seal, letter-heads, name, etc."

4. To Issue Shares at Discount

"RESOLVD that the Board of the Company be and is hereby authorised to issue 10,000 equity shares at a discount provided however the maximum rate of discount shall be 4% consistent with Section 79 of the Companies Act, 1956."

5. To Issue Further Shares (At Premium)

"Resolved that 20,000 equity shares of Rs.100/- each be and hereby are issued and offered for subscription on following terms and conditions:

(a) 15,000 equity shares shall be offered for subscription at a premium of Rs. 5/- each to the existing shareholders on the Register of Members of the Company on 30th June, 1968, and the balance of 5,000 equity shares be disposed of by the Board at a premium of Rs. 5/- each in such manner as they think most beneficial to the Company within M/A and A/A of the Company."

6. To Appoint a Director (Who Retires by Rotation)

"RESOLVED that Shri R. K. Shah who retires by rotation under Article 89 of the Company's Articles of Association, but who being eligible offers himself for reappointment, be and is hereby elected and reappointed a Director of the Company."

7. To Elect the Chairman

"RESOLVED that Shri S. D. Hazare, a Director of the Company, be and is hereby appoined as the Chairman of the Board of Directors and of the Company."

8. To Appoint a Managing Director and to Fix his Remuneration

"RESOLVED that subject to the approval the Central Govt. being obtaianed, Shri V.T. Patil be and is hereby appointed Managing Director of the Company for a period of 5 years commecinng from 1st April 1966 on the remuneration of Rs. 2500/ per month or commission at the rate of 5% of the net profits of the Company determined as provided for in Sec. 349 of the Companies Act, 1956. whichever is higher and on other terms and conditions contained in the draft agreement produced at this meeting and initialled by the Chairman for identification which draft agreement is here by approved."

9. To Shift the Registered Office

"RESOLVED that the Registered office of the Company be shifted from 21, Somaya Road, Kolhapur, in Maharashtra State, to 3712. Mahatma Gandhi Road, Shukrawar Peth, Kolhaur, in the same State with effect from 15th August 1964."

10. To Appoint Managing Agents

"RESOLVED that M/S Vijay and Bros. Pvt. Ltd., be and are hereby apointed Managing Agents of the Company under Sec. 326 of the Companies Act, 1956, with effect from the 1st Jan. 1962 under the terms and conditions mentioned in the agreement attached hereto and entered into with the Managing Agents, and as approved by the Central Government."

11. To Appoint Committee

"RESOLVED that a Committee under the Chairmanship of Shri A B. Chattarjee. Chairman of the Company, and Shri D. E. Fuley and Shri G. H. Ingawale. both Directors of the Company as its members, be and is hereby apointed to investigate the markets in Southern India for the products of our Company and to suggest means and methods for increasing sales in that area, and that Committee should submit its report within four months from this date."

12. To Issue the Prospectus

"RESOLVED that a Prospectus, the draft of which is approved at this meeting, be and is hereby issued offering 2,00,000 (two lakh) Equity Shares of Rs. 100/- each at par for subscription; and that the draft be signed by the Directors now present; and that the signed Copy be forthwith filed with the Registrar, and the Secretary be instructed to get printed ten thousand copies there of; and

That immediately thereafter the Prospectus be issued and also be advertised twice in large-circulated four dailies.

13. To Issue Debentures

"RESOLVED that 1,00,000 (one lakh) 9% Debentures of Rs. 500/- each. constituting a charge on the fixed assets of the Company, be and are hereby offered to the public for subscription at par, and be redeemable at par at the opinion of the Board but not before 1st April 1990 and not later than 31st March, 1991.

14. To Allot the Shares

"RESOLUED that 2,00,000 Equity Shares of Rs. 100/- each be and are hereby allotted to the persons whose names, descriptions, addresses, etc. are set forth in the 'Allotment Sheets' now produced before the Board and initialled by the Chairman, and that the Secretary be and is hereby instructed to prepare and issue the letters of regret with refund of application money to the applicants whose applications are rejected."

15. To Increase the Capital/To Effect Change in the Memorandum

"RESOLVED that the Authorised Capital of the Company be and is hereby increased from Rs. 20 lakhs to Rs. 50/- lakhs divided into 5 lakh Equity Shares of Rs. 10/- each Instead of 2 lakh Equity Shares of Rs. 10/- each and that accordingly the Authrised Capital clause in the Memorandum be altered, and that the Secretary be instructed to file an altered copy of the Memorandum of this Company with the Registrar, and to effect necessary alteration in the Copies of the Memorandum of this Company."

16. To Make a Call

"RESOLVED that a Call (First Call) of Rs 20/- per Equity Share be and is hereby made upon the Equity Shareholders of this Company, and that the same may be payable on or before 31st March 1962. at the office of the bankers of this Company, and that all calls unpaid by that date to bear interest at 9% from the due date until payment; and that Secretary be instructed to prepare and communicate can to Shareholders of the Company."

17. To Transfer the Shares

"RESOLVED that the Applications for Transfer Nos. 831 to 1011 as appearing in the Transfer Register, representing a total of 12,575 of Equity Shares be and are hereby approved and that the Secretary be instructed to record, and endorse the Certificates accordingly."

18. To Forfeit the Shares

"RESOLVED that 45 Equity Shares in the Company numbering 101 to 145 both inclusive, registered in the name of Shri X Y Azad of Poona, be and the same are here by forfeited for non-payment of the First call of Rs. 50/- per share, and that Shri X Y Azad be informed accordingly."

19. To Close the Transfer Book

"RESOLVED that the Transfer Books of the Company be closed from 13th march, 1965, to 27th March, 1965, both days inclusive, and that the Secretary be and is hereby Instructed to issue public notice accordingly."

20. To Appoint Auditors

"RESOLVED that M/S Roopchand and Company, Chartered Accountants of Kolbapur, be and they are hereby appointed the (first) Auditors of this Company at a remuneration of Rs. 7,500/- and that the Secretary be asked to inform them accordingly and to have their consent in writing."

21. To Remove the Director

"RESOLVED that Shri X Y Z a Director of this Company be and is hereby removed from his office from the Board under the provision of Article 98 (gross negligence) of the Articles of the Company, and that the Secretary be and is hereby instructed to communicate the same to X. Y. Z.

RESOLVED that Shri A. B. Chand, duly proposed and seconded by Shri C.S. Mantri and Shri S. K. Bharati respectively, be and is hereby appointed a Director, in place of Shri Zha, of this Company."

22. Agreement to Purchase Property

"RESOLVED that the draft agreement with Shri S. H. Marathe of Satara, for the purchase of the land and buildings thereon comprising the plot Nos. 19, 20, 21 and 22 Ogalewadi Road, Karad, be and is hereby approved, and that Shri L. K. Azad, Chairman of the Company, and Shri B. K. Raut, Director of Company, be and are hereby authorised to seal and sign on behalf of the Company."

23. To Recommend the Dividend

"RESOLVED that a dividend of Rs. 9.25 per Equity Share less tax and of Rs. 7.50 per Preference share be recommended to be paid to the Share-holders whose names appear on the Company's Register on 17th March, 1966."

24. To Permit the Directors to Borrow

"RESOLVED that the Board of Directors be and hereby authorised to borrow moneys from time to time for carrying on the business of this Company notwithstaning that the money to be borrowed, excluding temporary loans will exceed the aggregate of the paid up capital of the Company and in free reserves, provided the total outstanding amount at any time on account of principa,l shall not exceed Rs. 65 lakhs (Rs. Sixty five lakhs)."

25. To Increase the Remuneration of a Wholetime Director

"RESOLVED that subject to the approval of the Central Government, the basic salary payable to Shri V. K. Vinod, a wholetime Director of this Company be increased from Rs. 2,000/- p.m. to Rs. 2,500/- p.m. with effect from 1st June 1966."

26. To have Loan from the Bank

"RESOLVED that application be made to The Central Bank of India Ltd., Banker of this Company, for a temporary loan of Rs. 2,50,000/- for financing the working expenses of the Company."

27. To Open a Bank Account

"RESOLVED that banking account be opened in the name of the Company with The Central Bank of India Limited. Bombay, and that all cheques or other orders upon the said account be signed on behalf of the Company by one Director and the Secretary of the Company; and that all negotiable instruments be accepted, drawn, made and endorsed for and on behalf of the Company by one Director and the Secretary of the Company."

28. To Adopt the Seal

"RESOLVED that the Common Seal, a Specimen impression of which is affixed to these minutes, be and is hereby adopted as the Common Seal of the Company; and that the Common Seal of the Company be with the Chairman of the Company."

29. To Consolldate the Capital

"RESOLVED that the shares in the capital of the company be consolidated in such a manner that every ten, the existing

Equity Shares shall constitute one Rs. 100/- share, upon which the sum of Rs. 50/- shall be credited as having been paid up; and that the existing Equity Share certificates be called in and cancelled, and that new share certificates be issued in place thereof."

30. To Adopt the Directors Report

"RESOLVED that the Directors' Report, submitted to the members, be approved and is hereby adopted."

31. To Adopt the Auditor's Report

"RESOLVED that the Reports and Accounts, as audited and certified by the Auditors of the company, now before the meeting, showing the position of the affairs or the Company as on 31st Dec. 1965, be approved and are hereby adopted."

32. To Wind up the Affairs

"RESOLVED that the Company be wound up voluntarily, and that Shri B. S. Bajaj, retired Director of this Company, of 15 C M. Gandhi Road. Fort Bombay-1, be and is hereby appointed liquidator."

SPECIMEN—MINUTES

(1) Minutes of First Board Meeting

Minutes of the First Board meeting held at the Registered Office of the Company on Tuesday the 4th January 2006 at 11-30 a.m.

Present: Shri. A. B. Madan, in the Chair.
Shri. C. C. Narang
Shri. E. F. Oswal
Shri. G. H. Patil
Smt. I. J. Rasal
Shri. K. L. Sheth.
} Directots.

In attendance: Shri. R. K. Yadav, Secretary,
Shri. R. D. Pant, Solicitor.

(a) **Chairman.** Shri A. B. Madan was voted to be the Chairman of the meeting. Shri E. F. Oswal proposed the name of Shri A. B. Madan and Shrimati I. J. Rasal duly seconded the motion which was unanimously carried.

(b) **Certificates of Incorporation and Appointment of Directors.** Shri R. D. Pant, the Solicitor of the Company, produced before the meeting the Certificate of Incorporation No. 6927/65 dated 4th Nov., 2005, and a copy each of the Memorandum Association and Articles of Association as filed with the Registrar. The Secretary reported that all Directors present (named in the M/S and A/A as the Directors of the Co.) has signed the acceptance of office.

(c) **Election of Chairman of the Board of the Company.** Shri. C. D. Narang proposed the name of Shri A. B. Madan and Shri G. H. Patil duly supported the motion, and unanimously Shri. A. B. Madan was elected the Chairman of the Board of the Company.

(d) **Appointment of Managing Director.** Upon a motion of Shri K. L. Sheth, duly seconded by Shri E. F. Oswal, it was unanimously Resolved that Shri C. D. Narang a Director of the Company, be and is hereby appoined as the Managing Director for the term of five years from the date of incorporation at monthly remueration of Rs. 5,000/- plus other allowances admissible to other senior officers of the Company.

(e) **Quorum of Board Meeting.** In pursuant to the Article 36 of the Articles of Association of the Company it was Resolved that the quorum for the meetings of the Board shall be three directors present in person.

(f) **Appointment of Bankers.** It was unanimously Resolved that the current account in the name of the

Company be opened with the Bank of India Ltd., Laxmi Road, Poona Branch, and the said Bank be and is hereby authorised to debit the Company's account with all cheques and order drawn upon such account when signed for and behalf of the Company by the Managing Director and anyone of the other directors, that any negotiable instruments can be drawn, accepted or endorsed on behalf of the Company. The Secretary was instructed to deliver to the Bank a sealed copy of the resolution, signed by the Chairman and a copy each of the Memorandum and Articles of the Company and to submit them along with application form duly filled in and specimen signatures of all the Directors.

(g) **Appointment of Company Secretery.** It was Resolved unanimously that Shri R.D. Yadav be and is hereby appointed as Secretary of the Company for a term of five years from the date of incorporation at a monthly salary of Rs. 1,000/- plus other allowances agreed between the Company and the Secretary the copy of which is initialled by the Chairman and attached herewith, and subject to the terms and conditions stated therein."

(h) **Appointment of Auditors.** It was Resolved unanimously that M/S Chandrashekhar and Co., Chartered Accountants Laxmi Road, Poona, be and they are hereby appointed as the Auditors of the Company until the first Annual General Meeting of the Company & that their remuneration be fixed at Rs. 2,500/-; and the Secretary be and is hereby instructed to communicate the appoitment to the Auditors and to receive their acceptance in writing.

(i) **Appointment of Solicitors.** It was unanimously Resolved that Shri R. D. Pant of Laxmi Road, Poona be and is hereby appointed as the Solicitor of the Company.

(j) **Adoption of Seal.** The common seal of the Company was produced before the meeting and it was unanimously Resolved that the seal, an impression of which is given hereto, and is hereby adopted as the common seal of the Company; and that the Seal be kept in custody of Shri K.H. Narang, the Managing Director of the Company.

(k) **Issue of Prospectus.** Shri R. D. Pant, Solicitor of the Company, produced the draft of the proposed prospectus, and it was Resolved that the draft Prospectus as produced and initialled by the Chairman for identification be and is hereby approved and that it should be dated and signed by all the Directors present at this meeting; and further Resolved that it be printed forthwith, filed with the Registrar, issued to the public and advertised twice in four dailies; and that the arrangements as to the printing, filing, issuing and advertising, be looked after by the Managing Director, Secretary and Solicitor under the supervision of the Chairman of the Company.

(l) **Confirmation of the Prelimimary Contracts.** The Solicitor, Shri R. D. Pant. produced and read the deed of contract between M/s Jadhav Rajaram Desai and Brothers on the one part and the Company on the other part for the sale of the business including land, buildings and fixtures thereon of the said M/s Jadhav Rajaram Desai and Bros. to the Company; and it was unanimously Resolved that the said agreement, intialled by the Chairman for its identification, be and the same is hereby adopted and approved on behalf of the Company, and that the Seal of the Company be affixed thereto; and further Resolved that 5,500 Equity Shares of Rs 100/- each be allotted as fully paid to the Vendor in part payment of the purchase money for the business and property on completion of the purchase.

(m) **Next Meeting.** It was unanimously Resolved that the next Board Meeting be summoned on Monday 7th Feb., 2006 at 5.00 p.m.

There being no other business, the meeting terminated.

....

Chairman.

Dt.

(2) Another Example of the Minutes of a Board Meeting

Minutes of the Board Meeting held at the Registered Office of the Company on Saturday the 1st Jan., 2006 at 11.30 a. m.

Present: Shri. K. I. Gopal, in the Chair.

Shri. G. E. Chaware
Shri. A. L. Jadhav
Shri. H. E. Doshi
Shri. B. M. Sadashiv
Shri. O. P. Vasudev
Shri. M. Vithal
} Directors

In attendance: Shri Y. K. Rasal, Secretary.

(a) **Confirmation of the Minutes.** The minutes of the last meeting of the Board, held on 4th Dec. 1965, were read, approved, an signed.

(b) **Approval to Payments.** List of accounts due for payment were submitted, amounting to Rs. 60,020=07 np. These were approved and cheques were ordered to be signed.

(c) **Transfer of Shares.** Transfer Deeds No. 327 to 383 inclusive as appearing in the Transfer Register were submitted, together with necessary Share Certificates. The deeds were approved and passed, and the Secretary of the Company instructed to communicate the concerned parties accordingly.

(d) **Debtors of the Company.** The Secretary produced and read the list of debtors whose accounts were in arrear for more than six months. The Secretary was instructed to apply them for immediate payment and to report again during the next Board meeting.

(e) **Issue of Duplicate Certificates.** Applications Nos. 71 to 83 inclusive for the issue of certificates, as per details attached herewith and initialled by the Chairman, were approved and passed. The Secretary was asked to prepare the duplicate Certificates and Seal them and after receiving signatures of two Directors, to countersign and issue them to the concerned parties.

(f) **Next Meeting.** The next Board meeting was fixed for 5th Feb., 2006, at 11.30 a.m. at the Registered office of the Company.

....

Chairman.

Dt.

(3) Minutes or the Statutory Meeting

Minutes of the Statutory Meeting held on Tuesday the 4th Jan., 2006 at 2.30 p.m. at the Registered Office of the Company.

Present: Shri. S. D. Yadav, in the Chair.
Shri. B. K. Jadhav, Shri S. A. Natu, Shri B. O. Thakur, Shrimati P. K. Jaju, and Shrimati S. A. Desai, all Directors were present.

In attendance: Shri. D. K. Apparao, Secretary.
Shri. H. T. Mane, Auditor.
Shri. S. S. Sanas, Solicitor.

And other 120 members, a list of whom is appended were present.

(a) **Notice.** The Secretary read the notice convening the meeting.

(b) **List of Members.** The Chairman drew the attention of the members to the fact that the list of members of the Company is open for members inspection.

(c) **Chairman's Address.** The Chairman explained to the members, at length, the satisfactory position of the Company and outlined the immediate future plans and prospects of the Company.

(d) **Statutory Report.** The Chairman invited discussion upon the Statutory Report which was taken as read. Upon a motion from the Chair and duly seconded by Shri B. O. Thakur, a Director, it was unanimously Resolved that the Statutory Report, as circulate, be and is hereby approved and adopted.

(e) **Vote of Thanks.** A vote of thanks was accorded to the Chairman, who suitably replied and requested the members to take a round of the factory after the closure of the meeting and, then, the meeting was terminated.

....

Chairman.

Dt.

(4) Minutes of the Annual General Meeting of a Company

Minutes of the Tenth Annual General Meeting held on Friday the 16th September 2006, at 2-30 p.m. at Registered Office of the Company.

Present: Shri. B. D. Desai, in the Chair.
Shri P. D. Sawant, Shri R.D. Sohoni, Shri B. S. Jamadar, Shri D. P. Jain, Shri G. Y. Bhosale and Shri D. A. Deshmukh, all Directors, were present.

In attendance: Shri. S. K. Bhargave, Secretary, and Shri. S. D. Nagarkar, Auditor and full quorum of the members.

(a) **Notice.** The Secretary read the notice convening the meeting.

(b) Directors' Report and Audied Accounts. etc.: The Directors' Report and Accounts were taken as read, The Auditor read. his Report. Chairman invited the members to discuss over them.

(c) It was unanimously resolved that the Reports of Directors and Auditors and the Profit and Loss Account for the year ended 30th June, 2006, and the Balance Sheet as on that date be and they are hereby approved and adopted.

(d) As recommended by the Board, Shri D. S. Patil a Shareholder proposed and Shri K. L. Rao duly seconded and it was unanimously resolved that Dividends recommended to be paid by the Directors in their Annual Report, *viz.* 9% on the Preference Shares and 22% on the Equity Shares for the year ended on 30th June, 2006, be and is hereby approved and declared, payable forthwith to all members whose names appear on the Register of Members as on 16th sept 2006.

(e) Resolved that Shri R. D. Sohoni, the Director retiring by rotation but eligible for re-election be and is hereby re-elected as Director of the Company.

(f) Resolved that Shri B. S. Jamadar, the Director retiring by rotation but eligible for re-election be and is hereby re-elected as Director of the Company.

(g) Shri C. Y. Bhosale proposed and Shri D. P. Jain duly seconded and unanimously, it was Resolved that M/S. S. D. Nagarkar & Co., Chartered Accountants, Auditors of the Company having to continue in the office, be and they are hereby re-appointed as the Auditors of the Company till the next Annual General Meeting, and their remuneration be Rs. 7,500/-.

(h) A vote of thanks was accorded to the Chairman and the Board. The Chairman suitably replied and declared the meeting closed.

....

Chairman.

Dt.

(5) Minutes of Extra Ordinary General Meeting of Company

Minutes of the Extraordinary General Meeting of the Company held at the Registered Office of the Company on Thursday the 6th Jan., 2006 at 3-30 p.m.

Present: Shri. M. B. Azad, in the Chair.

Shri. N. D. Chaugule
Shri. O. E. Fulay
Shri. P. H. Gawande
Shri. S. L. Kedar
Shri. R. J. Ingle
Shri. V. M. Morbale.
} Directors.

In attendance: Shri. Y. K. Raghav, Secretary together with the required quorum of shareholders.

(a) The Secretary read the notice convening the meeting.

(b) "RESOLVED that the Directors be and they are hereby empowered to borrow from time to time money upto a limit of Rs. 2 crores (apart from temporary loans borrowed), remaining outstanding on account of principal at anytime for the purposes of the Company, notwithstanding, that the money to be borrowed together with the money already borrowed by the Company, will exceed the aggregate of the paid-up Capital and free reserves of the Company."

(c) A vote of thanks to be the Chairman was proposed and then the Chairman terminated the meeting.

....

Chairman.

Dt.

(6) Minutes of the Class Meeting of a Company

Minutes of the meeting of the Preference Shareholders of the Company, held at the Registered Office of the Company on Thursday the 6th Jan., 2006, at 2.00 p.m.

Present: Shri. M. A. Bahadur, in the Chair.
Shri. N. C. Deshmukh, Shri O. F. Ekbote, Shri. P. G. Hirave, Shri S. K Lugade, Shri R. I. Jondhale, all Directors Shri Y. R. Kurane, Secretary, Shri. T. S. Lahiri, Solicitor, and 91 Preference Shareholders. whose signatures on the Attendance sheet is appended.

(a) The Secretary read the notice convening the meeting.

(b) The Chairman explained the purpose of summoning the meeting.

(c) RESOLVED that the Capital Reduction Scheme of the Company as submitted to the High Court, Maharashtra, the draft which is now presented before the meeting, be and is hereby approved, and futther resolved that the paid up value of the Preference Share be reduced to Rs. 50/- Per share in consideration of increase of dividend rate from 7% to 10%."

(d) The Chairman then declared the closure of the meeting.

....

Chairman.

Dt.

(7) Minutes of Societies, Associations, Clubs, etc.

(a) Executive or Managing Committee. Minutes of the meeting of the Managing Committee of the Society held at its Registered Office on Saturday the 2nd Dec. 2006, at 3.30 p.m.

Present: Shri. A. W. Hawale, in the Chair.
Shri. N. T. Nawale
Shri. V. N. Bapat
Shri. R. D. Vipat
Shri. P. L. Jamale
} Members of the Managing Committee.
Shri. W. D. Chaware, Secretary.

1. The minutes of the last meeting held on 4th Nov. 2006 were read, and as there was no objection, were signed as correct.

2. The Financial Statement and Auditor's Report thereon were read by the Secretary.

3. The Annual Report, produced before the meeting and intialled by the Chairman, was approved and to be laid before the ensuing Annual General meeting of the Society.

4. RESOLVED that Shri A. W. Nawale and Shri P. L. Jamale, be and they are hereby elected as members of the delegation of our Society at the ensuing Maharashtra Cooperative Societies' Conference to be held at Poona in February 2007.

5. The date for the next meeting was fixed January 2007 at the same place and time.

....

Chairman.

Dt.

(b) Annual General Meeting of a Society. Minutes of the Annual General Meeting of the Society held at its Registered Office on Monday the 3rd Jan. 2006 at 2.00 p.m.

Present: Shri. A. W. Hawale, in the Chair.
Shri. N. T. Nawale, Shri V. N. Bapat, Shri W. D. Vipat, Shri P. L. Jamale, all members of the Managing Committee.

Shri. W. D. Chaware, Secretary, Shri P.H. Thakur Auditor. Alongwith 53 members of the Society whose details are annexed herewith.

1. The minutes of the preceding Annual General Meeting held on 4th January 2005, were read and approved.
2. The Chairman gave a brief account of the activities of the Society during the year under review.
3. The adoption of the Report of the Managing Committee, Financial Statement and Balance Sheet. and Auditor's Report was moved by Shri B. P. Telang, duly seconded by Shri T. P. Yadav, and was unanimously passed.
4. Shri A. W. Hawale moved the reappointment of Shri P. H. Thakur as Honorary Auditor, which was duly seconded by Shri A. J. Patange, and was unanimously carried.
5. The following six names were submitted, duly proposed and seconded, to the meeting as candidates for election to the Managing Committee:

   (i) Shri. V. N. Bapat

   (ii) Shri. K. S. Gawande

   (iii) Shri. A. W. Hawale

   (iv) Shri. P. L. Jamale

(v) Shri. N. T. Nawale

(vi) Shri. R. D. Vipat.

The voting was by ballot, and Shri K. C. Pant and Shri P. L. Alexander acted as tellers. After voting and counting the Chairman announced the result of the ballot and it was Resolved that Shri A. W. Hawale, Shri N.T. Nawale, Shri V. N, Bapat, Shri R. D. Vipat and Shri P. L. Jamale these five members be and are hereby elected on the Managing Committee of the Society.

6. A vote of thanks to the Chairman was proposed by Shri S. N. Bhide, seconded by Shri B. N, Jaju and carried unanimously. The Chairman responded and then terminated the meeting.

....

Chairman.

Dt.

❑

4

Posters

We daily see attractive posters on the walls to divert our attention to the short information depicted in it. It is a suitable mode of providing ample information regarding the subject, but drafting a poster is in itself a suitable and skilled art. Posters or phamphlets play a vital role in our daily life. Not it has been used in every sphere of life. Normally in the offices, business, films, schools etc., these are used. We can make our poster very much attractive and appealing by considering the following points:

1. Our poster should catch the glimpse of the reader at the first glance.
2. It should be meaningful, visual and clear.
3. It should make use of attractive vocabulary in the shape of slogans, proverbs and quotations.
4. Normally bold letters are used to highlight the text.
5. Only relevent informations are used.
6. Complete information regarding date, time, place etc. are given in the text.
7. Name of the issuing authority should be given in the end.

Following are given some posters normally used in day to day life:

1. Design a poster for your school fete. You may use slogans.

A COLOURFUL
AND
GRAND FETE
OF
ALOK MEMORIAL SCHOOL
ON SUNDAY THE 25TH OCTOBER 2007
IN
SCHOOL COMPOUND
From
10.00 A.M. TO 2.00 P.M.

MAIN ATTRACTIONS:

* Stalls	* Fancy Dress Show
* Sweets	* Oriya Song
* Lucky Draw	* New Handicrafts & Woollen Garments
* Cultural Programmes	* Puppet Show

Tickets Rs. 20/-, Rs. 30/-

Available at the School Office and
Cultural Secretary

Organised by :

Students' Union

2. Draft a poster advertising the opening of new school called Happy Academy. Highlight some of the facilities being provided.

HAPPY ACADEMY

An English Medium Preparatory School

16, Church Lane, New Delhi-12.

Admission Open for Pre-nursery, Nursery and K.G. Classes

Salient Features:

- Good site and spacious accommodation
- Trained and experienced staff
- Play-way method of teaching
- School transport available
- Latest Toy Games
- Atractive Library
- Fully Airconditioned
- Timings : 8.30 a.m. to 1.30 p.m.

Admission on the Basis of Interview

Registration Open

Contact between 9 a.m. and 12 noon any working day.

Principle.

3. As the President of Leo Club of Temple town, prepare a poster on behalf of Lions Club and Leo Club for 'Diwali Mela' to be held at Nehru Stadium, Chennai, mentioning some of the attractions.

DIWALI MELA : FUN FAIR

Most Colourful Diwali Mela Being Organised

by

LEO CLUB AND LIONS CLUB
TEMPLE TOWN

at Nehru Stadium-Chennai
From 10th October to 13th October
(3 p.m. to 9 p.m.)

Main Attractions:

* Stalls
* Mini-circus
* Swings & Merry go-rounds
* Cultural fetes
* Death well
* Lucky draw

Tickets: Rs. 20/- Available from Post Office.

PRESIDENT

4. The Red Cross Society, Delhi Blood Donation Camp at your school. Imagine yourself as Secretary of the District Red Cross Society and design a poster for your school notice-board.

THE RED CROSS SOCIETY
New Delhi
is organising a

BLOOD DONATION CAMP

AT Delhi PUBLIC SCHOOL, R.K. Puram
on 20 November, 2005

DONATE BLOOD

&

SAVE A LIFE

All Donors will be awarded Certificates

HON'BLE UNION
HEALTH MINISTER
GOVT. OF INDIA

will donate his blood & inaugurate the function
He will pose for a group photograph with the donors.

Secretary

RED CROSS SOCIETY, DELHI

5. Draft a poster, to be displayed in the market place, announcing sale of Sarees at Aga Khan Hall Preet. Vihar Delhi Mention some of the varieties available.

SALE SALE SALE
GRAND CLEARANCE SAREES SALE
AT
AGA KHAN HALL
PREET VIHAR DELHI

Main Attractions:

1. Chiffon
2. Banaras Zarikota
3. Garden Silk
4. China silk
5. Queen valvet and
6. Many other different varieties

Special 30% discount on all items
Offer open till stocks last.

ORGANISED BY :

Geeta Saree, Emporium
Deep Cinema, Ashok Vihar
Delhi.

6. Prepare a poster to Highlight Computer Diploma

Here's
A COMPUTER DIPLOMA

That's Recognised By The Ministry of HRD and AICTE

and PSUs and Banks and State Govt's and Multinationals and....

And of course all major Private Sector Companies. This is the DOEACC Computer diploma awarded by an independent body under the Department of Electronics, Government of India.

The courses offered are:

'O' Level (Foundation)
'A' Level (Advanced Diploma)
'B' Level (Graduation)
'C' Level (Post Graduation)

so, if you wish to be a Computer Professional, walk-in to one of our 60'0 Accredited Centres and INSIST on the DOEACC Course. For more details, contact our Accredited Centre, nearest to you.

DOEACC

(A Scheme of AICTE & DOE, Govt. of India)

Electronics Niketan, 6 CGO complex, New Delhi-110003
Phone: 4363330/1/2 Fax 4363335

INSIST ON THE "DOEACC" COMPUTER COURSE

7. Design a poster on eve-teasing a warning.

EVE TEASERS ! AVAIL IF YOU CAN

We have a unique pair of bangles for men who are fond of eve-teasing
Free Food and Free Lodging

NOBLE CITIZENS!
HELP YOUR MOTHERS,
SISTERS AND DAUGHTERS

Move Out with Respect in Congenial

Atmosphere

Stand against Ruffians with Guts

Provide Deterrent Social Atmosphere for them.
If you see a woman being harassed or teased, don't
Shy away ! Catch hold of them ! Bring them
to Police Picket.

Police Post, Police Station or
Police Van or Dial 100.

DELHI POLICE

WITH YOU, FOR YOU ALWAYS

8. Design a poster for your school library on the value of books and reading in our life today. You may use slogans.

Your Library Beckons you

To

SIT IN THE COMPANY OF MASTER MINDS ENRICH YOUR KNOWLEDGE

And

Explore New Areas of Interest
Cultivate the Habit of Reading Books
And See Yourself the Difference
Reading Makes a Man Perfect

Open during School hour on all Working Days

Avail Facilities of reading Books

Timings : 2.00 p.m. to 10.00 p.m.

Librarian

DELHI PUBLIC SCHOOL, DELHI

9. Design a poster warning the people of Delhi against the danger of pollution and appealing them to keep their surroundings clean.

POLLUTION
THE SILENT KILLER
More Dangerous Than Atom Bomb
LET US FIGHT IT

* Keep your vehicle pollution-free.
* Keep your surroundings clean.
* Don't smoke, let out no smoke.
* Perform Sacrificial Fire (Havan) in your homes.
* Grow terrace gardens and kitchen gardens.
* Grow more trees in your surroundings.

POLLUTION IS ENEMY OF ALL
All Religions-All Communities-All Castes-All Creeds

Issued by :

NATIONAL POLLUTION
PREVENTION ORGANISATION

10. Draft a poster for the Great Royal Circus, highlighting some of the major feats.

GREAT ROYAL CIRCUS REACHES YOUR TOWN IN THE LAWNS OF THE RED FORT ENJOY MIRACULOUS

FUN
&
FROLIC

ENJOY

MIRACULOUS

Manager
Royal Circus

Major attractions : FUN & FROLIC

* Death well
* Swings
* Walk on fire
* Rockets show
* Dance on rope
* Feats of animals
* Petrol burning on water
* Clowns with their hilarious jokes

Show Timings : 12.00 p.m. 6 p.m.

(Daily 4 shows)

Tickets available at :—

All post offices worth Rs. 50/-, 100/- and 150/-.

Special concession for students

Manager
ROYAL CIRCUS

11. You are making an effort to spread the message of Communal Harmony. Prepare a poster with catchy slogans to be displayed in the school premises.

FROM KASHMIR TO KANYA KUMARI

UNITED WE STAND
"DIVIDED WE FALL"
LET THERE PREVAIL
COMMUNAL HARMONY
PROGRESS
IS
Revoked if we
* Indulge in Communal Clashes

INDIA IS ONE GREAT NATION

* Unnecessary Communal Violence
Let's Unite & Remain Tolerant,
Sympathetic and Secular

UNITY IS STRENGTH
DIVISION IS DEATH

By courtesy from : Adarsh Vidhya Mandir,
R.K. Puram, Delhi

12. Design a postar for a Cultural Evening

MUSIC GIVES LIFE	**ENJOY A CULTURAL EVENING &**	LIVE IN MUSIC

STAY AMONG ROMANTIC ARTISTS
on
5th March, 2003 at SANGAM HALL OF MAGIC
Navodaya Vidyalaya, R.K. Puram, Delhi.

Chief Guest :

Minister for Development Human Resources
Govt. of India, New Delhi
The money will be sent to the Welfare
of SLUM CHILDREN

Entry through Ticket @ Rs. 25/-, Rs. 35/- Rs. 50/- Ticket available in :— School office & Post Office	G. Ram Gupta, Secretary, Organised by Cultural Association

13. You have started an English Coaching Centre. Experts, at your centre, enable students to speak and write correct English in 60 days. The course is meant for those students who have passed +2 exam. Make a poster to this effect.

WHAT AFTER PASSING + 2 EXAM.?

Utilise Your Summer Vacation
&

Learn to Speak and Write
CORRECT & FLUENT
ENGLISH
In 60 Days
at
LEARNWELL SCHOOL OF LANGUAGE
India's No.1 English teaching school
with a proven record of teaching English for more than
20 years to people from all parts of India

CONTACT: N-8, Ring Road, South Ext. Part-II, New Delhi.

14. Draft a poster on behalf of Y.M.C.A. Delhi for a Diwali Mela being organized in Amusement Park, Rohini Delhi, naming some of the attractions.

DIWALI MELA : A GREAT FUN & FROLIC FOR ALL
MOST EXCITING DIWALI MELA

Organised by

Y.M.C.A., Delhi
In Amusement Park, Rohini, Delhi.
From 1st October to 7th October.

Main Attractions:

* Stalls
* Cultural fetes
* Puppet show
* Swings
* Death well
* Lucky Draw
* Mini circus

Tickets Rs. 20/- available from your nearest post office.

15. Design a poster about the need for regular exercise. You may use slogans.

ALL WORK AND NO PLAY MAKES
JACK A DULL BOY

Make a Habit to Have Regular Exercise
This is the Dream of All,
Awake at the Nature's Call,
Get Strength,
and
Enjoy good Health,
Remain free from Ailment,
Lead a Life of Enrichment
IF HEALTH IS LOST, EVERYTHING IS LOST
EXERCISE IS BENEFICIAL FOR ALL

16. Write out a Poster on 'Drug Addiction'.

DRUG ADDICTION
A
GATE WAY
TO
DESTRUCTION,
AFFLICTION,
DEATH,
&
DEJECTION,
MANY HOMES RUINED,
LIFE DISTORTED,
SLOW POISON & DEATH
DON'T HUG THE DRUG

An Awareness Programme

SPECIAL ATTRACTIONS:

1. Film on various drugs
2. Cultural Programmes
3. Lucky Draw

Free Entry on 15th January, 2007
10.00 a.m. at
DIWAN HALL
PANCHSHEEL CLUB, Delhi

Organised by:

DIWAN EDUCATION TRUST, DELHI.

17. As a Secretary, Students Union. ABC School, Delhi, write out a poster to announce the staging of a play in your school.

THE MOST EXICITING
HISTORICAL
&
SENSATIONAL PLAY
—WALL OF DEATH—
AT
ABC SCHOOL, CAMPUS, Pritampura, Delhi.
ON
2nd October, 1997 at 8.00 p.m.

Tickets Available at :

4, School Office,
Union Office,
for Rs. 2/- 5/- and 10/- each.

Reena Gupta
Secreary,
STUDENTS UNION,
ABC SCHOOL, AGRA.

18. Design an attractive poster for an Anti-Smoking Campaign being held in your school on the occasion of World No-Tobacco Day. You may use slogans.

DO NOT SMOKE

SAVE YOURSELF AND OTHERS
Smoking saps your strength, stamina

And

Energy and brings ruin and death
SAY NO TO CIGARETTES
That is why...............?
Every Packet carries the warning

SMOKING IS INJURIOUS TO HEALTH

Every Cigaratte
Cuts
Yours life short
by 5 minutes

You want
to save your
precious life?

Issued by :

MINISTRY OF HEALTH
G.O.I., NEW DELHI

19. Draft a poster advertising sale of handicrafts, including pottery and cane furniture etc. organised by the Blind Welfare Society, Delhi. Mention how the proceeds will be used.

COME ONE/COME ALL
AND
Contribute Generously to a Noble Cause

Sale of Handicrafts
- Pottery
- Cane furniture
- Hand-woven carpets
- Bed-covers.

AVAIL OPPORTUNITY TO
HAVE USEFUL ITEMS
AT
BOAT CLUB-INDIA GATE
15th July to 25th July
10.00 a.m. to 5.00 p.m.

Organised by:

The Blind Welfare Society, Delhi.

The proceeds will be used for opening a school for the Blind.

20. Draft a poster on behalf of Ministry of Environment and Forests on the World Environment Day.

WORLD ENVIRONMENT DAY

&

20TH ANNIVERSARY OF

THE NATIONAL MUSEUM OF

NATURAL HISTORY

(Ministry of Environment & Forests)

Functions

Chief guest :

Shri Suresh P. Prabhu

Union Minister for Environment & Forests

Guest of honour:

Shri Babu Lal Marandi

Union Minister of State for Environment & Forests

A Special lecture on UN theme

"For Life on Earth-Save our Seas"

by:

Padmashree Prof. (Mrs.) K. Mohanty,

Vice Chancellor, Delhi University,

Venue: FICCI Auditorium, Barakhamba Road, New Delhi-110001

Time: 9.00 a.m. to 10.30 a.m.

Date: 5th June, 2006

Entry: On Invitation Cards only

Invitation Cards Available:

Reception, FICCI on 3 & 4th June, 2006, 10 a.m. to 5 p.m.

21. Draft a Poster on Free Pollution.

FREE POLLUTION OR POLLUTION FREE

YOU DECIDE

Delhi is one of the most polluted cities in the world, where millions of vehicles, constantly emit their toxic breath into the atmosphere, making an average Delhite, inhale smoke equivalent to 20 cigarettes, everyday. It's upto us to do something before our city, virtually turns into a gas chamber.

To help reduce pollution emission from motorcycles, Escorts Yamaha has organized free pollution check camps, where you can bring in your motorcycle of any make or model for a free check-up and you will be given an authentication report on the status of your motorcycle's breath.

Venues:

* 25-26th March,
  SK Automobiles,
  Rajdhani, Enclave.
* 27-28th March
  Satya Service Station,
  'L' Block, Hari Nagar.
* 29th March,
  MRG Motor Co.,
  Jhandewalan Ext.

EY

ESCORTS YAMAHA

Breathe Easy

Free Pollution Check Camps

March 25th to 29th 1997

Once again on tribute to the environment

say YES

EXCORTS YAMAHA MOTOR LIMITED

HELPING DELHI BREATHEEASY

22. The Director of Health Services, NCT Govt., Delhi, is organising an Essay Contest for the students of Delhi schools on AIDS Awarenesss. Design a suitable poster for the same.

THE DIRECTORATE OF HEALTH SERVICES
GOVT. OF NCT, DELHI

is organising an

ESSAY CONTEST

FOR BONAFIDE STUDENTS OF DELHI SCHOOLS
on

AIDS FREE INDIA—A HEALTHIER INDIA

WIN FIRST PRIZE OF Rs. 5000 and other Attractive Prizes

* Written Hindi or in English on one side
* It should not exceed 1000 words
* The decision of judge shall be final

LAST DATE: 5th AUGUST, 2004

Send your entries to :
The Director
Health Services
NCT Govt.
Secretariat
New Delhi

23. Draft a poster to school students to participate in Science Park.

FUN – FUN – FUN

Now since exams are over,
it is time to go to the

SCIENCE PARK

at Timarpur and enjoy

Open everyday between
9 AM & 1 PM (*Except Sundays*)

School students with identity cards will get free entry
in addition to Organised Group visits.

A Project of National Science Centre
Phone : 3371893/1936/1945

COME, LET'S HAVE FUN

24. Design a poster for promoting good health through 'Health Mela'.

GOOD HEALTH IS KEY TO PROSPERITY
ENJOY SOUND HEALTH
and
PAY A VISIT TO THE "HEALTH MELA"
on
5th August 200... at 4.00 p.m.
in
Sarvodaya Vidyalaya RAJA GARDEN DELHI
Chief Guest: The Mayor of Delhi

Special Features :

1. Lectures on yoga
2. Demonstration on the use of Herbs.
3. Exhibition on exercises
4. Lectures by eminent doctors
5. Free medical check up

Organised by:
Students Club
Sarvodaya Vidyalaya
Raja Garden Delhi

25. Design a poster advertising a Clearance Sale of household articles by a family going abroad. List some of the articles being sold.

SALE SALE SALE
GRAND CLEARANCE SALE

A family going abroad wishing to dispose of the following household articles. Prices indicated against each item.

1. Godrej Fridge 164 Litere	Rs. 3000/-
2. Double Bed	Rs. 500/-
3. Sofa Set (2 piece)	Rs. 1200/-
4. Kishan Lal Almirah	Rs. 1500/-
5. Bajaj Scooter (1994 Model Chetak)	Rs. 16000/-

Contact immediately:

P.K. Garg
15, Mall Road, Delhi

26. Draft a Poster for Hilarious Comedy.

On The Occasion of World Theatre Day

AT Ashok Theatre AND **tornado** Comunications

P R E S E N T

The Entertainers

in the

Gut Wrenching
Hilarious comedy

EK GHODA CHHEY SAWAAR

Adapted and Directed by
Ranjit Kapoor
on 27th March at 7.30 p.m.

Convention Hall, Ashok Hotel
Tickets: Rs. 150/
Buffet at special price at The coffee Shop

intercard

Special discount for dinner at Ashok Hotel's speciality restaurants for Intercard Members.

AT

Ashok Hotel
New Delhi. Ph: 6110101. Extn. 2295
Tickets available at Hospitality Desk,
Ashok Hotel

27. Write out a poster 'on 'Drug Addiction'.

DRUG ADDICTION

A

SLOW POISONING

AND

A DIRECT WAY

TO

RUIN

&

DEATH

MANY HOMES RUINED

SAVE YOUR LIFE & CHILDREN

It is a National Crime.

Special Attractions :

1. Film on the effects of Narcotics

2. Drug Addiction a sin

3. Cultural Programmes

4. Lucky draw

Free Entry on 26th January, 2007.
10.00 a.m.
GULMOHAR PARK
DELHI

Organised by
Gulmohar Education Society
Delhi

28. Draft a poster to beware the Public to protect from Cancer.

You don't have Cancer. This is what you believe. Not what you know!

This very belief can prove fatal for you.

Every year about 10 lac cases of Cancer are detected in India. And it is sad that about 5 lac Cancer patients cannot be saved from the disease.

Reason-detection of Cancer at an advanced stage.

To protect yourself from Cancer

1. Avoid drinking, smoking, chewing of betel, tobacco, panmasala, zarda etc.
2. Examine your breasts regularly or undergo a regular examination. Training for self examination of breasts shall be given at your nearest health centre during this programme.

Following symptoms are a warning of Cancer—

1. A sore that does not heal.
2. Thickening or lump in breast or elsewhere.
3. Obvious change in wart or mole.
4. Continuous indigestion or difficulty in swallowing.
5. Unusual blood discharge or bleeding.
6. Nagging cough or hoarseness of voice.
7. Change in bowel or bladder habits.

If you notice any of these symptoms for more than 15 days then don't delay and contact your nearest health centre immediately.

Cancer Control Campaign ↔ 31st March 2007

Ministry of Health, Govt. of Delhi

29. Prepare a poster on behalf of DSIDC about traditional treasures.

BHARTI

DELHI TEMPORIUM

Tastefully transformed Interiors for Truly Traditional Treasures

Experience the many splendoured heritage of unusual masterpieces in the newly renovated, airconditioned interiors of the Delhi Emporium.

10% TO 20% OFF

On an exciting range of following hand-crafted masterpieces from 25th to 29th March, 2007

* Brass Artware Minakari Products
* Wooden Inlay Work
* Sandal Wood Items
* Wall Hangings and Paintings
* Decorative Candles, Terracotta Items
* Paper machie and Zari Products
* Bed Covers, Table Cloth, Mats and Napkins and Cushion Covers
* Many more attractive Gift Items

DSIDC Baba Kharak Singh Marg,
New Delhi
Telephone: 3363287

30. Draft a poster for enhancing your Jute Products

DIVERSIFIED JUTE PRODUCTS

Your business. Your success.

Your future. Our support.

N.C.J.D.

Calling all NGOs, Weavers, Craftsmen, Entrepreneurs and Individuals who wish to profit from the growing Indiawide, worldwide popularity of an ever-expanding range of diversified jute products. From carpets and fashion garments to handicrafts and home furnishings.

Get all the support you need.
Where and when you need.

Jute Service Centre **1**

2 Raw Material Bank

Market Support **3**

4 Design Development

Jute Entrepreneurs **5**

Assistance Scheme **6** Special Financial Support For NGOs

You've got questions. We've got answers.

NCJD

National Centre for Jute Diversification
ICMARD Bldg. (8th floor), Block 14, Scheme VIII(M)
Calcutta-700 067. Ph : 351-3269/3270 (Telefax)

31. Draft a Poster on Dengu Prevention

DENGUE IS PREVENTABLE

Summer is approaching

BEWARE!

Eliminate mosquito breeding places

* Clean your water coolers once a week and mop them dry before reuse
* Put one tablespoon of petrol in coolers which cannot be so cleaned
* Empty all water containers/haudis daily and after refilling keep them covered
* Overhead water tanks should be covered
* Do not allow collection of water in & around house
* Do not keep unused/broken bottles, cups, pots and tyres that can hold water in open
* Put kerosene/petrol/diesel in any stagnant waste water which is not for human use
* Heads of Govt. departments, Local bodies, Public Sector Undertakings, Market Associations, Professionals & Private bodies are requested to arrange the above measures in their office buildings/premises
* Resident Welfare Associations are requested to co-operate with Zonal Health Officers of MCD who are holding meetings with them for elimination of mosquito breeding in domestic and peri-domestic areas

HAMARI DILLI - SWASTH DILLI

Health Department,

Municipal Corporation of Delhi

ACTIVITY

1. As the manager of "Excellent Coaching Centre" run by you, prepare the poster calling the attention of students desirous of attending IIT, PMT coaching to join your coaching centre.

2. Draft a poster advertising a clearance sale of household articles by a family going abroad. List some of the articles being sold. Use the address: R. K. Sharma, 34 Mall Avenue, Lucknow)

3. Draft a poster for a Science Exhibition going to be organised by the Science Club of your school. You are Ramesh of St. Paul Public School, Hissar.

4. Draft a poster in about 50 words on 'Save the Earth" on behalf of the Pollution Control Deptt. of your State Government.

5. Health Ministry Govt. of India has launched a special programme to eradicate Polio from India. Being the Pupil Leader of your school, draft a poster in about 50 words by inventing relevant details.

6. You are going to contest the election for the post of the President of the Student's Council of your school. Design a poster in not more than 50 words for your voters impressing upon them why they should vote for you. You may use slogans and other requisite pojnts.

7. Prepare a poster on kindness to animals to be displayed in the city at Public Places appealing to show kindness to animals.
8. Draft a poster on Dowry-a curse.

9. As the President of Leo Club of Temple Town, prepare a poster on behalf of Lions Club and Leo club for 'Diwali Mela' to be held at Nehru Stadium, Chennai, mentioning some of the attractions.

10. Prepare a poster advising the people not to take alcoholic drinks illustrating the dangers of consuming alcohol. Your illustration should be in conformity with the theme provided to you.

11. Your school Sharda Vidyalaya is organising a cultural evening to collect funds for the slum children. The Human Resource Development Minister has consented to be the Chief Guest. Draft a poster in about 50 words to be displayed in different areas of your locality. Imagine you are the Head Boy of your school. You may use slogans.

12. You are making an effort to spread the message of communal harmony. Prepare a 'poster with catchy slogans to be displayed in your school premises.

13. You are disturbed after visiting a blind school. In order to mobilize your friends and the school mates, you are planning to campaign for Eye Donation. Prepare a poster high lighting the need for eye donation and eye bank. (Word limit: 50)

❐

5

Writing of Invitations (Formal & Informal)

Letters of invitations can be divided in two categories:

(1) The formal letters of invitation.

(2) The ordinary or informal letters of invitation.

Characteristics of a formal letter of invitation:

(i) These letters are written in the Third Person.

(ii) The Simple Present Tense is used.

(iii) There is no signature.

(iv) The address is written at the bottom of the invitation on the right side. The date of writing is not given.

(v) The abbreviation RSVP *i.e.,* please reply, is written at the bottom.

(vi) In formal letters of invitation each of the following is written in a separate line *i.g.*

(a) the name(s) of the person(s) given in the invitation.

(b) the formal expresion; request the pleasure of the company if.

(c) the time as well as date of the event.

(d) the reason of the invitation.

Characteristics of the informal or ordinary letter of Invitation:

(1) It is written in the First Person.

(2) The salutation is usually dear and name.

(3) The date of writing is given. But the year is generally omitted.

(4) Different tenses are used as the sense demands.

(5) The complementary close is : yours sincerely.

(6) Inside address is not given.

(7) The writer's address is given in the usual place.

(8) The writer does not ask for a reply. But the last sentence suggests that a reply is expected.

Avoid use of such common place and clumsy expressions as the following:

(1) Just a line to tell you.

(2) Your kind remembrance just to hand.

(3) Hoping this will find you in good health.

(4) I am well and wish you to be in the same state.

(5) Soliciting the favour of an early reply.

(6) Your loving letter of the 14th May to hand.

(7) Respect to elders and love to youngers.

(8) The use of slang must be avoided.

(9) Close a personal letter with some expression of regard or affection as :

With best wishes,

With best wishes to all the home,

With love to yourself and respected mother,

With love and best wishes,

With kind regards,

With best respects to all,

With best respects to father and love to brothers and sisters

A. Formal Letters of Invitation.

1. **As the Principle of M.J. International School which is holding its Annual Day Function at 5.00 p.m. on 15th November 2005 in the school auditorium. Design an invitation card to be sent to the occasion.**

The Principal, Members of the Staff and Students of M.J. International School, Darya Ganj, New Delhi request your benign company on the Annual Day Function of the School to be Celebrated on 15th November 2005 at 5.00 p.m. in Mavalankar Hall of the School. The Hon'ble Education Minister has consented to be the Chief Guest on this occasion.

2. **Draft an invitation for dinner at home.**

MRS. AND MR. J.C. KAPOOR
INVITE
MRS. AND MR. R.K. MITTAL
TO
THE BIRTH DAY PARTY OF THEIR
SON ANIL KAPOOR
ON
SUNDAY, THE 1ST JANUARY, 1997
AT 7.00 P.M.
AT THEIR RESIDENCE
F-11 MODEL BASTI DELHI

3. **Vivek has come out successful in I.I.T. Entrance Examination. He has decided to throw a party for his friends. Write out an informal invitation giving details of venue, time and date.**

680/20, Panchsheel Colony
Sonepat
5th April, 1997
Dear Manik,

All of you know that I have come out with flying colours in the I.I.T. Entrance Examination. This will be a deciding step in my educational carrer. To grace the occasion I have arranged a very decent party at the Rosy Rosy, Gulmohar Park, Ashok Vihar, Delhi, on 10th April 2005 at 4.00 p.m. Please do attend and inform other friends to be present on the occasion.

Yours faithfully,
Vivek.

4. You are Miss Neha Mittal of 680/20 Panchsheel Colony, Delhi. You are celebrating your 15th birthday next week. Draft a formal invitation to a tea party. (Do not mention the invitee's name).

MISS NEHA MITTAL

requests the pleasure of the company of
at a

TEA PARTY

on the occasion of her 20th birthday
at 6.00 p.m.

On Sunday, 5th August

at her residence 680/20 Panchsheel colony, Delhi.

R.S.V.P.

5. Write a formal reply to your neighbour accepting the invitation to his brother's birthday party. Write names, date, time and place etc.

Mrs. & Mr. A.K. Joshi

of Ambala Cantt.
Thank

Mrs. & Mr. P.C. Sethi

for their Invitation
on
the auspicious occasion
of
the brithday of their younger brother

Mr. Atul Sethi

and
accept the same and promise to be there
on Sunday 5th March, 2007-at 5.30 p.m.
at their residence at
L-3, Mayawati Colony-Ashok Vihar, Delhi-7.

6. You have set up a cooperative store in your colony, Yamuna Vihar Delhi, you have decided to invite one member from each family settled there to its inaugural ceremony. Prepare a draft of the invitation letter for the purpose.

Messrs D.K. Mittal and Sons.

announce the opening of their new establishment

Mittal COOPERATIVE STORE

A-3, Yamuna Vihar, Delhi

INAUGURATION

On Sunday, the 2nd October at 10.00 a.m. by
Mr. S.L. Gupta, M.L.A. One member from
each family settled in Yamuna Vihar is

cordially Invited to Visit for all kinds of
domestic items : readymade Garments
Cosmetics, medicines and electrical Items.

**AVAIL INAUGURAL DISCOUNT OF 20%
ON ALL GOODS**

R.S.V.P.
Mittal Cooperative Store
Phone: 7427593

7. Write out an attractive invitation to be sent to all the parents/guardians for your school annual function:

The Principal and the staff of
Govt. Boys Composite Senior Secondary School Shahdara
request the pleasure of your company
on the occasion of the celebration of
Annual Function
on
Monday, 15th January, 2007 at 1.00 p.m.
Dr. A.K. Mittal, Director of Planning
has kindly consented to distribute the prizes

R. Mohan
Phone: 7291052
Light refreshment will be served
after the Programme

Note: Please bring this card with you **Principal**

8. You are Raj Kumar S/Shri M. Kumar of 10 Raja Ji Road, Delhi. Prepare a draft for an invitation card to be sent on behalf of your parents on the occasion of the wedding of your sister.

Shrimati and Shri Raj Kumar

request the pleasure of your company on the auspicious
occasion of the marriage of their daughter

REKHA

with

RANJIT

(Son of Shri R.K. Gupta of Kamla Nagar. Delhi)
On Sunday, 2nd February, 2005 at 9.00 p.m.
at their residence 10, Raja Ji Road Delhi

as per programme
Reception of Barat 8.00 p.m.
Dinner 9.00 p.m.
Doli will leave on 3rd Feb. 2005 at 5.00 a.m.

R.S.V.P.	**With Best compliments from**
M/s R.R. Garments	All Relatives
10, Raja Ji Road, Delhi	&
Phone : 591029	Friends

9. You are Apoorva, the president of the Rotary Club of Madras East. Draft a formal invitation in connection with the Literacy Month Celebration being organised by your club.

Miss Apoorva
President, Rotary Club, Madras East
Request the pleasure of the company of
Mr. & Mrs A. K. Shah
the Celebration of Literacy Month
being
Organized at Govt. Boys, Senior School, Rohini
on
30th January, 2008 at 11.p.m.
Under the Chairmanship of Director of Education
R.S.V:P.
Apoorva
Phone 3810198

10. Write a formal letter of invitation to a friend of your daughter inviting her to your daughter's birthday.

Mrs. and Mr. S. Kapoor
request the pleasure of the company of
Miss Neha
on the occasion of the 17th birthday of their daughter
Shalu
at 7 p.m. on October 20,
E-27, Rajouri Garden,
New Delhi-110027

11. Indian Airforce is celebrating the 64th Air Force Anniversary. You are the Public Relations Officer. Draft a formal invitation for all retired Air Force Officers.

AIR FORCE DAY CELEBRATIONS

INVITATION TO RETIRED AIR FORCE OFFICERS

To celebrate the 64th Air Force Anniversary, the Chief of the Air Staff will host a reception for all retired Air Force Officers at 20.00 hours on 05 Oct. 2007 at Air Force Officers Mess, Dr. Zakir Hussain Marg, New Delhi.

All retired officers with their spouses are cordially invited.

R.S.V.P. 3015478
3377608
3377609 Dress-Formal

B. The Informal (Ordinary) Letters of Invitation

1. Write an informal letter of invitation to your friend inviting him to your son's birthday party.

125/20, Panchsheel Colony,
Delhi-131001
25th December, 2005.
Dear friend Rohit,

I have much pleasure in inviting you to the 15th birthday party which we are giving for our son Ashish at 6.30 p.m. on 5th January, 2005. We very much hope that you will grace the occasion with your benign presence. It will not be out of place to mention that Sohan and his party is coming from Haryana to entertain us.

Yours sincerely,
Ashu Sharma.

2. Write a reply to informal letter of invitation accepting the invitation.

A-5, C.C. Colony,
Ashok Vihar, Delhi-52
25th December, 2005.
Dear friend Mahesh,

Thank you very much for your kind invitation for 5th January 2005. I shall be extremely happy to be with you on this auspicious occasion. I will be well in time. If there is any service for me, please do ring me immediately.

Yours sincerely,
Rohan

3. You have arranged a picnic on Sunday, the 25th January 2008 at Bhadkal Lake, Faridabad. Write an informal invitation to your friend, Sohan to join you.

120 E, Kamla Nagar, Delhi-7
15th January, 2005.
My dear Sohan,

We have arranged a picnic at Bhadkal Lake Faridabad on Sunday the 25th January 2008. I shall be very happy if you accompany us. Our party will consist of ten members and we shall be there by 10.00 a.m. I would request you to join us at my house well in time.

Yours sincerely,
Mohan.

4. Write a reply to the above invitation refusing to join the party.

E-120, Mohan Nagar, Delhi-7.
5th January, 2005
My dear Mohan,

Thanks for your kind invitation. But I am sorry to inform you that I would not be able to enjoy your picnic. This morning I have to go to see my elder brother in his house at Ambala. You know that father is out of station in Bombay. So it is my foremost duty to proceed to Ambala in the morning of Saturday.

I hope you will excuse my absence without any ill-feeling.

Yours sincerely,
Sohan.

5. You are Manoj. You have been invited to attend a birthday party of your close friend. Respond to this invitation.

681/20 Panchsheel Colony
Sonepat
8th Sept., 200...
Dear friend Varun,

I am really very thankful to you for extending me an invitation at your birthday party to be celebrated on 18th Sept., 200... at 5.00 p.m. at your house. I will be there well in time and grace this occasion among your family members.
I send my best wishes on your twenty first birthday.
With deepest respect to your parents.

Yours faithfully,
Manoj

6. Class XI students have newly joined their classes. Your class XII students have decided to have a welcome party for them. Write out an invitation giving details of venue, time and date.

Dear Friends,

All class XI students are cordially invited to join their seniors for a get-together being held on 25 July, 2008 in the Common-Room at 11.00 a.m. This is to welcome the freshers to Senior Secondary Class. Do come.

All Students of Class XII

FOR PRACTICE

1. **You have received an invitation from the Manager, 'Youth Club, I.I.T., Powai, Mumbai to attend the Premiere of the play called 'Desh ki Pukar' Write a letter of regret giving atleast three reasons for your not being able to attend the programme.**

2. **You are Arun. You have been invited to attend the wedding to your friend's sister during summer vacation. Respond to the invitation accepting the invitation.**

3. **You are Akshay. You have been invited to participate in a seminar of 'Fundamental Rights of Children', organized by the Lions Club of your district. Respond to the invitation by writing a letter to the Secretary of the club.**

4. **You are R. Kumar S/o Shri S. Kumar of 30 Park Street, Kanpur. Prepare a draft for an invitation card to be sent on behalf of your parents on the occasion of the wedding of your sister.**

5. **You are Manoj. You have been invited to attend a birthday party of your closest friend. Respond to his invitation.**

6. **You are AV. Raman of Hyderabad. Prepare a draft reply expressing your inability to attend the birthday party of a friend.**

10. You are Rahul. You have been invited by the youth club of your locality to act as one of the judges for an inter school group song competition organized by the club. But unfortunately, you cannot accept invitation due to previous engagement. Write to the Secretary of the club regretting your inability to accept the invitation.

11. You are the Head Boy/Head Girl of your school. The students of Class XI want to organize a farewell for the outgoing class XII. Write an informal invitation for the same inviting the teachers for the function.

❐

6

Report Writing

WRITING A REPORT

Here we will study the reports writing used in schools magazines, newpapers etc. Writing a report needs careful, systematic and logic presentation of a written document that contains proper analysis and examination of all the relevant facts. It should serve a very specific purpose including a particular situation.

People adopt different methods to apend a report. Some use only titles and sub-titles whereas others use a paragraph form. To be more specific, a report should contain the following elements.

1. The writing purpose.
2. The time and date of the occurrence.
3. The venue of the event.
4. The fact, point, data on which it is based.
5. The party, people or the organization involved in it.
6. Cause.
7. Results.

Let us see the following reports:

REPORT

1. You are a member of the team which represented your school in the Maltova Quiz Contest and won the team trophy. You have been asked to read out a report about the event in the school assembly. Write the report in not more than 100 words.

A REPORT ON MALTOVA QUIZ CONTEST

Kanpur : 6th March, 2005

A Maltova Quiz Contest was organised in Govt. School Kanpur to win the final trophy on 5th March, 2005. Near about ten participants form two neighbouring schools participated in it. This contest was to test the general knowledge of the school children of Secondary and Senior Secondary students. The participants were divided in groups. One was to speak in its favour and the other side was to speak in its opposition. There was a set of three judges to announce the result. The questioner put a variety of questions on science, literature, music and general knowledge. He was an expert from Delhi. The students of the rival team had a tough competition. Our school team was well equipped with all the answers. The students answered very sharply and answered almost all the questions. Thus they secure 75 points while the rival team could get only 60 points. The judges declared the result and offered the trophy to our team. It was a great event for all of us.

2. Your school has celebrated the World Environment day on 5th June. Write a report in 125 words to be published in yours school magazine. You are Vishal.

SEMINAR ON WORLD ENVIRONMENT DAY

Delhi : 6th June 200...

By Vishal, Student Editor

The students of Govt. School Roop Nagar No.2 arranged a seminar on 5th as the world environment day in which more than 20 students participated in the discussion. The participants had written papers as well as interacted with the experts on suggesting the ways to control the spreading pollution in every nook and corner of the city. They accepted the fact that our environment is under the attack of constant pollution through various agents like water, soil, air and noise. Consequently the participants agreed on the fact that we are near to the point of extinction. It was pointed out in the discussion that over population has posed a serious problem to our environment. They opined that every item is under the impact of pollution and nothing is safe, pure and fresh. They viewed that we must plant trees and saplings on all the open spaces. The use of CNG should be made compulsory in all the vehicles with noise resistant horns. The RWASC should educate the masses on the harms of pollution through interaction, exhibitions and seminars.

3. Deepika a student of Mark Public School has been asked to write a report for the School Magazine on the inauguration of literacy week by Minister of State for Education. Write her report in not more than 100 words.

STATE MINISTER INUGURATES THE LITERACY WEEK

A historic literacy week was inaugurated in Mark Public School, Dehradoon by the Minister of State for Education on 16th January at 11.00 a.m. The chief guest was given a hearty welcome. He was led to the dias and there he unfurld the national flag. After this ceremoney, he inaugurated the Literacy week. This week would last upto 1st February. A large crowd of illiterate villagers were awaiting for his message. He raised the slogan, 'Each one, teach one'. He taught a class of 25 villagers for about half an hour. He advised the educated masses to spare at least one hour daily from their schedule so that their bretherns could get at lest elementary knowledge of reading, writing and simple arithmetic. He encouraged them to volunteer themselves for this noble cause. School students, teachers and the educated men among the masses volunteered themselves and took a pledge to teach the illeterate people. In this way the inauguration was followed by an immediate action plan.

4. You are a Press Reporter from the Hindustan Times. You visited the victims of Tsunami Waves in the coastal areas of T.N., Kerala, Andhra, Pondicherry and Andamans. Prepare a report in about 125 words.

A REPORT ON TSUNAMI DISASTER

Delhi : 28th Dec., 2004

By H.T. Correspondent

The Christmas Night of 25th Dec. will remain the most lamentable night in the Indian history : On one side the people were celebrating the Christmas, while on the other side the Indian Ocean was bringing havoc in the coastal areas of Andhra, Kerala, Tamil Nadu, Pondicherry and the islands of Andamans and Nicobar. The sea quake was so violent that it devastated the area completely. The residents were rendered homeless with a great loss of property, humanity, animals and crops. A few villages were swept away completely and nothing was known about their whereabouts. In the Coastal area of Tamil Nadu, Kerala, Andhra and Pondicherry the estimated loss expected to more than 5322 crores. Near about 162 Km. of National Highways, 462 km. of state and district highways along with 17 bridges were completely damaged. In the Andaman the estimated loss had came around 2500 crores whereas colosal damage to public and private infrastructure, defence installations, power supply system, roads and hospitals is still remains unestimated. The tourism industry has been hardly hit. The earthquake has marred the Coastal areas of Thailand, Indonesia, Srilanka as well. The World Bank has offered a loan of 3 billion to rehabilitate the people. The Government of India is doing its best in providing the victims with food, money and other possible and as well as sheltering places to the victims.

5. A Report on 'Electioneering in Your Town for a Newspaper.

Mumbai : 10th February, 2007

By Kapoor Atul, Times Correspondent.

We have set up a democratic system in India. So elections are held in one or the other corners of the country. We lay, a great stress on free and fair elections. In Delhi, the election commission declared polling. More than 500 candidates filed their nomination papers for the election of councillors. So they were given different symbols. For more than fifteen days, the candidates arranged meetings and put forth their charter of manifesto. They tried to woo the voters through their oily and sweet slogans. They circulated hand-bills among the residents. The candidates held corner meetings under a certain code of conduct. The election campaign stopped 48 hours before the actual conduct of the election. On the election day tight security arrangements were made. The voters appeared in great numbers to cast their votes. The polling started at 8.00 a.m. and continued till 4.00 p.m. In the presence of the contesting candidates or their agents, their result was declared on the same day.

6. During the Kargil conflict the Arts Club of your colony had organised various cultural activities to collect funds for the victims' families. As the Secretary of the club, write a report for your News Letter about these activities and how you utilised the funds collected.

A REPORT ON COLLECTION FUNDS FOR KARGIL VICTIMS

Delhi : 5th March, 2000

By Mr. Yash

Pak intruders captured Indian Territory along the line of control. Their intrusion was detected on May 6, 1999. Accordingly a war started on the line of control compelling the Pak intruders to withdraw its forces. The conflict continued for about two months and heavy casualties were reported on both the sides. All the Indians showed unity and raised funds for the victims' families. Different organisations, clubs, societies, government offices and from a labour to high ranking man contributed all possible helps. Our colony organised a charitable cultural programme in the shape of songs, dramas and one act play to raise money. This fund was used to buy medicines, food packets and other material help to the affected families. Even cash was also handed over to these families whose sons have shed blood for the sake of motherland.

7. You are a Newspaper Reporter. Write a report, in about 100 words, on the visit of an important dignitary to your locality.

New Delhi : March 5, 2007

By our special correspondent P.C. Kaul

It was the occasion of Prime Minister's routine visit to our locality. He arrived at 5 p.m. in an open car accompanied by many Union Ministers, the Chief Minister of Delhi, the Lieutenant Governor of Delhi and other high officials of Delhi Administration. On that day our locality wore a festive outlook. Every road, street, lane and by lane, foot-path and corner were thoroughly swept clean and decorated. He went from lane to lane, met people of all creeds and communities. He enquired about their problems. He directed the local councillor to pay frequent visits and redress their grievances. He also met petty shop-keepers and businessmen. He listened to their problems sympathetically and patiently. He assured them of his government's assistance. Finally, he advised the people to live in peace and cooperate with the Government to remove poverty, illiteracy and social evils. The people of the locality assured him of their all cooperation. His short visit relieved one and all.

8. You are Shrey working for India Today. Last week, you attended a seminar on 'Pleasures of Eye-Donation', organized by the Young Buzz of your district. Write a report of this seminar in not more than 100 words for publication in The Times of India.

A REPORT ON EYE DONATION

Delhi : 27th June, 200...

From Mr. Shrey, Correspondent from India Today

Last week a seminar on pleasures of eye-donation was organized by the Young Buzz of Rajouri Garden district in the Community Hall of the locality. Approximately one hundred people participated in one day seminar. It was advocated that we must sacrifice our life for the sake of others as the service of humanity is the best service of God. In India, many people suffer from eye-sight. They are either blind by birth or have loss of visibility. Many people lost their eyes in illness or in some accidents. While we are on our last legs we can donate our healthy eyes to the benefit of others. It was a general consensus that this would provide the donor a lot of pleasure. All the participants registered their names with the Medical Superintendent of the Civil Hospital Delhi to donate their eyes when they die.

9. You are Savant of Lala Lajpat Rai Memorial Sr. Secondary School, Poona. Your school has just celebrated its Silver Jubilee on completion of its meritorious services to the cause of education. Now write an article in not more than 100 words on the programmes that your school conducted on this occasion to be published in the Times of India.

SILVER JUBILEE CELEBRATIONS

Lala Lajpat Rai Memorial Sr. Secondary School, Poona is doing a yeoman's service to the cause of education since

2005. It celebrated its Silver Jubilee function on 5th August 1997. All the old and the present students participated in the function. This celebration was inaugurated by Hon'ble President of India because he himself had been a meritorious student of this institutions. He praised the all round progress of the institution where the teachers have taken an oath to impart their knowledge and wisdom to the cause of students' community. He revealed that most of the students of this institutions are serving the nation and they have got prestigeous ranks either in Government or in private organisations. He spoke that institutions like Lala Lajpat Rai Memorial are very rare in India. Certain students spoke about their career development through this institution. They spoke highly of the Principal and the teaching staff. The President gave prizes to all the brilliant students. A cultural programme was presented to entertain the guests. Everybody left the institution with words of praise.

10. You have witnessed a train accident where the Delhi-bound Goa Express derailed. Write a report in 125 words to be published in Naveen Times, Goa. You are Rohan of Goa.

A REPORT ON TRAIN ACCIDENT

Goa : 5th August 200....

By Mr. Rohan of Naveen Times

A very ghastly accident took place yesterday at 6.30 a.m. when a passenger train collided with Delhi-bound Goa Express near Panaji. According to an eye-witness, the passenger train was given a clearance on the wrong track while the Goa Express was coming. All of a sudden, the passengers felt a heavy jerk causing the first three compartments derailed. Other victims cried mercilessly and were tracing their near and dear ones. The farmers from the nearby fields came to help the injured. The engine driver and his helper were killed instantly.

More than 150 passengers were seriously injured. The station staff and the Red Cross ambulance arrived in no time and took the passengers to the Railway Hospital. The Railway Minister announced a payment of rupees 20,000 each to the victims of the train accident. A railway inquiry has been instituted. It will be in the fitness of things that we should do our duty honestly and deligently leaving aside no error.

11. Write a report, in about 100 words, for the Local Newspaper on the Republic Day Celebration is held at your school. (Use Model Senior Secondary School ABC city) as the fictitious name for your school.

REPUBLIC DAY CELEBRATIONS

ABC City : 26th January, 2005

From our special correspondent—Mr. A. Gupta.

Republic Day was celebrated at Model Senior Secondary School Salem today with great pomp and show. The Chief Justice of India was the chief guest on the occasion. He reached in time, and was taken to the platform to unfurl the National Flag. He told about those innumerable volunteers who sacrificed their lives for the cause of motherland. He paid a glorious tribute to hounour them. He stressed the need of discipline and moral values in life. He exhorted them to cultivate the ideals of the great national leaders. Earlier he was introduced with the staff members and the school managing committee. A colourful cultural programme was presented by the students. The highlights of the programme were patriotism, devotion and loyalty to the country. All praised the programme very much. We took a pledge to serve our motherland till we have life.

12. You are the co-ordinator of your school Junior Red Cross Group. Prepare a report on its activities of this academic year, to be published in your school magazine.

ANNUAL REPORT OF JUNIOR RED CROSS GROUP

Delhi : 5th August, 2007

By Miss Kavita, Junior Red Cross Coordinater

The Junior Red Cross Group of this area is doing a Yeoman Service for all. During the year 2003-2004 it achieved a rewarding success in its mission and created awareness among the people about their health and hygiene by organising seminars, workshops and camps. In the Blood Donation camp more than 500 volunteers donated their blood which made the group perplexed. Throughout the year the group arranged training workshops in First Aid, HIV/AID, Eye donation, cleaning, A week long exhibition was arranged during the winter break at the Community Hall in Karampura. A team of doctors from WHO conducted a seminar which was attended by more than two hundred residents. The slum-dwellers were given comprehensive awareness about water-borne diseases and the precautionary measures to be taken in this regard. In the coming year, the group has planned to conduct more activities.

13. You are Rohit of Vivekananda Sr. Secondary School of Banglore. Your school has recently Conducted a charity show in aid of the flood affected people of Andhra. As cultural secretary of the students' council of your school, write a brief report in not more than 100 words on this activity of the school for publication in "The Hindu."

ANDHRA ADVERSELY HIT BY FLOODS

Banglore : 5th August, 2005

A hectic survey of flood hit areas of Andhra was arranged by the Government officials and other local agencies. It was seen that the Government and other social organisations were trying to provide all possible facilities to the victims. A knee deep water could be seen everywhere in the areas of Raj Nagar, C.C. Colony, Pandit lane, Rajaji Square and King's Marg. The residents told that the drainage facilities for the outlet of water were only in names. The officials go on sleeping but they awake a little near the rainy season. People are in need of immense help and relief. So to provide all possible assistance, the students of Vivekananda Sr. Secondary School Banglore organised a charity show in the school compound for three days to raise money in aid of the flood victims. The show lasted for 3 days in the first week of August. Students and general public responded to the show in great number. Tickets were sold in good quantity. They collected one lakh rupee to support the worst people of Andhra. The money was immediately sent to Prime Minister's Relief Fund to help the affected people.

14. 'Each One Plant One' campaign was organised by you to celebrate, Vanamahotsva Day on 10th November. As Secretary of your school, Armada Public School, Delhi, write a report in 100-125 words for your school magazine. You are Anant of Delhi.

EACH ONE PLANT ONE

Delhi : 10th March, 2005

A Vanmahotsava Day was organised in Armada Public school in which the motive was 'Each One Plant One'. Every one planted a tree. Chief Minister of Delhi was the Chief Guest. He spoke on the importance of trees. He told that the trees maintain ecological balance in the nature. They provide medicines and timber for our survival. Many people depend on the trees to earn their livelihood.

An exhibition was also arranged in the school by the students stressing the need of tree plantation and their utility to the society. Various solgans regarding the 'Importance of Trees' were displayed. We should organise such functions to make the public aware of the wonders of trees.

15. Write a report on : "Environmental Pollution is a Health Hazard."

New Delhi : 5th August, 2005

From our special correspondent.

Population is a way of vitiating the environment through adding impurities in it. Our environment is constantly polluted through different objects.

—Smoke and noise pollute the air, sewage pollutes the water and solid wastes (garbage and junk etc.) pollute the land. Population explosion, urbanisation and industrialisation are its major reasons. Industrial units and sewage of big cities drop their wastes in the rivers. This results into spreading of chemicals which are harmful for the water. Plants, animals and human beings die by using the polluted water. Often it causes cancerous diseases like cholera, jaundice and diahorrea etc. The smoke of the factories and vehicles create health problems. We regularly breathe or inhale this polluted air. Headache, nausea and many other diseases of lungs and heart get birth. This is a serious health hazard to all of us. We should use anti pollutant materials in our vehicles. Noise makes our hearing power impaired. We would be on our safe side if we are very conscious about pollution.

16. You participated in a career counselling programme organized by Careers India. You had the opportunity of listening to professionals from various fields like food technology, fashion technology, media management etc. Write a report of the programme for Career Times. You are Vivek.

A REPORT ON CAREER COUNSELLING PROGRAMME

Delhi : 23rd June, 2005

By Mr. Vivek

One day career counselling programme was organized in our school by Careers India, Education Academy New Delhi on

22nd June. Students from nearby schools and other youths of locality attended the lectures given by expert professionals in the fields of food technology, fashion technology and media management. Students of Art stream showed their interest in media management. Some decided to be journalists, editors and social educationists. The girl students were hankering after the food technology and fashion designing though the boys were taking keen interest in both the courses. After the workshop was over, an exhibition was arranged having complete information including books, institutions and other details. Some of the parents put questions for further avenues in other fields for their wards. It was a nice programme. It was wound up by the expert lecture of the Director Counselling, Ministry of Education Delhi. He gave a message 'Let us not be a parasite on the society'. All praised the programme very much as it was an eye-opener and educative to aware the students and the parents for their future prospects.

17. You are Madhu, a staff reporter of the Times of India. You have been asked to cover the incident of a day light robbery when the inmates were present, in a house in the outskirts of Delhi. Write a report in about 100 words.

A REPORT ON DAY LIGHT ROBBERY

New Delhi : 10th August, 2007

By a Staff Reporter, Mrs. Madhu

Three unidentified armed youths robbed a businessman's house in Najafgarh Colony situated, in the outskirts of Delhi. They robbed a golden colour Fort Ikon car, jewellery, money and stereo. It had been learnt that the robbers had guns in their hands. West district police had sounded an alert in the area. The car owner had a jewellery shop in Chandni Chowk. He, his wife and the other members of the household were present in the house enjoying their dinner. It was a broad day light robbery. It had been learnt that they entered from the back door in the street, cut off the wire and took away valuable articles. Nobody raised a voice for fear of being shot dead. Their small ten years servant was found strangled and tied with the cot. The police is investigating the case.

18. A.K. Singh a Staff Reporter with Daily Hindustan in Agra reports about a road accident involving a lorry and a Maruti car. Write his report including details of numbers of people injured and the extent of damage caused to the colliding vehicles in not more than 100 words.

FROM OUR STAFF REPORTER A.K. SINGH

Agra : 5th August 2005

A very fatal accident took place yesterday on Agra Delhi road at 12.00 p.m. It was a serious and sudden collision between a lorry and a maruti car. The maruti car was running at a break neck speed. It was coming from Delhi while the lorry containing 40 passengers took a sudden turn from the bus stop towards Delhi. The maruti car struck directly in the mouth of the lorry. The driver breathed his last on the spot. The four other passengers had serious injuries on their bodies. The passengers sitting in the lorry got a heavy jerk and some of them got bruises on their bodies. The victims were taken to the hospital. The police came and registered a case. It was a very shocking accident.

19. Your school has celebrated 'Library Week'. As the Head Boy/Head Girl of your school, write a report on it to be published in your school News Letter.

REPORT ON LIBRARY WEEK

Delhi : 3rd March, 200...

By Mr. Yash

A library week was celebrated in Hindu Senior Secondary School, Sonepat with the close cooperation of the students. The school library was tastefully decorated and arranged with books, magazines, papers, charts and innumerable written material in the hall. The school counsellor was guiding and awaring the students about the utility of books and adopting books both as a hobby and career in life. The books are our everlasting friends and enable our souls by removing darkness and superstitious ideas from our minds. Such types of weeks play an important role in our life. They inculcate the habit of learning and bring us near to the genius people. Not only this, they bring punctuality, regularity and develop a balanced personality in a man. They provide current information about different countries and bring us close to them. In reality, such weeks serve a befitting knowledge, gate for all.

20. Recently you have celebrated the Golden Jubilee of your school, Noida Public School, Noida. Write a report in about 125 words to be published in your school magazine. Sign as Vinod of Class XII.

REPORT ON GOLDEN JUBILEE CELEBRATIONS

Noida : 10 the October 200...

By Vinod of Class XII

Golden Jubilee Celebrations of Noida Public School drew a special attention of all and sundry after the completion of its 50 years of meritorious services to the cause of education. The whole campus looked like a newly-wedded queen. The Golden Jubilee was celebrated on 8th October under the chairmanship of his Highness, the Governor of Uttar Pradesh as he was the ex-student of this school. The students decorated a huge pandal to depict various themes and concepts through quotations and charts. An exhibition on environment preservation was arranged by the Eco-Club. The Chief Guest declared the programme open. The Principal delivered a speech which highlighted the contribution of the institute in the cause of education and social service during the past 50 years. The school alumni also shared his moments in the school. The Chief Guest acknowledged the meritorious services and retorted his pride to be the ex-students of this institution. He gave away prizes and awards to the students and the teachers. The programme concluded with the singing of National Anthem.

21. You are Ritu. As a special correspondent of a leading local daily, you are sent to cover a Three Day Book Fair organised by the Book Publishers and Distributors in the city. The Book Fair also organised a series of competitions for school students. Write a report in about 125 words for publication in a local daily.

REPORT ON A THREE-DAY BOOK FAIR

Delhi : 16th April, 2005

By Ritu, a Special Correspondent

A three Day Book Fair was organised by the Book Publishers and Distributors of India in the Pragati Maidan on 3rd April, 2007. Leading publishers and distributors of good repute participated in it. They had set up their books on different subjects, languages, designing, science, medicine, law, computer and architecture. There were even attractive designs, multi-coloured pictures, fine printing and hard bound library covers. Books on language and literature printed by J.P.H. Mansarover Garden were selling like hot cakes. Students liked the Interactive Grammar by Dr. R.K. Mittal and many schools purchased it as their reference book. The interactive sessons with the authors were quite illuminating and a rewarding experience. Children books were also available detailing the system of education in foreign countries. Comics and Cartoons were in great demand. In short the Book Fair created a new enthusiasm for learning and awakening among the book lovers.

22. You are Sundresh of Rajeev Gandhi Memorial Sr. Secondary School, Allahabad. Your school has just inaugurated its new computer wing, constructed with generous grants from the Rajeev Gandhi Foundation. Write a report in not more than 100 words for your school

magazine on the programme organised by the school on this occasion.

A NEW COMPUTER WING IN RAJEEV GANDHI SCHOOL

Allahabad : 3rd March, 2005

Due to the mounting pressure from the public and the students, the management has got a rewarding success for the construction of a new computer wing in the institution. It was inaugurated by the state minister for Education in the 1st week of March. The new wing has two different workshops with all the modern computerised facilities. There are five lecture rooms for the students to get themselves trained in Hardware, software and other allied fields. From the ensuing academic session, near about 200 students can be benefitted by getting admissions in various courses. This will provide a help in removing unemployment from the minds of modern youth. They would become bright professionals. For all the construction work and the availability of equipments, the credit goes to the Rajeev Gandhi Foundation Trust which is kind enough to release generous grants for the institution in achieving a long cherished vision.

23. You are Rajesh working for the Sunday Magazine. Last week, you attended seminar on the importance of 'Blood Donation', organised by All India Medical Institute, Delhi. Write a report of the seminar in not more than 100 words for publication the magazine you represent.

A REPORT ON BLOOD DONATION

New Delhi : 5th March, 200....

From our own Correspondent Mr. Rajesh

Yesterday a seminar on 'The Importance of Blood Donation' was organised by the All India Medical Institute of Medical Sciences, New Delhi. Near about 30 delegates of good repute from different states and 400 doctors attended the seminar.

The Union Health Minister pointed out the importance of blood for our life. He revealed that a single drop of blood can save the precious life of a dying man. The Medical Superintendent stated that by donating blood they were not inviting any ailment or deficiency of any kind in the body. It is the mental or psychological whim that a donor possesses in his or her mind about some weakness. A healthy man can donate blood after every six months and he will remain in a perfect trim. Other eminent doctors, too, stated that they should save and protect their blood and utilise it at the proper time. The seminar concluded that masses should be educated to donate blood.

24. You are Mukul of Laxmi Bai Sr. Secondary School, Gwalior. Your school has recently organised a Blood Donation Camp on the occasion of its Silver Jubilee celebrations. Now write a report in not more than 100 words as an editor for year school magazine on this widely acclaimed activity.

REPORT ON BLOOD DONATION CAMP

Gwalior : 10th Feb. 2005

From Our School Editor Mukul

On the auspicious occasion of Silver Jubilee Celebrations in Laxmi Bai Sr. Secondary School, Gwalior, a Blood Donation Camp was organised by the school authorities on 9th February. The Principal Secretary to the Health Minister inaugurated the function at 10 a.m., by donating his blood. A long queue of ex-students of this school was waiting for their turn to donate the blood. There were five doctors and ten nurses to collect the blood. It looked nice to see the high dignitaries standing for blood donation. They were praising both the academic and other fields of the school. They were speaking that this institution was a boon for the area which is meant for an all round development of the boy. Its students always get top positions. The camp lasted for 4 hours. The donors were issued certificates. People were leaving the place in high spirits.

25. As Apoorva, a newspaper correspondent, prepare a report in 125 words on the traffic conditions prevailing in your locality.

A REPORT ON TRAFFIC CHAO IN SUBHASH PARK

Agra : 10th August 2007

By Apoorva, Our Correspondent

Subhash Park of Agra is a very busy place round the clock and not a single moment passes even in the biting cold, when one cannot fail to witness a passer-by. But during the peak hours, the area creates a scene of utter chaos and confusion. The entire stretch upto Prem Vihar is very narrow and the unending stream of buses, vans, cars, auto-rickshaws, bicycles and pedestrians result in traffic jam. It causes a great inconvience to the public, students and the office-goers in the morning. Even in the afternoon, the traffic remains jam due to rush of the school students. More often there occurs accidents. The traffic crawls rather than moving smoothly. The traffic congestion fills the air with shrill voices of horns and this irritates temper. During the rainy season the situation becomes all the more troublesome. Even the traffic police tries its best to ensure smooth flow of traffic but there remains disturbance. The Residents have seen the Traffic Commissioner many a times but there is no solution.

26. You have attended a seminar on how to decrease the burden of studies on school going children. Write a report in 100-125 words for your school magazine. You are Ravi/Raveena of Guru Nanak Public School, Delhi.

REPORT ON DECREASING THE BURDEN ON SCHOOL CHILDREN

Delhi : 5th March 200...

By Ravi, Editor School Magazine

Since long our Government has been thinking to decrease the burden of studies on school-going children. Consequently it happened to attend a seminar on this aspect on behalf of Guru Nanak Public School Kanpur. The seminar was organized by the experts of N.C.E.R.T., S.C.E.R.T., C.B.S.E. & Ministry of Human Resources at the Jubilee Hall of Kanpur University. It was attended by more than 100 persons and lasted for three days. The experts debated the school going children should be free from the burden of books and variety of subjects. They pointed out Indian children are more burdend than the foreign students in relation to their physique. They should learn reading, writing, arithmetic and other national and moral values through play way method and creative working. Instead of burdening them with books for their homes, all work need to be completed in their respective institutions. In addition to this, proper attention has to be given for their harmonious development. While leaving the school, a child should feel freeness so that he can participate in other games and physical activities at home. They opined and fixed age and mental development formula for their progress in studies. It was commonly agreed to provide one or two books of a few pages for small children. These books are to be written keeping in view the debated facts and the new books will be available in the coming session.

27. To mark the importance of women in the society "On International Women's Day", different women activities organised this day in the capital. Being a reporter from Times of India News Service, you attended one of the programmes. Draft a report in about 100 words.

A REPORT ON INTERNATIONAL WOMEN'S DAY

New Delhi : 9th March, 200...

By a Staff Reporter

From workshops to burning of effigies and seminars to puppet shows, women activists organised a wide range of programmes in the capital to mark International Women's Day on Monday the 9th March. The joint action front for women organised a function in which Union Human Resources Development Minister and other leaders participated. There the bill on women's reservation in Parliament echoed in everybody's mind. The minister announced "the bill on reservation has already been introduced in this budget session of parliament and will go through". The member activists demanded 33 per cent reservation for women in all spheres, free education for women up to graduation, equal pay for equal work and an end to sexual harassment among other things. Though participants expressed jubilation at the progress women have made in several fields but the crude statistics of crime against women and low literacy among women bothered many.

28. You are Rahul of Laxmi Bai Sr. Secondary School, Meerut. Your school has recently organised a Blood Donation Camp on the occasion of the Republic Day Celebrations. Now write a report as a cultural secretary for your school magazine on this widely acclaimed activity.

BLOOD DONATION CAMP IN LAXMI BAI SCHOOL

Meerut : 27th January, 2005

Maharani Laxmi Bai School has been celebrating the Republic Day function since India got her independence. Every year a varitiey of programmes are exhibited to the guests. This year a Blood Donation camp was inaugurated by the Health Minister of Delhi Government. He was the first to donate the blood. Near about 200 people from the area participated in the camp. People started pouring early in the morning. They donated their blood. The chief guest made the pubic aware about the importance of blood donation. He stressed that single drop of blood could save the life of a departing soul. He unfurled the flag and witnessed the cultural programme. Then he spoke about the sacrifices of innumrable volunteers to the name of freedom for our motherland. In the end donors were given fruits and certificates for this sacrifice. He stressed the need of blood donation. People were impressed on hearing his speech.

29. You have taken part in an inter-school oratorical competition conducted by the government of India on the topic 'Women Empowerment' and won the First Prize at the State level. Write a report of this, to be published in your school magazine. You are XYZ, student of Class XII of ABC school, Vadodara.

A REPORT ON AN INTER-SCHOOL ORATORICAL COMPETITION ON 'WOMEN EMPOWERMENT'

Delhi : 5th August, 200...

By XYZ, ABC School, Vadodra

The Government of India is drafting a National Policy for the Empowerment of Women. In order to know the views of the younger generation on this issue, an inter-school oratorical competition was conducted at the State level by the Ministry of Human Resource Development in the Tagore Hall. I had the honour of representing our school. There were fifteen participants from various schools of Delhi. A panel of three judges was formed to adjudge the best speaker. In his inaugural address, the Secretary of the Ministry of H.R.D. declared that aim of the policy was to ensure educational, political and economic empowerment of women. Some speakers dwelt on the subjection of women by men in a male-dominated society; others advocated reservation for women at various levels. In my speech, I asserted that education should be the cornerstone of any agenda for the empowerment and equality of women since information and life-long learning skills lead to income-generating opportunities, health care, elimination of violence against women and all forms of gender-based discrimination. My speech was adjudged the best and I won the first prize.

30. You are Vivek working as a news correspondent for "The Indian Express" at Mumbai. You were invited by the organisers to cover the much awaited programme of Pop Star Michael Jackson in Mumbai. Write a report on this historic event giving necessary details in not more than 100 words for the benefit of the fans of Michael Jackson.

Mumbai : 3rd March, 2005

From our news correspondent Mr. Vivek

Last year in December 2005 a much awaited dance programme of Pop Star Michael Jackson was organised in Mumbai. Michael Jackson, being a popular figure in the field of dance and music, was in the headings of the different newspapers for his shows in India. After a long awaited uncretainty, Mumbai Corporation ascented to hold his show. Tickets were sold like hot cakes more in advance. When he landed with his band of singers from the aeroplane, a tight security was at work to the cine-star and his people. He exhibited his feats before the public and the audience enjoyed them. Rather all were fascinated over his actions. Their necks were craned and did not know when to leave their seats. It was an enchanting magic for the public. People praised him from the core of their heart. No untoward incident was reported occurred in the city. It was a grand success.

31. You are Shrey working for the Indian Express. As a Press Reporter, you were much worried about Price hike of essential commodities. Write a report in not more than 100 words and suggest measures to sort out the problem.

A REPORT ON PRICE HIKE

Delhi: 5th January, 200....

From our Press Reporter Mr. Shrey

It is a matter of grave concern for all of us that the prices of essential commodities are increasing day-by-day. Not a single day passes, when we don't hear about the price hike. The petty vegetables like potatoes, onions and brinjals etc. are becoming dear in the seasonal days. The availability of pulses is also a thing of anxiety. You can well imagine how a poor worker can make his both ends meet. It is hard for him to earn a square meal per day. The wheat and rice are also not available at the ration shops. Taking a cup of tea is going to become a drink of gods. It looks as if the hoarders and black marketers are earning a lot of profit. At this difficult time government should check ration supply. It should take steps against hoarders. The price line should remain under control. Vehicles on the move and more ration shops need to be opened where one can get items at the reasonable price.

32. You attended a seminar conducted by Swami Krishnananda. The seminar was on the benefits of Yoga for heart ailments and the need to practise it for good health. Write a report about it for your newspaper.

A REPORT ON ATTAINING GOOD HEALTH

Delhi : 5th January, 2005

Mr. Alok Gupta

A seminar was conducted by Swami Krishnananda in the Community Hall of South Avenue New Delhi on 3rd January in the morning hours of the day. More than 100 participants came to attend the seminar which was specifically arranged for the patients of heart attack, hypertension, diabeties and blood pressure. Swami Krishnananda not only delivered a lecture but also taught the use of yoga and other 'asanas'. He demonstrated them and stressed the need of practice in case we want to remain healthy and need a long life. According to him, diseases like heart ailments and blood pressure are very minor. They can be cured permanently through yoga. He stressed the importance of morning walks and minor exercises daily. One can keep fit and eniov a healthy life through yoga.

The participants praised the seminar and took yoga to remain healthy.

33. Write a report on A Popular Television Programme.

New Delhi : 5th March, 2005

Television, being the great wonders of science, has brought the distant world very closer. It is a system of sending pictures and sounds by electrical signals. People can perceive them on a television set in their homes. It is a good source of entertainment. It has an educative value that imparts scientific and allied informations. In the presentage we can't forget its impact on our life. One can enjoy a variety of programmes round the clock. Films, serials, songs, scientific information, geographical facts, business matters and counselling serials go on as per schedule. Among these programmes I like "The India Today" programme very much. It is a clear mirror that presents the actual functioning of the government ministers; officers and other public servants. It not only enlightens us with their actions to dodge the public but also presents specific informations about their misdeeds. I daily watch this programme and leave behind all other routine work. I like this serial very much because it is a resource advancer method.

34. You are Vishal As a special correspondent of a leading local daily, you are sent to cover a two-day cultural fiesta organized by the Rotary Clubs of Delhi for the city school students, in commemoration of the centenary year of the Rotary. Write a report in about 125 words for publication in the local daily.

REPORT ON CULTURAL FIESTA

Delhi : 12th March, 2005

By Vishal—a special correspondent

Rotary Club of the city organized a two-day cultural fiesta for the city school students at the club's cultural centre. It was to commemorate the centenary year of the Rotary.The programme lasted for two days *i.e.* on 10th and 11th March in which students from different schools participated in music, dance, songs, dramas, one act plays and fancy dress competition. It was a very adventurous programme as it encouraged the audience to labour hard to uplift the nation. It held the public spell-bound and they never had a dull moment. The elite audience applauded the splendid items. The Valedictory Function was presided over by Mr. Arun Kumar —Who was the Chief Rotract. He distributed prizes and shields to the students and other members of the club who had rendered a yeoman service for the society. In his winding speech, he stressed the importance of such clubs for the national development. He indicated that such clubs serve as a good platform for all round development of our personality. As the Rotary Club has completed its hundred years, a get-together programme was also arranged. The Chief Rotract gave a new slogan of "Health, Wealth and Work for all."

35. A Report on 'An Exhibition' for a Newspaper.

Delhi : 5th March, 2005

Report from Miss Radha Gupta.

Exhibitions are the mirrors of progress before all of us. They provide new horizons and standards and work as an eye-openers. Every year exhibitions and trade fairs are organised by the Government. This year a specific industrial exhibition was held in Talkatra Garden, Madras. It attracted a throng of visitors from all over the country. It impressed the onlookers that India has made an exemplified progress in the field of industry. People could be seen taking interest in all the items nicely placed in the pavilions. The machinery section, was the busiest one. Agricultural implements of Punjab were in great demand. Some of the stall-keepers were distributing hand-bills to popularise their items. People were walking here and there in an enthusiastic mood. Small children were busy on the merry-go-rounds. Sections containing chemicals too were attracting a huge rush. The refreshment cormer was a busy site to see. We had certain necessary purchases and got out of the exhibition in the evening.

36. You are Umesh. As the President of a voluntary organistion, you have visited a slum area of your city that was destroyed in a massive fire. Write a report on the tragic situation of these homeless people to be published in a magazine.

A REPORT ON FIRE IN A SLUM AREA

Delhi: 7th January 200...

By Umesh

Last week our NSS Group visited the slum area of Kidwai Nagar in our city which had been destroyed in a massive fire about five days ago. It is almost difficult to explain in words the pathetic condition of the slum dwellers which has become from bad to worse after their homes have been almost gutted by the fire. These people have been forced to live on the footpath in the chilly cold and the city government has made no arrangement. It is touching to see their miserable condition. Some of them have lost their wards and belongings completely. Their wailings can melt the heart of anyone. Some voluntary organisations have came to their rescue but there needs concrete steps by the Government. They need money, material and sheltering places. We must not forget that human life is very precious. It is our duty to provide it safety.

37. Arun watched a Cricket Match between the teams of India and Pakistan. He noted down the following points in his note-pad for writing a report for a newspaper. Use these points and write a report in about (100 words) in the space provided.

A REPORT ON A CRICKET MATCH PLAYED BETWEEN INDIA AND PAKISTAN

10th March, 2005, New Delhi.

The young as well as old generation get great pleasure in witnessing or either hearing a running commentary about a cricket match. Most of us have such a fondness that they even fail to participate in their daily important business. Yesterday on 9th March a well organised and enthusiastic one day cricket match was played between the teams of India and Pakistan at the Ferozshah Kotla grounds. The match started at 10.00 a.m. Shri Arun Mittal was working as an umpire. The match was to be exhibited on the T.V. so I switched on my TV at 10.00 a.m. and the team of India started the batting. It was a very brisk game. The team of Pakistan bowled and fielded well. The players were very enthusiastic and did their best. The onlookers were clapping and the team scored 150 runs. The lunch started at the end of India innings. After the lunch the match was becoming quite exciting. Just then Sachin Tendulkar scored many runs and his bating was remarkable. Everybody praised his courage and clapped. He was declared the man of match. India won the match and Pakistan lost It.

38. Recently your school Amethi Public School, Amethi had organised the C.B.S.E. Table Tennis Tournament at the National level. Write a report in 125 words to be published in the C.B.S.E's CEN BOSEC. You are Apoorva, the Sports Secretary of your school.

REPORT ON C.B.S.E. TABLE TENNIS TOURNAMENT

Delhi : 5th January 200...

By Apoorva, Sports Secretary

The C.B.S.E. Table Tennis Tournament at the National Level was held at Amethi Public School, Amethi. There were ten leading teams all over India which have come after defeating their rivals at the district level. So there was neck to neck as well as enchanting competition among the participants. The girls Singles Final Match was between Govt. School Agra and Govt. School Kangra. The first set was won by the girl of Govt. School Kangra and the second was won by the girl of Govt. School Delhi. In the final set, girls of Kangra defeated her rival with 10-15 points. In the boys single final, the encounter was between Vaish School Rohtak and Vidya Mandir Mumbai. The opening of Vidya Mandir boy was disastrous and lost first set with 11-15 points. But in the last two decisive sets it exhibited excellent spirit and stamina by winning the last sets with 11-6 and 11-5 points. The Vaish School boy exhibited a lot of zeal in his shots. It was an adventurous game.

39. Write a report on 'In Air Crash' for a Newspaper.

Simla : 5th March, 2005

By our special correspondent Mrs. Seema Sharma

Many airlines were in operation to transport and back from Simla to Delhi. The Indian Airlines had to start its first flight to Delhi on Wednesday on 'Vijay' a newly remodelled aeroplane. It was supreme, safest and suitable to the conveniences of all. All the passengers were in high spirits. A great throng of people including the press photographers and newspapers had gathered to see its first launching. The weather was all fair. The captain, the pilot and the other service men had undaunting courage. Nearly 50 passengers boarded the plane at 10.00 a.m. It started as scheduled and press photographs took snaps. As it rose in the sky, it started revolving. The signals emitting red lights. The crowd was perplexed to see a sudden and fantastic change. The safest plane was about to fall leaving all at the death door. It fell at a height of 100 feet in the vicinity of the aerodrum. The smart pilot handled the situation very carefully and saved all. All the passengers praised him.

40. You are Ritu. As a special correspondent of a leading local daily you are sent to cover a two-week Book Fair organized by the book publishers and distributors in the city. Write a report in about 125 words for publication in a local daily.

REPORT ON BOOK FAIR

Delhi : 15th November, 2005

By our special correspondent Ritu

A two-week Book Fair commencing from 1st November to 14th November was organized at Pragati Maidan by All India Association of Book Publishers and Distributors. The publishers and distributors have well arranged their pavilions by keeping books and other printed materials on all subjects and on different languages. The entry was by tickets. Some foreign book publishers also participated in it. Lovers of literature, librarians, academicians, scholars of medicine, law, engineering, agriculture, electronics, computers, fashion designing, dress and weaving materials were visiting the fair in great number. A heavy rush was seen on all the working and other days. The Minister for Human Resources and Development inaugurated the fair. Such kinds of fairs provide a good deal of information on what is happening in the remotest part of the world. These are the literary tools that pave a way for first hand knowledge and information.

41. You are the correspondent of a newspaper. Write a brief report for your paper on a violent student demonstration. Sign yourself as Sumit.

STUDENT'S DEMONSTRATION

Delhi—4th March 2005

From our special correspondent Sumit.

The University Students in the South campus held a violent demonstration before the Vice-Chanceller's office. They were having hand bills in their hands. They raised slogans to change the fee structure and examination pattern from the university. They were demanding to fulfil their outstanding demands. They raised slogans and disturbed the general discipline. Other students came out of their classes and hampered the traffic. The roads were jammed and the police had to open tear gas shells and fired in the open. There was no casualty. This demonstration completely brought the educational work to a stand still. Ultimately the vice chaneller appeared in the crowd and received their memorandum. He assured the students to think over their rightful demands.

42. You are Roshan Secretary of Cultural Club, Hyderabad Public School, Hyderabad. As a member of N.G.C. (National Green Crops), write a report, in 100-125 words for your school magazine, about the activities organised by your club for greening of the environment.

A REPORT ON GREENING THE ENVIRONMENT

Hyderabad : 5th January, 200....

By Rohan, Secretary Cultural Club

Hyderabad Publc School is in the habit of organising cultural, social, national, educational first-aid, health awareness and other multiple activities through its students. This year the N.G.C. Wing of the cultural club did a commendable service by greening the environment. The students planted trees and green saplings in the surrounding areas of Hyderabad. They even took a vow to care for these trees till they had proper growth. They formed groups, selected open sites and other vacant lands for planting trees of different kinds. In order to create awareness among the massess the club organized camps seminars and workshops stressing the need to plant more and more trees as they provide life, health, freshness, rain and protect our soil and environment from pollution. In the school, too, a green nursery has been set up under the careful guidance of our Horticulture Incharge. Here the different varieties of plants, saplings and flowers will be grown by the students. It is underway that an advertisement may be added in the local dailies awaring the people for free supply of plants and other green saplings. This will help our campaign in greening the environment.

43. You are Anita. As a representative of your resident welfare association, you have attended an awareness camp on "Keeping the Campus Clean". Write a report in about 125 words for publication in your association's newsletter.

REPORT ON KEEPING THE CAMPUS CLEAN

Delhi : 5th January, 2005

By Anita a representative from Resident Welfare Association

The Health Unit of Delhi Corporation organized an awareness camp in Kamla Nagar on keeping the campus neat and clean. More than 100 representatives from nearby associations of different areas attended the camp. It enriched their knowledge on keeping their environment clean. Different experts on cleanliness stressed the importance of keeping hale and hearty as a sound mind dwells in a healthy body. They told that life in unhygienic surroundings gives a call to so many fatal diseases which very often results in loss of life, money, time and energy. They advised to keep our streets and drains neat by using cleanliness modes. Insecticides need to be sprayed at least once in a week. We should not let the water collect in the pits as these become the breeding points for the mosquitoes. The damaged roads, streets, and drains should be repaired immediately. We should wash our hands before eating. This camp opened their eyes. May the government arrange such health awareness camps now and then in every locality so that all and sundry can benefit from them.

44. Your school has recently celebrated its Golden Jubilee, organising a number of inter-school competitions and awarded the prizes at a gala function. As the Secretary

of the Cultural Club of "your school, write a report in 125 words, suitable to be published in your school magazine. Your are Sumit.

REPORT ON CELEBRATING GOLDEN JUBILEE

Delhi : 3rd March, 200...

By Mr. Sumit, Secretary Cultural Club

Lala Lajpat Rai Senior School, Pilani celebrated its Golden Jubilee on completion of its 50 years service to the cause of education. The old and the young students participated in the function. Dr. R. K. Mittal, Chief Patron of the school inaugurated the function and spoke highly of the institution. He impressed the need of moral and vocational education so that the future generation should not be a parasite on the society. He revealed that the pious soil of this institution has produced many academicians, lawyers, engineers, players, magistrates and ministers. He paid great tributes to the teachers who have dedicated their lives to the nation. His speech filled the students with zeal, inspiration and enthusiasm to work the masses. A variety of cultural programmes were conducted by the students to celebrate this grand day. All the programmes were exciting and a mass gathering clapped on all the occasions. To make the day more memorable, a Blood Donation Camp was organised by the cultural club of the school in which more than 200 students donated their blood. The function came to a close with a light refreshment.

45. While you were waiting for a bus, a scooterist hitting a cyclist and running away to escape the wrath of the people. You went to the police station and lodged a report. Write out the report in such a way that it will help the police catch the offender.

Delhi : 25th August, 1997.

Yesterday, I was waiting for my Route No. 512 at Adarsh Nagar bus stand. There stood a huge rush of passengers. A poor cyclist was passing on the road at a fairly good speed. Soon a scooterist appeared at a breakneck speed. He hit the cyclist who fell on the ground. The scooterist did not stop and he took to his heels to save his skin. People gathered round the cyclist. He got severe injuries. The blood was profusely coming from his 'wrists and thighs. He was taken to the Adarsh Hospital for immediate medical aid and I went to the Police Station and lodged a report. The scooterist was driving without a helmet. He was a youngman of 25 years with cream shirt and a new black coloured scooter with a faint number DDH-2909. The constable on duty registered a report. I hope that the police would arrest the scooterist in no time.

46. You were a member of your School Quiz Team which won the C.B.S.E. Quiz Contest at the National level. Draft a report about it to be published in your school magazine in about 125 words. You are Rohan.

A REPORT ABOUT CBSE QUIZ CONTEST

Delhi : 11th August 200...

By Rohan, a member of School Quiz Team

I feel proud and happy to have been a member of our School Quiz Team which won CBSE/ Bournvita Quiz Contest at the National/Regional level. The Quiz Contest was organized in Govt. School, Simla on 10th August, 200.... More than 12 teams participated in the contest.

This contest was to test the general knowledge of the school children of Secondary and Senior Secondary level. One was to speak in its favour and the other side in its opposition. There was a set of three judges to announce the result. The questionnaire had a variety of questions on science, literature, music and general knowledge. He was an expert from Delhi. The students of the rival team had a tough competition. Our school team was well-equipped with all the answers. The students answered very sharply and answered almost all the questions. Thus, they secured 75 points while the rival team could get only 60 points. The judges declared the result and offered the trophy to our team. It was a great event for all of us.

47. You are the correspondent of a newspaper. Write a brief report for your paper on an earthquake in your area. Sign yourself as Anand Kumar.

EARTHQUAKE HITS AMBALA CITY

Jabalpur : 22nd May, 2005

From our own correspondent Anand Kumar

Jabalpur—All of a sudden early in the morning of 22nd May, violent conclussions of earthquake were felt at about 4.30 a.m. The duration of the earthquake was for about ten to fifteen seconds. Everything was moving. People came out of their premises. They were crying 'save! save!' within no time, everything stopped moving. There was a great loss to the property of the poor people. A few kacha houses were damaged. All the activities came to a stand still. The local bus stand fell on the ground which destroyed the buses. Near about eighty people lost their lives. It was a very dangerous earthquake. Cracks also appeared in many buildings. Municipal office was completely devastated. The estimated loss was more than 100 crores.

48. You are Veena. As a representative of your resident welfare association, you have attended a workshop on physical fitness. Write a report in about 125 words for publication in your association's news letter.

REPORT ON A WORKSHOP ON PHYSICAL FITNESS

Delhi: 10th March, 2005

By Veena, Our special representative

Panchsheel Residents' Welfare Association organized a day long workshop yesterday in its Community Hall on "Physical

Fitness." Representatives from other associations attended the workshop and gave suggestions in this regard. This workshop included yoga experts and naturopaths to advise the people. They revealed the miraculous results of yogas, asanas, and pranayams in healing incurable and fatal ailments. They demonstrated them before the public and retorted their uses. They pinpointed that every man can survive more than a century or more in case he becomes addicted to such exercises. They all advocated that morning walk is a panacea for hundred and one diseases. They stressed the need of open air & pure food. We should keep ourselves away from junk and tasty foods duly available in the markets as these give a clear call for ill-health. Let us keep ourselves hale and hearty by keeping ourselves fit.

49. Suppose that you are a Newspaper Reporter. Writer in about 100 words an account for your paper of a fire in a cloth market.

New Delhi—5th March, 2005

By Our Special Correspondent Anand Kumar

A devastating fire broke out in a crowded Cloth Market in Katra New Adampura Nai Sarak, at about 8 a.m. Twenty-five shops were completely gutted. The cause of the fire was not known. The fire started from one shop but soon it spread to the other shop nearby. The flames began to rise sky high. The other shop-keepers pulled down their shutters. There was great confusion. People ran helter-shelter. Within half an hour the city fire-brigade arrived. The fireman fought the flames bravely and could not control the fire till 2.00 p.m. More water tanks and sand trucks were called for. The Military and Police showed remarkable courage and controlled it at 4.00 p.m. The area was very tense. It was all cloudy. The shopkeepers were weeping profusely. The P.M. reached there and assured all possible help. A judicial enquiry was ordered to probe into the cause of fire. However, the property worth Rs. 2,000 crore was destroyed.

50. Your school celebrated the Teacher's Day on 5th September. Prepare a report in 125 words to be sent to CBSE. Sign as Deepak of Jindal Public School, Indore.

A REPORT ON TEACHER'S DAY

Indore : 6th September 2007

By Deepak, Student of Jindal Public School

Yesterday Hindu Public School celebrated the birthday of Dr.S. Radhakrishnan as the day is celebrated as a Teachers' Day in all the schools of India. On this day, the school students run the school like all the other working days. On this day, Miss Priyanka headed the school with a team of 30 students to work as lecturers and teachers. The morning assembly was conducted with the speech of pupil principal. She stressed the importance of a teacher who burns himself like a candle and gives light to all. Then the school started in accordance with the fixed timetable. There was perfect discipline and regularity in the school. The pupil teachers were taking their classes with perfect trim and the students were busy in their work. In the last period, the worthy principal held a meeting of her staff in which the student teachers revealed their experiences. The school came to a close after a light refreshment among the staff members.

51. You are Sweta as a representative of your resident welfare association, you have attended a workshop on Art and Handwork. Write a report in about 125 words for publication in your associations newsletter.

WORKSHOP ON ART AND HANDWORK

Kanpur : 5th April, 2005

From a Representative of Pancsheel Residents Welfare Association

An educative-cum-knowledgeable as well as vocational workshop on 'Art and Handwork' was organised by the Lions

Club in the Community Hall, Subhash Chowk, Kanpur on 4th April at 10.00 a.m. Mr. Ashok, the Chief Lion inaugrated the workshop by lighting an earthern lamp before the Goddess Saraswati. The Lion's Club has invited representatives from different welfare associations to make them aware about the Art and Handwork activities that can be learnt by the residents during their spare time and thus they can bring a good improvement in their economic culture. It is a good resource to use one's leisure also. There were artists and handicraft engineers who provided handsome information, written material and different modes to start our own industry on a small as well large scale in the houses. Ladies were much lured towards the handicraft items while the gents desired to learn art in small items made from paper, earth, plastic, cloth, straw and pulp etc. It was a good event and the participants praised this workshop and showed deep interest in setting up their work.

52. You are Arun Mittal from Bharathi Pharmacy College Doddi Banglore. You organised a team of ten students to visit the holy cave of Amarnath. The natural calamities did not support your team to procced to the place and you had to stay half-way. Your team visited the affected people. Write a report giving it a suitable title in about 100 words. Pose yourself a reporter from the Times of India News Service.

'YATRA' IS FROZEN AS 51 PILGRIMS DIE OF COLD

Srinagar : August 23, 2005

The Times of India News Service

At least 51 pilgrims to the cave-temple of Amamath have died of cold since Thursday as more than 85,000 pilgrims are stranded along the route due to snow and heavy rains.

(Meanwhile, a report from Jammu said that the Amamath pilgrimage was officially frozen till the clearing of weather as heavy rain continued to lash the entire Jammu region on Friday. The rains led to six deaths in house collapses and inundation of 75 villages by swollen rivers.)

The Himalayan mountains in south Kashmir have witnessed an untimely snowfall and incessant rains since Thursday, causing disruption in the annual pilgrimage to the high-altitude abode of Lord Shiva, which began a week ago. The authorities here said more than 65,000 pilgrims were stranded along the 46-km. route between Phalagam; base camp for the trek, and the cave situated at a height of 14,000 feet. Of them, at least 40,000 are held up at Sheshnag and Panchtarni, high altitude points along the trekking route.

Reports say that 51 of them have died due to cold since Thursday. However, the authorities fear that the toll may rise.

They say the evacuation of the standed pilgrims by helicopters is not possible due to bad weather. The dead are being cremated on the spot. The pilgrims have come from different parts of the country.

53. You have witnessed a major clash between two political parties near your house in Aligarh. Prepare a report in 125 words to be published in the National Herald Lucknow. Sign as Ramola.

A REPORT ON CLASH BETWEEN TWO POLITICAL PARTIES

Aligarh : 20th May 200...

By Ramola, Editor National Herald

Yesterday a pitched battle was witnessed between two political parties on a very simple abuse. All of a sudden a youth appeared in the street where some people were standing. He passed some indecent remarks on some lady who was the sister of a person standing there. He belonged to some other political party. On hearing the remarks, a very violent protest started between the members of other political party. In no time, members of both the parties gathered in the street and there arose a clash which finally ended in pitched battle between the fighting group. The members resorted to stone-pelting. The situation worsened when they attempted to blaze the two state transport buses but the police failed to control the situation. Five people died on the spot and twenty one were taken to the hospital. The government declared state of emergency in the area. The situation is very tense.

54. You are the survivor of a train accident. Write a report of what happened in about 100 words.

REPORT ON TRAIN ACCIDENT

On 5th July, 2005, I was an eye-witness to train accident on the Delhi-Bhopal line. I was travelling by the T.N. Express. I was fast asleep when I felt a jerk and was thrown away aside. The train had stopped. When I woke up I heard cries and shouts all around. It took me a few minutes before I learnt that our train had collided with a goods train coming from the opposite direction. The engine and four bogies were derailed. Luckily, there was no loss of life. Only a few passengers sustained minor injuries. There were a lot of cries. People were shouting help! help! They were given first-aid. Only two passengers were admitted to the Government Hospital. After an hour a relief train arrived to take the passengers. People took a sigh of relief and proceeded to their destinations with troubled faces.

55. Your school has arranged a programme on Life Skills for Class X and XII. Experts invited on the occasion delivered speeches on motivation, stress management, goal setting and inter-personal relationship, which were of immense help to the students in acquiring leadership qualities. Write a report in 125 words, sign as Pallavi, National Public School, Hyderabad.

A REPORT ON ACQUIRING LEADERSHIP QUALITIES

Hyderabad : 10th April 200...

By Pallavi, Student Reporter

In the present era, we are passing through the most competitive age in which we need to develop diversified skills and capacities. Many times we lose golden opportunities which may bring challenging rewards in our life. But very often we lack knowledge about our life management. In order to make aware about the need of life skills, National Public School Hyderabad invited a team of experts in this field. They delivered speeches on motivation, stress management, goal setting and inter-personal relationship which are of immense help to us in acquiring leadership qualities. One of the experts advocated the need for patience, perserverance, positive thinking and behavioural science to understand our vital life so as to become a goal achiever. The programme ended with vows to live an opportunistic life.

56. You are Sweta. As a special correspondent of a leading local daily, you are sent to cover a fund raising programme organised provide a New Computer Laboratory for the school in your town, organised by a non-governmental organisation in the city. Write a report in about 125 words for publication in the daily.

FUND RAISING PROGRAMME FOR A COMPUTER LABORATORY

Delhi : 5th April, 2005

By Sweta

Rajiv Dramatics, a non-government social service organisation, arranged a thrilling cultural night in ABC School on 3rd April in order to collect a huge amount from the on lookers. The entry was the tickets worth Rs. 50 each. There the reputed film actors participated in the programme and thrilled and entertained the public with their songs, actions, mono act and dancing. Their fun and frolic kept in audience spell-bound. The ceremony was inaugrated by the State Education Minister who donated a cheque of Rs. 50,000 to the Principal for arranging relevant material for the Computer Laboratory. More than 2 lacs of rupees were collected on that day. It was a nice programme to see. In reality the Non-Government organisations have become a boon for the institutions and public as their roles do a miraculous service for all.

57. You have witnessed a road accident on Mathura Road, Delhi. You are Amit, a reporter of the New Indian Express, Delhi. Write a report on the accident in 125 words to be published in the newspaper.

A REPORT ON ROAD ACCIDENT

Delhi : 5th August 200....

From Mr. Amit, Editor New Indian Express

A very fatal road accident took place on Mathura Road Delhi at 11.30 a.m. It was a sudden and serious collision between a lorry and a Maruti car. The Maruti car was running at a break-neck speed. It was coming from Delhi near Ashram while the lorry containing 40 passengers took a sudden turn from the bus stop towards Delhi. The Maruti car struck directly in the mouth of the lorry. The driver breathed his last on the spot. The four other passengers got serious injuries on their bodies. The passengers sitting in the lorry felt heavy jerks and some of them got bruises on their bodies. The victims were taken to the hospital. The police came and registered a case. It was a very shocking accident. We should be very careful while driving our vehicles so that any mishap can be avoided well in time.

58. You are Amit. As a special correspondent of a local daily, you are sent to cover the inauguration of a Trade Fair where international agencies have put up their

stalls for the exhibition and sale of their products. Write a report in about 125 words for publication in the newspaper.

A REPORTER OR TRADE FAIR INAUGURATION

New Delhi : 15th November, 200...

By Amit

Every year on the eve of Children's Day, the Trade Fair Authority of India organises a trade fair for one week. It has a decorative assembling of pavillions from all the states, union territories and the foreign countries. They exhibit their items and important products in the stalls and people from every nook and corner visit the fair and purchase items of their interest. Industrialists, farmers, businessmen, educationists and engineers etc. take keen interest and get good knowledge to boost their products. This year the exhibition was inaugurated by the Prime Minister of India at 9.00 a.m. There was a great rush of people, politicians, ministers, students and the others. The stills of computer, electronics and herbal medicines were put up at the fair. It looked as if the whole India had shown her presence in the fair. Such fairs and exhibitions help exhibit the new inventions and progress of the nation.

59. You are Rohan as a representative of your resident welfare association, you have attended an awareness camp on 'Keeping the City Clean'. Write a report on the camp and also about the suggestions given in the camp on connection with keeping the city clean for publication in your association's newsletter (about 125 words)

REPORT ON KEEPING THE CITY CLEAN

Sonepat : 5th April, 2005

By Rohan—a representative of Nidhi Resident's Welfare Association

A one day Keeping the City Clean Camp was organised by the Friend's Club of the city in a Manav Sewa Hall of

Panchsheel Colony on 3rd April to make the people aware about the importance of keeping the city clean and methods to remain healthy and wealthy. More than 50 representatives from different welfare associations assembled in the camp and heard the lectures delivered by eminent health care experts, doctors health officers and media-men. All of them stressed the need for keeping the surroundings and the environment neat and clean as unhealthy surroundings give a birth to a lot of fatal diseases. During the rainy and summer season, they gave the suggestions to safeguard our bodies and eyes neat and clean. They told the importance of keeping a pure water bottle while beaming from the houses. It was advised to drink water before we depart. Uncleaned and uncovered items should not be purchased. Sprinkling of DDT and other insecticides as well as use of nets, and the up keep of the desert coolers remained the talk of the day. They advised to clean the hands as and when we put to them for eating. It was a very specific programme and opened the eyes of the people who undertook a vow to spread the message of cleanliness everywhere.

60. You have attended the Hero Honda Awards function for the film stars. Inventing relevant details, prepare a report in 125 words to be published in The Times of India, Delhi. You are Raju, a special correspondent of the newspaper.

A REPORT ON HERO HONDA AWARDS FOR FILM STARS

Delhi : 5th August 200....

From Raju,

The much awaited 5th Hero Honda Awards function was organised for the film stars at the famous Ashoka Auditorium at 6.00 p.m. The auditorium presented a dazzling look and was tastefully decorated to welcome the film stars and the onlookers. The Minister for Broadcasting hailed the occasion. A large number of gathering cheered the film stars and their beloved leader. The awards were given for the best films in Hindi and other regional languages. Shah Rukh Khan and Rani Mukherjee were awarded for showing their talents as the best actor and the actress respectively. Other awards included for the best director, character actor, movie director, and the best singer. When the awards were given, the audience cheered up. Winding up the function the minister praised the role of music, action and facts in life. People ran to get the autographs of their favourite stars. It was a memonible scene for all.

61. You are Apoorva, Student of the Science Club of Ajay Public School, Darjeeling. Draft a report on the activities of the Science Club during the academic year, in about 125 words, to be published. in your school news letter.

ACTIVITIES OF THE SCEINCE CLUB

Darjelling : 30th December, 2005

By Apoorva, Cultural Secretary

Science club organised many activities during the second term. The astronomy wing took about 120 students to Nehru planetarium on 2nd October, 2004 to study about various planets and their orbits etc. They also spent a night out to have a telescopic view of various celestial bodies especially the Mars. The environmental wing conducted several activities like air monitoring, pollution control and tree plantation drive etc. They made posters and banners and organised activities like street, plays, discussions etc. A science exhibition was organised on 12th November, 2005. Mr. S.P. Mohan Deputy Director, North Zone was invited as the chief guest to inaugurate the exhibition. In his speech he praised the hidden talent of the participants and encouraged them to be more innovative and resourceful. Various models, projects and charts were displayed during the exhibition which was a great success. All the activities of the science club were conducted and well appreciated by all.

62. You have witnessed a fire accident in a busy market place. As a reporter of the National Herald Delhi, draft a report in 125 words. You are Rohan.

A REPORT ON FIRE ACCIDENT

Delhi: 3rd August 2005

From Mr. Rohan

A very devastating fire broke out yesterday in the busy market of Sadar Bazaar in the early hours of the morning. It was learnt that a timely alarm was given by the night watchman Mr. Guntur as soon as he saw the rays of smoke emitting out from a godown of timber. The fire brigade was rang up and residents from the neighbouring streets came out with their buckets full of water but the fire could not be brought under control In the twinkling of an eye, the whole market came in its spate. The fire brigade arrived and tried to extinguish the fire. The residents were crying mercilessly. After four hours, the fire came under control. Ten shops were gutted and the damage estimated was about more than rupees twenty crore. It is believed that the fire was caused by a short-circuit. Luckily there was no loss of life. A local inquiry has been probed by the administration.

63. You are Beena. As a representative of your school, you have attended a workshop on creative writing. Write a report in about 125 words for publication in your school newsletter.

A REPROT ON CREATIVE WRITING

Narela : 5th April, 2005

By Beena, School Representative

The Friend's Club of Sonepat organised a workshop in the Community Hall of Narela on 3rd April, 2004. It was a good workshop on Creative Writing in which several well known artists and more than 50 students from different schools of the adjoining areas participated in it. They prepared posters, charts and pamphlets on 'Indian Shining' by sketching India in multiple phases. The students seemed to be much keen on preparing charts. The workshop lasted for three hours and the students exhibited their hidden talents. Such workshops give a rent to show their secret energies by participating in such type of activities. The writers interacted with the students and the same left a deep impact on their ideology. The Principal of Students Vocational College, Shimla was the Chief Guest who advised the students to be creative and search activated mind as the present India needs the services of people who have artistic and creative nature in them. The best students were awarded cash prizes of Rs.100 each. Eleven students from Senior class, 10 students from Middle and 15 students from Primary classes were encouraged with prizes. After the workshop, a light refreshment was served to all.

64. You are Rohit. As a special correspondent of a leading local daily, you are sent to cover a cultural fiesta, organised by the Lions Club of Mumbai in connection with a fund raising programme for the construction of a building for an orphanage in Mumbai. Write a report in about 125 words for publication in the daily.

REPORT ON FUND RAISING PROGRAMME FOR CONSTRUCTION OF AN ORPHANAGE BUILDING

Mumbai : 25th April, 2005

By Rohit, a Special Correspondent

The Lions Club of Mumbai organised a Cultural Fiesta on 3rd April in Reena Banquet Hall, Rajaji Road Mumbai at 3.00 p.m. In order to raise funds for the construction of an orphanage building in the city. As we all know that Mumbai is a metropolitan city of India. One can see so many orphans roaming here and there in a very piteous condition who need shelter for their dwelling. In this connection, the club invited many artists, singers and dancers of the Mumbai Film Nagri to entertain the audience. The entry was the sale of tickets worth Rs. 100. More than three thousand tickets were sold and many people had to leave without tickets. It was a nice programme to see. When Lata Mangeshkar stood up, people clapped. Her voice was really inchanting. The mono act role play of Amitabh Bachchan put everyone into the peels of laughter. Shabana Aazmi too presented a nice song and people cried for recitation. The programme lasted for three hours but one knew about the passing of the time. All praised the Lion's Club for its success.

❑

7

Factual Description and Process Writing

A Factual Description entails an accurate, systematic objective and logical description of a person, object, scene, event, incident, or a process. It requires a constant writing ability that occurs to a student after a long practice of studying, reading and putting into black and white correctly. For writing a good description, one needs to be carefully in search of new ideas, observation, alertness and objectivity. The facts should be presented in such a systematic way so as to give a coherent view to the reader. While describing an event, a process, or a place all the relevant details, facts and figures that contribute to it should be given logically in a very cemented way. The passage should show unity and continuity. It should look to the reader that he himself has involved in it. It should aim at accurate and objective statement of facts. We can use certain linking words such as: so, therefore, because, as well as, both end, next, consequently, which, whether, although etc.

We can divide the description in the following catagories.

1. Factual description of Persons
2. Factual description of Objects
3. Factual descriptions of Places and Scenes.

4. Factual descriptions of Events.

5. Factual descriptions of Processes etc.

A few examples of all the above catagories can be studied for our ready reference.

1. Attempt a factual description of your house in about 125 words.

MY HOUSE

My house is very beautiful and spacious. Though not very big, it is well-ventilated and well lighted. It has a small coourtyard in front and a backyard which is about 12 ft × 12 ft in size. A row of plants and seasonal flowers adores the front courtyard. The main gate is painted black and silver. The walls allover the house are painted white. The white marble flooring with green strips in the sides compliments the wall very well. The decor of the house is simple yet elegant. The kitchen has easy to use drawers and cupboards. All the windows and the doors are made of teak wood and are freshly polished. In short, my house is a haven of delight and comfort.

2. Describe in about 125 words an Exciting Match.

AN EXCITING MATCH

Friendly matches fill in us the spirit of co-operation, fellow, feeling and friendliness. Yesterday a one day cricket match was played against the famous cricket eleven of Young Friend's Club. It was a very exciting match. Luckily we won the toss and our captain chose to go in for batting first. Our first wicket fell when the score was only twelve. Then the skipper of our team Meenu went for batting. He struggled hard and stayed on the wicket for one hour. He then hit ten fours and two sixers. Our score reached at fifty. Then there was a sudden set-back. The wickets started falling one after the other. The whole team was dismissed for two hundred and ten. The rivals too had a poor start. But their skipper was a very courageous challenger. He was caught at eighty. After that their wickets also started falling. They were all out for one hundred and ninety eight. We won the match but they did not lag behind.

3. Delhi is the Capital of India. People from every nook and corner arrive to see their relatives or otherwise. Travelling by bus is the cheapest mode of travelling but when one travels in an overcrowded bus, it becomes all the more troublesome. Write a description when you had to travel in an overcrowded bus.

TRAVELLING IN A BUS

Travelling in a crowded bus is an exciting experience. One has to wait for long time at the bus stop before one is able to get a bus. One is really lucky if one gets into the bus without getting one's shirt torn or pocket picked. The real ordeal begins after getting into the bus. Usually the bus is already packed full. So, there is no question of getting a seat. One has to rely on one's feet and bear with the jostling and elbowing of the other passengers. When the bus is about to reach one's destination, one has to make one's way, inch by inch, to the front door. The driver would not stop the bus unless he is informed in time. Then one has to hurry while getting down. One never knows when the conductor would blow the whistle and the bus would move on. In the overcrowded bus, one gets completely perspired and exhausted. There is no alternative but to travel in the bus.

4. Life without entertainment is monotonous and dull. The cable T.V. presents a variety of programmes round the clock. Write a paragraph on 'Cable T.V.'.

CABLE T.V.

The saying 'All work and no play makes Jack a dull boy' holds true for all people and for all times and climes. Man needs recreation and variety in life that appeals to his senses and relaxes him after the day's monotonous routine. Television has become the easiest means to achieve the maximum entertainment due to the 'Cable TV'. It is a system in which signals are sent along the wires to the TV sets attached to the different houses after having been transmitted to central receiver. Thus we have been able to have a number of channels like Star TV, BBC, ESPN, DISCOVERY, ZEE TV,.... and so on, with access to a special antenna (dish antenna). In the cable TV, a three metre dish antenna is wired to a number of houses. A monthly fee is charged from each of such households. The different programmes are relayed via communication satellites. We can watch programmes all the twenty four hours. Today life minus cable TV is almost unthinkable. In today's busy world this provides a faster access to the vast world of entertainment.

5. Attempt a factual description of the scene of your school morning assembly in about 125 words.

MORNING ASSEMBLY

The Morning assembly in my school begins with a prayer followed by five minute meditation. The students stand in rows class-wise. The assembly presentation is done section-wise on a theme stated in students' handbook. The students read out quotations, deliver speeches or enact a role play on the given theme. The assembly concludes with the Nation Anthem. Sometimes certificates and trophies are distributed to prize winners of various inter-school competitions. The principal, Mr. S.K. Gupta also addresses the students from time to time either on important occasions or to disseminate information about different issues. A uniform check also takes place after the prayer session. A solemn and peaceful atmosphere prevails during the assembly.

6. Manjit wants to know the process of planting a sapling. He approaches his Botany teacher. The teacher

decides to explain the process to him. Write the process description in not more than 80 words.

PLANTING A SAPLING

Planting a sapling is a delicate process which requires intense care and attention. First of all, seeds are sown at a suitable spot which gets light and air in abundance. The seeds sprout forth and tender plants appear. These tiny plants are uprooted and taken to the place where they are to be transplanted. While transplanting them, sufficient space is left in between for their growth. The whole process requires careful handling.

7. You happened to travel by train. In the compartment, you might have witnessed different activities going on in great haste. In about 100 words, describe 'he atmosphere in a railway compartment.

THE ATMOSPHERE IN A RAILWAY COMPARTMENT

A second-class railway compartment is a world in itself. Here one comes across all types of people. The atmosphere in the compartment varies from situation to situation. When it is packed full, atmosphere is tense. Those who are occupying seats are not willing to accommodate those who are standing. When the train is in motion, the atmosphere is a bit relaxed. Those who fail to get seats, somehow or other, adjust themselves. Often one comes across petty shop-keepers, fruit-sellers and tea vendors etc. People on long journey often purchase items from them. It is an atmosphere of fun and frolic. Generally, one can see the paper sellers and card players. They create a lot of humdrum and confusion. When the train is about to arrive at a station, there is a scene of excitement and activity in the compartment. Those who want to get down start pushing towards the door with their luggage.

8. Describe in about 125 words the utility of weekly Bazars.

WEEKLY BAZARS

Weekly bazars are gradually becoming very popular in big cities. Normally they are organised on the weekly off days of the regular markets. These markets do not have any names but are known by the days of which they are organised such as the markets held on Monday are called 'Som Bazars' or Monday Markets.

Two factors make these markets popular. First, the prices are quite low, and secondly, one can engage in the pleasures of hunting for a bargain without any shame. The regular visitors to these markets say that they can pick up small household articles at one place. These markets are becoming very popular with the housewives. They have their nuisance value too. They block traffic in already congested lanes and streets. Those living near these markets complain of noise and garbage. More serious is the sale of goods of inferior quality or harmful goods. Despite the problems, these markets have come to stay.

9. Examination is a contagious bug for all of us. When one appears for the paper in the Examination Hall, his face and expressions are worth-reading. The scene in the Hall is all the more interesting and exciting. You have an experience of witnessing a scene in the Examination Hall. Write your answer in about 100 words.

SCENE IN THE EXAMINATION HALL

The dread of examination hangs heavy on the minds of the examinees. Examination is a curse. The faces of the examinees are worth-reading. They have a look of utter despair and confusion. A learned examiner, a scholar and a teacher have rightly remarked that we have been examinees as well as examiners and we can easily describe the scene of examination. We are in the examination hall and the paper of English is before us. There is a pin drop silence in the examination hall. The seats are arranged in rows. Everybody is busy. The good students are doing their papers and their faces show that they are satisfied. Idlers are looking out for an opportunity to copy. The invigilators are busy to check all corrupt methods and the big clock is reminding the candidates.

Be quick-Be quick-Be quick
Tick-Tick-Tick

When the time is over, the students run to see their friends to discuss the questions. Some look disappointed and others leave the hall with a cheerful note.

10. You happened to visit the most crowded market place in your town in the evening. Write a factual description of the people, activities and things you saw there in not more than 100 words.

ACTIVITIES AND THINGS IN THE MOST CROWDED MARKET PLACE

A market is a place where people come to purchase their day to day items of domestic use. In the market one can find a variety of articles from cheapest to dearest depending on our purchasing power. A crowded market place presents a lively scene in the evening. People from all walks of life are seen wandering about. Window shoppers are seen walking about leisurely looking at the things displayed in the show cases. Some are actively busy in making purchases. Shopkeepers do roaring business. This is also an opportune time for evil-characters to indulge in their activities. Eve-teasers pass vulgar remarks on girls. The pick-pockets show the skill of their hands and relieve some passers-by in the crowd of their purses. The swindlers are also very active. All these activities go on till the shutters are down. Then the market presents a deserted look.

PROCESS WRITING

1. Describe in about 100 words, the process of applying for admission to a school.

To get one's ward admitted in a reputed school is a difficult task. But in a Government School it is easy in prescribed admission form. The form can be had from the school office. First of all one has to interview the Principal. On his satisfaction one has to fill on this form a student has to write his name, his father's or guardians's name and address, the date of his birth, nationality, the name of the examination's passed and the class he seeks to join. Additional information regarding his father's or guardian's income from all sources, the game in which he is interested and the extra-curricular activities in which he would like to take part, his hobby, etc. may also be given. Then a student gets his admission form checked by the class teacher. After that he presents himself before the Principal. If the Principal is satisfied, he allows him. This formality being over, the student goes to the office and deposits the admission form and the fees for admission the dealing clerk. Thus, he is admitted.

2. Describe in about 100 words, the process of washing clothes.

First of all, dirty clothes to be washed are collected at one place. Then the cotton clothes are separated from the clothes made of synthetic fibres. The white clothes and coloured clothes are also washed separately. Then we take a bucket full of water. We mix a certain quantity of some good quality detergent powder in the water. We mix it well for the powder to dissolve. Next we-dip dirty clothes into this solution and leave them in the bucket for about half an hour. The cotton clothes are left for a little longer period. Then the clothes are shaken well in the solution. We rub and squeeze them properly. On the very dirty parts, we rub a little dry powder. Then the clothes are rinsed two or three times in clean water in separate bucket. The process is repeated till the soap or the powder is out off the clothes. Finally, we bring the water out of the clothes. Now we hang them in the sun on a cloth line to dry up.

3. Describe in about 100 words, the process of opening a Savings Bank Account.

Saving in life is a future asset and it can be done safely through a Bank. For this one needs the banking services to operate an account. The process of opening a Savings Bank Account is very simple. Go to a bank and ask the clerk on duty at the Savings Account Counter to give you a prescribed and printed form for opening an account. You must take with you two photos and a ration card. You are required to enter your name and address in it. You can give the name of the nominee, You have to put your signature at two or three places on it. This is termed as your specimen signature. Account can be opened in the name of an individual, single or jointly, a minor with his guardian—father or mother. But the person concerned must be known to the Bank or should be introduced through some account holder of the Bank. Each applicant is required to sign a declaration to the effect that he or she has read and accepted the rules for the conduct of Savings Bank Deposit Account. After you have opened as account, you are given a Bank Pass Book with your name, home address and account number written on it. You can withdraw the amount by filling a withdrawal form.

4. Describe in about 100 words that you do everyday before coming to school.

Education plays an important role in the life of a student. He has to become ready for the school well in time. It require, patience, time and punctuality and so many other preparation. I am an early bird. I get up at about 4.30 O'clock early in the morning. Then I hurry through my daily routine. I am almost free by 5.30 a.m. Then I go out for a morning walk. I come back at about 6.15 a.m. After that I scan the newspaper while having my breakfast. In the meantime, there is the sound of the horn outside my house. It warns me of the arrival of the school bus. But I am still at the breakfast table. So I rush out of my house with my satchel. My mother runs after me to the bus with my lunch box. This, in short, is my daily routine in the morning before coming to school.

5. Sheetal's younger sister Seema is leaving for the Boarding School. She wants to know the method of preparing tea. Sheetal decides to explain the process to her. Write the process description in not more than 100 words.

METHOD OF PREPARING TEA

Tea is a modern hot drink that has become a fashion of our life. None of the party goes without tea. Tea making is a very simple process involving a few things. First of all, pour a required quantity of water in a kettle and place it on the stove. When the water begins to boil, add a piece or two of cardamom for flavour. After the water has boiled for a minute or two, put one or two spoonful of tea-leaves in it. Then we stir it gently. After that pour the boiled water in a tea pot and cover it with a lid. Similarly, we must boil the milk separately and pour it in a milk pot. Sugar cubes are kept in a small pot. Now the boiled tea water is poured in the cups with sugar cubes. Milk is added to make it more tasty. It is stirred and tea is ready for enjoying. It is ready to be served among our friends and relatives.

6. Books widen our world of knowledge. These ennoble our soul and enhance our wisdom. Describe, in about 100 words, your experience of borrowing a book from the library.

The previous day I was going to take part in inter college debate. The topic was 'Co-operative Farming in India'.

I needed some good books on the subject. I borrowed a library ticket from my class-mate, who is a member of Delhi Public Library, and went there.

There is an open shelf system. Books on various subjects are arranged in spearate shelves. I stood bewildered. I could not know in which shelf the books on 'Cooperative Farming in India' would be found. I went to the librarian and requested for help. He gave me the number under which the books on 'Co-operative Farming' were placed. Now I easily traced the book. I took two books and came to the counter. The librarian issued me the books. The man at the gate checked the books and allowed me to leave the library. This hardly takes some time to get the book issued.

7. Describe in about 100 words how a telephone trunk call is booked.

I am devoid of telephone facilities at my house due to non-availability of telephone facilities in the city. So I have to go to the telephone booth for booking a trunk call to talk with my son who is studying in U.S.S.R. We have to communicate with our relatives, friends or acquaintances living at far off distance places. So we have to book a trunk call with the telephone exchange. The process of booking the trunk call is quite simple. We simply give our own telephone number and the number on which the trunk call is to be booked to the operator on duty at the telephone exchange. He rings us back to ascertain that the call is booked for the right number. Then we have to wait patiently till we get a call from the telephone exchange that the booked number is on the line and we can talk to the person we want to.

8. Describe in about 100 words the process of getting a suit of clothes stitched.

A suit brings a touch of awareness and personality cult in a man. For a decent and durable suit-length we first go to a cloth merchant, choose the cloth according to our taste and pocket and buy the required length for our suit. Then we look for a tailor who knows the latest cuts and designs of dresses. Then we step into the tailor's shop and have a look on the stitched clothes hanging around. Next we hand him over the piece of cloth. The tailor takes the measurements of different parts of our body with a measuring tape, and notes them down in a diary. He gives us a slip and the dates on which we have to come for a trial. On the appointed date we visit the tailor's shop for the trial. If we are satisfied with his stitching, we ask for delivery date otherwise we suggest the minor changes. The tailor gives us another date for the final delivery. We again to go to his shop and collect our garments and pay the amount.

9. Describe in about 100 words, the process of applying for a post in an office.

First of all the person who seeks a job for a particular post is required to read and consult the 'Situations Vacant', columns of a newspaper regularly. If there is a vacant post for which the candidate has the required qualifications, he writes to the concerned office making a request for supplying a prescribed form for the post. On receiving the same, he fills it carefully and earnestly. He is required to give his bio-data in the application. He may be required to attach with the application form attested/authenticated copies of his certificates and testimonials in support of his qualifications and experience, if any. Sometimes, he is required to send a postal order of certain amount along with his application form. If he is considered a suitable candidate, he is called for an interview on the appointed day and time. For his success all depends on his performance and qualifications he possesses.

10. Travelling in a DTC bus is the cheapest mode of conveyance to go to and fro for the students and other passengers. The students can avail certain travelling

concession. Describe in about 100 words, how a bus-pass is made for students.

A bus pass is issued to students at concessional rates. First of all, the interested student has to obtain a prescribed form from the transport office. The form can also be had from the DTC van that comes to every school and college on a specified date. Then a student fills it and gets it verified from the Principal of his school or college. He affixes his passport size photograph on the form. Then he deposits the form the due amount with the bus pass making authority. The man at the counter scrutinizes the form. After scrutinizing the from, the offical on duty issues the bus-pass. The date of its issue and expiry and bus route are also specified on it. In this way a DTC bus pass is obtained.

11. Describe in about 100 words how you prepared yourself for joining a wedding party.

A wedding party is a festive occasion that comes once in a while in one's life. It is an occasion of meeting old friends, relatives and have new acquaintances, etc. So one has to be extra cautious about one's dress and outlook. In the last month, I was to join my friend's marriage. I went for a hair cut and hair dressing a day before the marriage. I got my new clothes stitched from a tailor at Connaught Place. I bought a new pair of shoes for the occasion. I got them polished by a shoe-maker for extra shine. Then I took my camera and put in a fresh roll of film. I took two spare rolls of film with me. I wanted to take photographs of all the important ceremonies. Then I hired a maruti and reached my cousin's house. When I got down from my maruti, all eyes were fixed on me. So I was filled with pride.

12. Tell your friend in about 100 words, the process of taking a photograph.

Taking a photograph with a camera is an art. It needs great attention. In case we do not go through the whole process, the snap may be spoilt. First we load the camera with the film carefully to avoid any exposure to light. Then we operate the advance lever to bring the film to the correct number, and set the aperture. Next we observe the correct distance and direction of the light, focus the lense on the person or object to be photographed. But before taking the photograph, we must make sure that the camera does not face the sun or any other source of light. When we are satisfied with everything, we remove the shutter cap and release the shutter. We also make it sure that we give the correct exposure. After taking the photograph, we are required to change the number of the film for the next exposure by operating the film advance lever.

13. Describe in about 100 words how you prepared for today's examination.

I am a studious student. I keep my studies up to date. So I prepared myself for today's examination. I went through the question papers of the C.B.S.E. of the last ten years. I also consulted the Sample Question Paper issued by the C.B.S.E. from time to time. Thus I came to know the type of questions generally set in the examination. I made an extensive and indepth study: A couple of days before the examination I revised some selected and expected questions thoroughly. This morning I glanced at the main points of important questions only. Thus I was satisfied that they were at my finger-tips. When I entered the examination hall, I had no fear of the examination. I left all hesitations and I occupied my seat peacefully.

FACTUAL DESCRIPTION OF PLACES AND EVENTS

14. You are Kiran Yadav of Sarvodaya Vidyalaya and your school has recently built a well planned auditorium to hold academic and cultural programmes. The editor of your school magazine has asked you to write a factual description

of the auditorium for the School Magazine.'Write Kiran's description in not more than 100 words.

OUR SCHOOL AUDITORIUM

The Government of Madras has built an auditorium in Sarvodaya Vidyalayn Madras. It was inaugurated by the Education Minister on last Saturday. It is situated near the main entrance with special, architectural designs. It has four gates for entrance respectively. It is fully air conditioned with a seating capacity of 2000 students. The chairs have been arranged in a dignified way for the audience. The stage is well equipped with modern techniques of electricity etc. The dazzling tubes and lights add to the scenic beauty of the auditorium. At the main entrance the Goddess Saraswati, encourages a message of learning. It has been named after Rabindra Nath Tagore and is called "TAGORE AUDITORIUM." This auditorium can also be used for other activities too. We should maintain its dignity and decorum.

15. Computer Education.

Thanks to the master genius who gave a gift of computer to the humanity.

Charles Babbage, an Englishman, is Known as the Father of Computers. He invented a machine that could take in informations and sort them in the form of tables. This first machine was called 'Difference Engine'. By 1970, researches promise to add new dimensions to the capabilities of computers. From a humble beginning a decade ago, the Indian computer Industry has gone a long way. The computers have vide applications which can be broadly divided:

1. Scientific applications—specially for engineering sciences, oceanography and geology.
2. Basic Applications: used by business and government houses. This helps in calculation of wages, leave record,

tax code and funds etc. Sales accounting, sales analysis and stock control can be done with great accuracy. In the present complicated set up, the use of computer has become a boon for all.

16. T.V. Advertisements.

Science and modern invention have brought a glorious revolution in our life. With their help, the genius brains have opened a new gate way for all of us. In a twinkling of an eye, one can get himself acquainted with far off happenings. Education has increased our knowledge and our out-look has broadened. Advertisements form a part and parcel of our new advancements. Earlier the advertisements used to take place through paper and radio etc. Now these have been replaced by T.V. though other methods do not lag behind. Government earns a lot of revenue through advertisements. Advertisements help us in many ways. Our energy, time, money and exertion are saved. One can analyse the facts himself. We are saved from making so many enquiries because everything is presented lucidly on a T.V. screen. We can get ourselves acquainted with so many new items. It should be the endevour of the authorities to delete the adverse facts that may spoil our character.

17. Role of T.V. in Building up Modern India.

With the progress of science and technology, new inventions have come out. Television is among them. The television plays a very vital role in educating all of us. It is a running screen on which one can see what is happening across the sea and in far off countries. When the new researches and inventions are on the screen of the television, one gathers a heap of knowledge and technical know how. The television has helped a lot in advancing our various fields like education, scientific, architecture and medical. India is a fast developing country. She needs knowledge and experiences. All these things are going on in the developed countries. When our learned men witness them on the television, they get a first hand knowledge. This helps us in advancing, progressing and making improved things. It is the television that has renovated Indian skill and knowledge. We are very much indebted to the master minds for this astonishing technique.

18. Inflation.

When a nation proceeding on a path of progress, inflation is bound to occur. It is causing a great concern for all. The prices are daily on great hike and have become beyond the control of the government. In reality, inflation is an increase in the purchasing power in relation to the goods available for purchase. In the state of inflation, the prices of the commodities get an artificial rise and there comes an increase in the instance of paper-money. Shortage of goods, black marketing, hoarding, Government policies and population explosion are the major causes of price-like. Shortage of commodities cause inflation and the supply becomes less. During the period of inflation, manufacturers and businessmen earn a huge profit but the common man is put under pressure. His budget becomes unbalanced thereby putting him in great difficulty. It is for the government to check inflation and thereby save the consumers from its adverse effects. The flexible policies should be left out.

19. One day you got a chance to visit Rohtak. You have to go by a local bus. Your journey was very difficult. You noted certain inconveniences in your diary. Write your experiences of travelling in an over crowded bus. Your ideas should not exceed more than 100 words.

EXPERIENCES OF TRAVELING IN AN OVER-CROWDED BUS

It was Sunday, I had to go to Rohtak on business. I reached the bus stop. There was a maddening crowd. I bought the ticket. I got into the bus. It was packed to its full capacity.

There was a lot of elbowing and jostling. There was no room to stand even. So, I kept standing on one foot. The plight of the ladies and the small children was still worse. Babies, in their mother's arms, were crying and weeping. The passengers were feeling as if they were in an inferno. The condition of those hanging on the foot-board was quite miserable. They felt like falling. Those inside felt suffocated. I was feeling all the time giddy. Getting down the bus seemed to be more difficult than getting into it. However, I managed to get down after fifteen minutes struggle. I thanked my stars when I reached Rohtak.

20. The Day I Like Most and Why.

Life is a great anxiety but in the midst of anxieties, very few memorable occasions come in our life. At that time we feel extremely happy and lucky. Yesterday was the day which infused me with high spirits and specific achievements. It was my birthday and there was great hustle and bustle in the house since morning. Early in the morning, my elder brother Ashok came from U.S.S.R. after getting his successful degree in M.D. He offered me heaps of gifts. So far my mother has not entertained him when the bell rang at the door. There was a special gift parcel from my maternal uncle of America. It contained a golden wrist watch. I liked it very much. In between, my great chums Mohit and his parents approached with sweets and gifts. Everybody in the house was in a gay mood. All offered me prayers and enjoyed the tasty meal. The songs were in great echo. Everybody graced the occasion. May God shower His blessings on all and grant rare opportunities to enjoy!

❒

8

Essay-Writing and Report-Writing

ESSAY-WRITING AND REPORT WRITING (Sub-Titles)

Here, you are asked to write a report or a composition in points instead of giving full details. So, you are expected to give the sub-titles only under which you would write the report or the composition.

SOLVED EXAMPLES

1. Give only the sub-titles of a composition you would write on the most humorous person you have met.

THE MOST HUMOROUS PERSON YOU HAVE MET

1. Introduction.
2. Name (invent some funny name), boast of high birth and early life.
3. Appearance and manner of dressing.
4. His muddleheadedness and absent-mindedness.
5. Fond of telling stories in which he figures as the hero.
6. Qualities, if-any, you admire.
7. Conclusion.

2. Supply sub-titles under which you would describe the plight of the physically handicapped children in your locality.

HANDICAPPED CHILDREN

1. The nature of their physical disabilities.
2. Families they belong to.
3. Attitude of their families towards them.
4. Attitude of other children towards them.
5. Establishment of an Institution to import them various trainings.

3. Give the sub-titles under which you would express your ideas on National Integration.

NATIONAL INTEGRATION

1. Fissiparous tendencies at work in India.
   (a) Communalism.
   (b) Casteism.
   (c) Regionalism.
   (d) Linguism.
2. Loyality to the country should over-ride all other considerations.
3. Uniting effect of the Chinese aggression and the war with Pakistan.

4. Give only sub-titles of a review you would write or a book exhibition you have visited.

BOOK EXHIBITION I HAVE VISITED

1. Venue and duration
2. General lay-out

3. Variety

4. Topical interest

5. Visitor's response

5. Supply sub-titles under which you would write an essay on:

INDISCIPLINE AMONG STUDENTS

1. Student indiscipline—an alarming problem students indulgence in rowdyism and vandalism.

2. Causes:

   (a) Loosening of the grip of parents on children.

   (b) Lack of accord between the teacher and the taught.

   (c) Defective system of education.

   (d) Lack of stress on moral instruction and character-building activities.

   (e) Interference of power politics in educational institutions.

   (f) Insufficient arrangement of games and sports and other facilities.

3. Its remedies.

6. Supply sub-titles under which you would describe your ideas about teacher-pupil relationship.

TEACHER-PUPIL RELATIONSHIP

1. Teacher-pupil relationship in the past.

2. Need to improve relations in the present times.

3. Causes for deterioration.

4. How harmonious relationship between the teacher and the taught can he developed?

7. Give the sub-titles of a composition you would write on the novel you have liked most.

THE NOVEL I HAVE LIKED MOST

1. Title and the author.
2. Theme.
3. Writer's handling of the theme.
4. Plot construction.
5. Character delineation.
6. Message.

8. Give five sub-titles (of equal scope for expansion) of a review you would write or a book you have read.

A Book I have read :

1. Title, the author his other works, his place in literary world.
2. Theme.
3. Handling of the theme.
4. Character delineation.
5. Message.

9. Give only the sub-titles of a composition you would write on advantages of living in a big city.

Advantages of Living in a Big City:

1. The fascination city life exercises on most people.
2. Educational facilities
3. Medical facilities
4. Means of recreation

5. Modern of amenities

6. Better chances of getting employment and earning money.

10. Supply sub-titles under which you would describe your ideas about the road traffic in Delhi.

ROAD TRAFFIC IN DELHI

1. Introduction: Road traffic—the problem of every big city—the result of growing industrialisation and urbanisation.

2. Causes of ever growing road traffic in Delhi:

(a) Delhi—the capital of India.

(b) Influx of people coming to Delhi in search of jobs etc.

(c) Inadequate finance allocated to the construction and maintainance of roads.

(d) Indifferent attitude of civic authorities.

(e) The growing number of vehicles.

(f) Apathy of the public to the traffic police and traffic rules.

3. Hazards: Road accidents, a common features.

4. Conclusion: How to cope with the problem:

(a) Adequate arrangement to traffic police.

(b) Creating aswareness in the public to obey the traffic rules.

(c) Widening the roads.

(d) Construction of flyovers.

11. Give only the sub-titles under which you would describe the person who has impressed you most in life.

The person who has impressed me most:

1. Name, birth and early life.

2. Appearance and manner of living.

3. His qualities I admire.

4. His gentlemanliness and neighbourliness.

5. Conclusion.

12. Under what sub-titles or main points you would organise an essay on 'The Year of the Handicapped'.

THE YEAR OF THE HANDICAPPED

1. 1981—the year of the handicapped.

2. Special attention to the handicapped children.

3. Their problems.

4. Change in the attitude of society.

5. Sympathy and understanding.

6. Need for special institutions.

7. Appreciation of their activities.

8. To make them feel wanted.

13. Supply sub-titles under which you would describe your Ideas on Eve-teasing.

Eve-teasing :

1. The problem of eve-teasing.

2. Factors which give rise to this problem :

   (a) the impact of films.

   (b) girls themselves responsible.

   (c) spirit of adventurism among boys.

3. **Remedies:**

   (a) Wide publicity to cases of eve-teasing through mass media.

   (b) girls-to change their ways and manners.

   (c) cultivating the spirit of true heroism among boys.

   (d) enforcement of law against eve-teasers.

14. Give five sub-titles (of equal scope for expansion) for a report you would write of your visit to a hospital for inspection.

Visit to a Hospital for Inspection:

(i) Visit-sudden and unexpected.

(ii) Inspection of the hospital building.

(iii) Inspection of the Stores.

(iv) Inspection of the Wards.

(v) Meeting with the staff.

(vi) A chat with the patients.

15. Supply sub-titles under which you would describe your ideas on family planning.

FAMILY PLANNING

1. The need of family planning.
2. Disadvantages of having unplanned families:
   (a) For children.
   (b) For parents.
   (c) For the nation.
3. Some devices of family planning.
4. How to implement family planning programme.

16. Supply sub-titles under which you would describe your ideas on the dowry system.

THE DOWRY SYSTEM

1. Dowry system—an ancient custom.
2. Dowry in the past and now.
3. The commercial character of present day marriages.
4. Miserable plight of the girls in the middle class families—before and after the marriage.
5. Remedies:

   (a) Adequate legislation.

   (b) Intensive propaganda, by social welfare organizations.

   (c) Anti-dowry drive by young boys and girls.

   (d) Popularising female education.

   (e) Opening new aveanues of employment for girls.

17. You have to describe the National Exhibition of Books. Give the sub-titles only under which you would describe the exhibition.

1. **Title:** National Exhibition of Books.
2. **Period:** 25th Feb. to 12th March.
3. **Place:** Pragati Maidan, Mathura Road, New Delhi.
4. **Organised by:** National Book Trust of India.
5. **Inaugurated by:** The Minister of Education.
6. Stalls set up by publishers from all over the country and a brief description of each.

18. You have to describe the Annual School Function. Give the sub-titles only under which you would write it.

ANNUAL SCHOOL FUNCTION

1. Annual School Function—an important event; its significance.
2. Held on—invitations—the choice of the chief guest.
3. Preparations and seating arrangement.
4. Invitees—arrival of the Chief Guest, guard of honour, welcome.
5. Principal's annual report.
6. Prize distribution.
7. Presidential address-vote of thanks.
8. Light refreshment.

19. Supply sub-titles under which you would describe your views on the quality of Television Programmes in Delhi.

QUALITY OF TELEVISION PROGRAMME IN DELHI

(i) Delhi Doordarshan, the most important relay centre of T.V. programmes.

(i) Various programmes relayed.

(iii) Their quality:

(a) Presentation.

(b) Entertainment value.

(c) Educational value.

(iv) Their impact.

(v) Overall assessment.

20. You have to write a composition on a Circus Show. Give the sub-titles only under which you will do this.

A CIRCUS SHOW

1. Circus comes to town, wide publicity.
2. Desire to visit.
3. Programme.
4. The pandal.
5. Interesting items.
6. Jokers and their antics.
7. Enjoyment.

21. You have to write a composition of the festival. Give the sub-titles only under, which you would.

1. Name of the festival and the community which celebrates it.
2. Cultural background of the festival.
3. Way of celebration.
4. Its significance.
5. Evils, if any, attached to it, the spirit of the festival.
6. Conclusion.

22. Give only the sub-titles of a composition you would write on a one-day international cricket match.

A ONE-DAY INTERNATIONAL CRICKET MATCH

1. Day, the rival tearms and the venue.
2. The toss.

3. Highlights of the performance of the team that came into bat first.
4. Stipulated overs.
5. Performance of the other team.
6. Last moment's and the final result.

23. The Annual Sports Day was a great success. You have been asked to write a report on it. Give the sub-titles only under which you would write the Report.

1. Event : Annual Sports Day at our school

2. Date : 20th Dec., 1988

3. Place : School Stadium

4. Chief Guest : The Mayor of Delhi

5. Invitees : Parents of the children of the School, students, local worthies

6. Programme : (a) Flag hoisting

(b) Oath-taking ceremony

(c) March past by the participants

(d) Meet declared open the Chief Guest.

(e) Highlights of various events, some new records established

(f) Meet declared closed

(g) Prize distribution.

7. Chief Guest's Address

8. Refreshment : To the Chief Guest, invitees and participants

24. Give only the sub-titles of composition you would write on a film you have liked.

THE FILM I LIKED MOST

1. Name, cast, story.
2. Characters.
3. Dialogues.
4. Sets, music, dances.
5. Comedy, tragedy.
6. Society shown—village or city, modern or old.
7. Ideas and lessons.

25. You have to write a composition on a historical building. Give the sub-titles only under which you would do this.

A HISTORICAL BUILDING

1. Name of the building and location.
2. Historical background—who built it and what was the occasion.
3. The exterior of the building.
4. The interior of the building.
5. Its historical significance.

26. Your school recently celebrated the Founder's Day. You have to write a vivid description for the school magazine. Give only the sub-titles under which you would write the description.

1. Event : Founder's Day Celebration

2. Date : 15th Dec., 2005

3. Place : Assembly Hall of the School

4. Arrangement and Decorations

5. Chief Guest and the Invitees.

6. Programme : (a) National Anthem.

(b) Annual Report read by the Principal

(c) Variety Programme

(d) Distribution of Prizes.

7. Presidential Address

8. Vote of Thanks

27. You have to write an essay on a cricket match. Give the sub-titles only under which you would write it.

A CRICKET MATCH

1. Day, the rival teams and the venue.
2. Inspection of the pitch by the captains—the toss.
3. Performance of the team that came into bat first.
4. Position at lunch interval.
5. Performance of the other team.
6. Position at tea break.
7. Last moment's and the final result.

28. Give only the sub-titles of a composition you would write on a city you have visited.

A CITY I HAVE VISITED

1. Delhi—the capital of India and its significance.
2. Its ancient glory.
3. New structures.
4. Big markets and shopping centres.

5. Means of recreation.

6. Medical facilities.

7. Educational institutions.

8. Conclussion.

29. Supply sub-titles under which you would like to tell us what you expect from your parents.

WHAT I EXPECT FROM MY PARENTS

1. Introduction—parents-children relationship.
2. Proper care and attention by way of food, clothing, education and health.
3. Affection but not over-indulgence.
4. Keep respectable distance but care enough to understand my problems.
5. Be an object lesson for me, my ideal in everything.
6. Sow the seeds of gentlemanliness.
7. Conclussion—my final devotion.

30. Give five sub-titles (of equal scope for expansion) for a report you would write on a children's painting competition.

A CHILDREN'S PAINTING COMPETITION

1. The occasion.
2. The participants.
3. Their performance.
4. The committee of judges and its verdict.
5. The prize-distribution ceremony.

❐

9

Messages

ILLUSTRATIVE EXAMPLES

1. Read the following telephone conversation between Sonu and Mr. Ahuja. Mr. Ahuja is leaving for Bombay within fifteen minutes and shall not be able to meet Mr. V.P. Singh. He leaves a message for him. Write this message, using not more than 50 words.

Sonu : Hello, is it 2245732

Mr. Ahuja : Yes.

Sonu : Could I speak to Mr. V.P. Singh?

Mr. Ahuja : He is not here at the moment However, he shall be back after sometime. May I know who is speaking?

Sonu : I am Sonu, uncle. Mr. V.P. Singh is our neighbour. Mrs. Singh is here. She tells me that Mr. Singh is wanted immediately at home. Some relatives from Hyderabad have come here, especially to meet him. They would be leaving in about 4 hours from now.

Mr. Ahuja : All right, I will ask Mr. Singh to reach home at the earliest.

Rajiv : One minute, uncle. Kindly tell uncle Singh to meet Mr. Joshi also on way home. He knows Mr. Joshi, the retired high court judge.

Mr. Ahuja : Anything else?

Sonu : No, thank you very much.

Mr. Ahuja : All right.

Answer

MESSAGE

Mr. V.P. Singh 15 Aug., 2005

There was a telephone from your neighbour's son, Sonu. You are wanted at home. Relatives from Hyderabad have come and are leaving within 4 hours. Meet Mr. Joshi, the retired High Court Judge, on way home. This is urgent.

Mr. Ahuja

2. Read the following telephone conversation between Rekha and Mohan. Mohan is about to leave house and will not be able to meet Rashmi. He leaves a message for her. Write this message, using not more than 50 words.

Rekha : Hello! May I speak ro Rashmi ?

Mohan : Sorry, Rashmi is not here at the moment. May I know who is speaking please?

Rekha : I am Rekha, a classmate of hers. When is Rashmi expected back ?

Mohan : In an hour or so.

Rekha : My aunt, who is a dress designer in Bombay, is here with us for a few hours and Rashmi is very keen to see her. My aunt says that she can see her at 5 p.m. today at my place.

Mohan : Thank you for the message. I'll convey it to Rashmi.

Rekha : Thank you. Bye.

Answer

MESSAGE

Rashmi 12 Sept., 2005

There was a telephone call from your classmate, Rekha. She says that her aunt, who is a dress designer, has come from Bombay. You may see her at 5 p.m.

Mohan

3. Read the following telephone conversation between Mrs. Khurana and Vineet. Vineet is about to leave for school within five minutes. In the space provided write the message that Vineet leaves for his mother, using not more than 50 words.

Mrs. Khurana : Hello! Is that Mrs. Aggarwal?

Vineet : Oh, No! Vineet speaking here, Aunty.

Mrs. Khurana : How sweet, dear ! There is something urgent, wanted to talk to your Mom about.

Vineet : But she is not home. She's gone to drop Tanu at school. I'm also leaving for school within five minutes.

Mrs. Khurana : Well, then could you please leave message for her?

Vineet : Yeah! Certainly.

Mrs. Khurana : Mrs. Suri, Mrs. Dutta and I were to meet her today at your place at 3 p.m.

Vineet : Yeah. I know that.

Mrs. Khurana : Would you please tell your mother not to wait for us since Mrs. Suri is suffering from fever and Mrs. Dutta has some relatives to attend to. We shall now meet on Saturday.

Vineet : O.K. Aunty, I'll convey that.

Mrs. Khurana : Thank you, dear.

Answer

MESSAGE

Dear Mom 14 Sept., 2005

Aunty Mrs. Khurana rang up to tell that she along with Mrs. Suri and Mrs. Dutta won't be arriving at 3 p.m; today, because Mrs. Suri is laid up with fever and Mrs. Dutta is expecting some relatives. They will be coming on Saturday.

Vineet

4. Read the following telephone conversation between Amrita and Rita. Ritu is about to leave home and will not be able to meet Arun. She leaves a message for him. Write this message using not more than 50 words.

Amrita : Hello, is that Kiran ?

Ritu : Speaking.

Amrita : It's Ritu here. You know there's good movie on, 'My left Foot. It's running at Alpana. How about seeing it tomorrow?

Ritu : Yes, not a bad idea.

Amrita : Let's go to the evening show. Where should we meet?

Ritu : Let's meet at Wimpy's Comer, at 5.30. Is that okay?

Amrita : Fine, Look, Vijay's coming along too, Why don't you ask Arun to join us ?

Ritu : I'll do that. He is not at home at the moment, But I'll ask him to ring you this evening. Please don't buy the tickets until he calls.

Answer

MESSAGE

Arun 13 June, 2005

Ritu rang up at 11 a.m. Invited us to see the film 'My Left Foot' at Alpana, tomorrow, evening show. Vijay's also coming. I promised to join. Meeting at Wimpy's comer at 5.30. Please ring Ritu this evening. Tickets will be bought only when you ring.

Amrita

5. Read the following telephone conversation between Sumit and his neighbour's brother, who lives in Amritsar. Sumit is leaving for college and will not be able to meet his neighbour. Sumit leaves a message for him. Write this message using not more than 50 words.

Mukesh : Is this four seven three one eight nine?

Sumit : Yes. May I know who is speaking, please?

Mukesh : Mr. R.K. Mehta lives in your neighbourhood. I'm his brother Mukesh from Amritsar. Will you please deliver my message to him?

Sumit : Most gladly.

Mukesh : Tomorrow, I am coming to Delhi by Shan-E-Punjab.Please ask my brother to come to the Railway Station with a car as I'm coming with a lot of luggage.

Sumit : I'll convey your message to Mr. Mehta.

Mukesh : Thanks a lot. Bye.

Answer

MESSAGE

Mr. R.K. Mehta 17 July, 2005

Here is a message for you from your brother Mukesh from Amristar. He is coming tomorrow by Shan-E-Punjab. He wants you to come to the Railway Station with a car as he's coming with a lot of luggage.

Sumit

6. Read the following conversation between the receptionist Neha Kapoor and a caller from a hospital. The caller wants to talk to Mohan Rakesh but he is, at present, not in the office. He will be back only at 5 p.m. and Neha will leave the office by then. She leaves a message for Mohan Rakesh. Write the message using not more than 50 words.

Caller : Is this Delhi University Registrar's Office, please?

Neha : Yes.

Caller : May I speak to Mr. Mohan Rakesh, Assistant Registrar, please?

Neha : I'm afraid Mr. Mohan Rakesh is not in the office at the moment.

Caller : Could I leave a message for him? It's rather urgent.

Neha : Sure.

Caller : His father has met with an accident and he is, at present, in Ram Monohar Lohia Hospital.

Neha : I'm sorry to hear that. I hope it's nothing serious?

Caller : He has broken his leg which is in plaster. He, otherwise, is all right. Please ask Mohan Rakesh to reach the hospital immediately. His wife has already gone there.

Neha : I sure will.

Caller : Thank you. Bye.

Answer

MESSAGE

Mr. Mohan Rakesh 14 Sept., 2005

There was a telephone call for you at 2.30 p.m. Your father is in Ram Monohar Lohia Hospital with a broken leg put in plaster. Don't worry. He is all right. Reach the hospital immediately.

Your wife is already there.

Neha

7. Read the following telephone conversation between Radha and Sunita. Sunita is about to leave home and will not be able to meet her mother. She leaves a message for her. Write this message, using not more than 50 words.

Radha : Hello! Can I speak to Mrs. Mehta ?

Sunita : She is not home. Is it Ritu speaking?

Radha : Oh, Yes. Sudha, where is your mummy? I've a message for her.

Sunita : Mummy has gone outside and will be back after half an hour. What's the message?

Radha : Well, the message is from my mother. She was to visit you this evening, but she won't be able to come.

Sunita : What's the matter? Is aunty all right?

Radha : Oh, mummy is quite O.K. Actually my uncle and aunt have arrived from Simla. Mummy will be busy attending to them.

Sunita : I'll inform my mother. Bye.

Radha : Bye.

Answer

MESSAGE

Mummy 13 May, 2005

There was a telephone call from Radha. She has conveyed her mother's message that she won't be able to visit us today evening as they have received some unexpected guests.

Sunita

8. The following is a telephone conversation between John and David. After this call, Mr. John receives an urgent telephone call from Mumbai. Before leaving, he leaves a message for Mr. Leslie. Write the message in not more than 50 words in your answer sheet.

David : Hello ! Is it Ahmedabad 632392 ?

John : Yes, it is.

David : Can I talk to Mr. Leslie?

John : Sorry, he is not in the office. May I know who is on the line?

David : I am David, a friend of his.

John : Would you like me to convey him a message?

David : Yes. Inform him that the interview scheduled for 5th October has been postponed to the 7th. So he can reach Delhi by 6th evening. The inconvenience is regretted.

John : I will surely convey this message to him.

David : Thank you!

Answer

MESSAGE

Mr Leslie 3 July, 2005

There was a telephonic call for you from David in your absence. He informed me that the interview scheduled for 5th October has been postponed to the 7th. Please reach Delhi by 6th evening.

John

9. A girl is missing. The Police is trying to find her. They ask her mother about her. Read the conversation between the Policeman and her mother. The Police has to draft a message to be broadcast over the T. V. about the missing girl. Draft the message for them in not more than 50 words.

Policeman : Would you please tell me something about the missing girl, her name, her age?

Mother : Her name is Vineeta. She is about 14. She is in Class IX.

Policeman : What is her full name?

Mother : Vineeta Rao.

Policeman : Can you describe her? How tall is she?

Mother : About 5 ft. 2". She is very thin.

Policeman : What colour is her complexion?

Mother : She is fair-in fact almost pale.

Policeman : What is the colour of her hair, Her eyes?

Mother : She has reddish-brown hair, cut very short. Her hair is very curly. Her eyes are light brown.

Policeman : What was she wearing? When was she last seen?

Mother : Her school friends saw her at the school gate. She was walking towards the bus. Today our driver had taken leave, so she had to return on her own. That was at about 2 pm.

Policeman : So she was in her school uniform?

Mother : Yes, it is a red and white checked shirt with a white blouse and red tie.

Policeman : Thank you m'am. We will do our best to find your daughter.

Answer

MISSING PERSONS

Vineeta Rao, 14 years old, 5 ft. 2" tall, this but fair complexioned having short curly reddish brown hair and light-brown eyes, studying in class IX. Last seen at her school gate at 2 pm, in a red and white checked shirt, white blouse and red tie. Please inform the police about any information relating to her where abouts.

10. Karan had the conversation given below with his mother's friend, Sheela. Since he was going out immediately afterwords he left a message for his mother. Read the conversation and write out the message in not more than 50 words.

Sheela : Hello, this is Sheela speaking. Could I please speak to Usha?

Karan : I'm afraid she is not at home, aunty.

Sheela : When is she likely to come back?

Karan : Not before six in the evening. Could I give her a message?

Sheela : Yes, please. Could you tell her that I have been able to make the appointment with the editor of the magazine, The Child's Universe. We have to meet her at 10 am tomorrow. Since Usha doesn't know the place I will come and pick her up at 9-30. She should bring the manuscripts she wants to show Mrs. Shekhar,—that is the editor's name.

Answer

MESSAGE

Mama 26 March, 2006

Your friend Ms Sheela informed on telephone that she has got the appointment fixed with Mrs. Shekhar, the editor of *the Child's Universe.* She wanted you to be ready with the Manuscripts tomorrow. As you do not know the place, she would come to pick you up at 9.30 a.m. to be with Mrs. Shekher at 10 a.m.

Karun

11. Gopal had the conversation given below with his brother Girl's tutor Mr. Guru. Since he was going out immediately afterwards he left a message for his brother. Read the conversation and write out the message in not more than 50 words.

Mr. Guru : Hello, this is Mr. Guru speaking. Could I please speak to Giri?

Gopal : I'm afraid he is not at home, Mr. Guru.

Mr. Guru : When is he likely to come back?

Gopal : In about one hour. Could I give him a message?

Mr. Guru : Yes, please. Could you tell him that I won't be able to make it today. I was supposed to come at six. However, I can come in at six tomorrow. If that is inconvenient, he should call me at home after eight at night today to fix another time. Will you see that he gets the message?

Gopal : Yea, sir. I will.

Answer

MESSAGE

Giri 20 Feb., 2005

Your tutor Mr. Guru informed on telephone that he wouldn't be able to come to you today at six. However, he would come at six tomorrow. In case it doesn't suit you, you may call him at home after eight tonight to fix another time.

Gopal

12. Now we send messages through S.T.D. and rarely use telegrams. Money paid in S.T.D. call is not on number of words but the minutes and seconds you spend on the telephone. Prepare a message of not more than fifty words to say that you need a house on rent in Mumbai. Message will contain the details of the house, locality and maximum rent to be paid. Put your message in a box.

Answer

MESSAGE

18 April, 2005

A two-bedroom flat on rent in a good colony is needed in a sub-urban area of Mumbai, preferably near Airport for two years on company lease. Maximum rent payable not to exceed Rs. 16,000 per month. Please contact me on phone 6731906. Caller

13. You receive a telephone call from your father's office in his absence and have the following conversation with the speaker. Write the message in your answer sheet to give to your father when he returns home.

Mr. Hair : Hello. Is this 5721625 ?

Yourself : Yes please, whom do you want to talk to?

Mr. Nair : Could I please talk to Mr. Mahajan ?

Yourself : I'm afraid Daddy is not at home. Do you have any message for him ?

Mr. Nair : Yes, please tell him that the meeting fixed for tomorrow *i.e.* 20th January has been cancelled.

Yourself : It has been cancelled ?

Mr. Nair : That's right. Please also tell him that we shall let him know as and when the next date is fixed ; have you got it ?

Yourself : Yes, uncle,l've noted it down and shall tell Daddy when he comes back.

Answer

MESSAGE

Daddy 16 March. 2005

Mr. Nair called from your office on telephone stating, that the meeting scheduled for tomorrow *i.e.*, 20th January has been cancelled. He also informed that they would let you know as and when the next date was fixed for the meeting.

Rahul

14. Write a message to be left at the desk of Shami, about a telephone call received for her when she was away. Write the message in about 50 words in your answer sheet.

Kishore : Hello ! Is it 5789533? Could I talk to Shami, who works in the Sales Department ?

Receptionist : Sorry, Shami has not yet arrived.

Kishore	:	Could you convey to her that her brother is quite serious in Bhubaneshwar and she should leave for Bhubaneshwar immediately? He is in hospital in an intensive care unit. He met with an accident.
Receptionist	:	Oh. so sad. Should I convey anything else?
Kishore	:	Yes, She should bring both her children. I am sure you will do this favour.
Receptionist	:	Yes, sure. I pray for his speedy recovery. By the way, may I know who I am talking to ?
Kishore	:	Oh ! Sorry ! I was in a hurry and did not introduce myself. I am Kishore, a neighbour of Shami's brother.

Answer

MESSAGE

Shami 21 March, 2005

Your brother's neighbour Kishore had called from Bhubaneshwar informing that your brother has met with an accident. His condition is quite serious. He is, at present, admitted in hospital in an ICU. Please leave for Bhubaneshwar at once alongwith your children.

Receptionist

15. Chitra called Mrs. Shanna, a furniture shop owner. Since she was not available, her assistant, Ganga answered. The following is a conversation between Chitra and Ganga. As Ganga was going out immediately afterwards, she left a message for Mrs. Sharma. Read the conversation and write the message in not more than 50 words.

Chitra	:	Is that 'Royal Furniture' ?
Ganga	:	Yes, it is.

Chitra : Could I speak to Mrs. Sharma?

Ganga : Sorry; she is not here at the moment.

Chitra : When will she be back?

Ganga : Not before six in the evening. Can I take a message for her?

Chitra : Yes, please. Could you tell her that she has to deliver the furniture ordered by me for my new house only on the 25th of May and not on the 20th. Ask her to keep them ready by 9.00 A.M. on the 25th of May. I will be sending a pick-up van and so she does not have to arrange for the same.

Ganga : Yes, I will inform her.

Chitra : Thank you.

Answer

MESSAGE

Mr. Sharma 18 May, 2005

Chitra telephoned to inform you that the furniture ordered by her for her new house should be delivered on the 25th of May and not on the 20th. She wants the furniture to be ready by 9 a.m. on the 25th. She would be sending a van to pick up the furniture.

Ganga

16. You are Sonal, who has arrived at the New Delhi Railway Station to board the Shatabadi Express to Amritsar. You hear the following announcement. Write a message to be sent to your father through your driver.

This is for the attention of all the passengers to board the Shatabadi Express bound for Amritsar scheduled to arrive at 6.55 a.m. The Shatabadi Express has derailed 20 kilometres from

ABC city. Please note that the Howrah Express that leaves the New Delhi Railway Station at 8.30 a.m. will carry all the passengers to their destination. You are requested not to buy a new ticket. Your ticket for the Shatabadi Express holds valid and at par for the Howrah Express. Special coaches are being attached to the Howrah Express to accommodate passengers of Shatabadi Express.

MESSAGE

Father　　　　15 May, 2005

The Shatabadi Express bound for Amritsar has derailed 20 kms. from ABC city. So I will board the Howrah Express leaving the New Delhi Railway Station at 8.30 a.m. for Amritsar. No new tickets are needed as the tickets for the Shatabadi Express hold valid for the Howrah Express. Rest on meeting you.

Sonal

17. Noted below is a telephonic conversation between Leena and Reena. Read it carefully. As Reena is also to leave she writes this message and puts it on Seema's table. Write the message in not more than 50 word in your answer sheet.

Leena : Good morning! Leena here. May I speak to Seema, please ?

Reena : Good morning! Sorry Leena, Seema is not here at the moment.

Leena : May I request you to convey my message to her on her return ?

Reena : Sure, please tell me.

Leena : My brother has brought the chemistry book she wanted for her examination. She may collect it soon.

Reena : I will convey it to Seema.

Answer

MESSAGE

Seema 16 March, 2005

There was a telephone for you from Leena. She has left a message for you. It is, that her brother has brought the chemistry book you needed. You may collect it soon.

Reena

18. You are Rashmi and had an appointment with your friend Ritu to visit an exhibition at 6.00 p.m. But you have been held up by your parents for preparing dishes for the unexpected guests. Draft a message to be sent to Ritu giving your excuse for not keeping the appointment, in not more than 50 words in your answer sheet.

Answer

MESSAGE

Ritu 13 June, 2005

I apologise to you for not keeping the appointment to visit the exhibition. Some unexpected guests arrived before the time of my appointment and I was detained by my parents to prepare supper for them.

Rashmi

FOR PRACTICE

1. Read the following telephone conversation between Sridhar and a Caller named Rita. Dinesh is about to leave home and will not be able to meet Geeta. He leaves a message for her. Write this message, using not more than 50 words.

Caller : Is this Mr. Srinvasan's residence ?

Dinesh : Yes, it is. Whom do you wish to speak to ?

Caller : May I speak to Geeta, please ?

Dinesh : Sorry, she's not here at the moment. She's out visiting an aunt. May I know who's speaking, please?

Caller : This is Rita. What time is she expected back?

Dinesh : By this evening, I think. Would you like to leave a message?

Rita : Yes, could you please tell her I am having a small get together of friends tomorrow evening at my place. I would like her to come at four thirty. Also could she tell Asha to come, rather could she bring her along. You See, Asha has no phone and I haven't been able to contact her. Sorry to bother you.

Dinesh : Not at all, I'll tell her everything.

Rita : Many thanks. Bye.

Dinesh : Bye.

2. Read the following telephone conversation between Girish and a caller named Raghvan. Girish is about to leave home and will not be able to meet Asha. He leaves message for her. Write this message using not more than 50 words.

Caller : Is this five four one three one seven one?

Girish : Yes.

Caller : May I speak to Asha please?

Girish : Sorry, she's just gone out. May I know who is calling, please?

Caller : This is Raghvan. We're in the same class. Could I leave a message for her, please?

Girish : Sure.

Raghvan : Please tell her, I have got two tickets for the play 'Ek Tha Gadha' for this evening at the Shri Ram Centre.

Girish : I'll tell her.

Raghvan : Please tell her to reach there six fifteen sharp.

Girish : I will.

Raghvan : Thanks a lot. Bye.

Girish : Bye.

3. Read the following telephone conversation between Rekha and Suman. Suman is about to leave home and will not be able to meet Alok. She leaves a message for him. Write this message, using not more than 50 words.

Rekha : Hellow. Am I speaking to Sunita? .

Suman : Yes, Sunita speaking.

Rekha : It is Rekha this side. You know there is Gemini Circus on at Ramlila Ground. What about seeing it tomorrow?

Suman : Yes, it is a good idea.

Rekha : Let's go to the evening show. Where should we meet?

Suman : Let us meet a Janter Manter, at 5.30. Is that all right?

Rekha : Fine. Look Rohit is coming along too. Why don't you ask Alok to join us ?

Suman : I will ask him. He is not here at the moment. but I will tell him to ring you this evening. Please wait for call before buying the tickets.

4. Read the following telephone conversation which took place when Mahesh was staying with his uncle. Write the message from Mahesh to his uncle, using not more than 50 words.

Seshu : Hello ! Hello! This is Seshu from Lucknow. Can I speak to Mr. Rao please? I am a friend of his son, Madhav Rao.

Mahesh : This is Suresh Rao. My uncle's not here at the moment. We heard about the earthquake. Is Madhav all right?

Seshu : Yes, Yes, He's okay now. But he had bad fall during the earthquake and he broke his left leg. It was a multiple fracture, but there's nothing to worry about now.

Mahesh : Is he in hospital?

Seshu : Yes, he's at the Tata Memorial Hospital here, would you please inform his family?

Mahesh : Of coures I will. Thank you for calling.

5. Read the following telephone conversation between Neelam and Mr. Chopra (from Carrier Aircon Ltd.) Mr. Chopra wants to talk to Mr. Rajpal, but he is, at present, not in office. He will be back only at 5 p.m. and Neelam will leave the office at 4 p.m. Neelam leaves a message for Mr. Rajpal. Write the message, using not more than 50 words.

Mr. Chopra : Is it Registrar's Office.

Neelam : Yes please.

Mr. Chopra : May I speak to Mr. Rajpal, the Deputy Registrar. I am Chopra from Carrier Aircon Ltd.

Neelam : He is not here at the moment. He has gone out and will be back around 5 p.m.

Mr. Chopra : In that case, will you kindly convery him a message?

Neelam : Yes, of coures, I shall also be going out for a important work at 4 p.m. But I shall leave the message on his table. What is it ?

Mr. Chopra : He had lodged a complaint that his air-conditioner is not functioning properly and I had told him that our mechanic will come to him today. But due to some unaviodable problem, the mechanic will not be able to come today, but tomorrow.

Neelam : Alright I shall leave the message for him.

Mr. Chopra : Thank-you very much.

6. Read the following telephone conversation between Rohit and Bhanu. Bhanu is about to leave home and will not be able to meet his brother, Rahul. He leaves a message for Rahul. Write this message, using not more than 50 words.

Rohit : Hello! Is that Yogesh ?

Bhanu : Speaking.

Rohit : Good God ! How lucky I am ! please take a message for your brother Rahul who works at the airport. I want to fly to Calcutta this evening. The time is very short. Ask Rabul to buy an air ticket for me.

Bhanu : Where should he deliver you the ticket?

Rohit : He should meet me at the Check-in Counter for Calcutta.

Bhanu : O.K. It will be done.

Rohit : Thank you. Bye.

Bhanu : Bye.

7. Read the following telephone conversation between Vineet and Rakesh. Rakesh is about to leave home and will not be able to meet Alok. He leaves a message for Alok. Write this message, using not more than 50 words.

Vineet : Hello! Is that Rakesh?

Rakesh : Speaking.

Vineet : It is Mohan here. Rakesh, you know India International Trade Fair, 2007 I suggest visiting it tomorrow.

Rakesh : Oh ! it is a wonderful idea. Why not make it today?

Vineet : Not today as I am busy. Let's make it tomorrow. Rajat is coming with me. You bring Alok with you.

Rakesh : He is not at home at present, but rest assured, he will be happy to be with us.

Vineet : Then it is settled. Please wait for us at Gate No. 4 at 1 p.m. tomorrow. In case, you reach earlier, please wait for us. If we reach earlier, we shall look for you.

Rakesh : Fine. We shall reach in time positively.

Vineet : All right, Bye till then.

Rakesh : Bye.

8. Read the following telephone conversation between Pankaj and Rahul. Rahul is about to leave home and will not be able to meet Ravi. He leaves a message for him. Write this message, using not more than 50 words.

Pankaj : Hello! May I speak to Ravi.

Rahul : Sorry, Ravi is not here at the moment. I'm Rahul, his brother, speaking.

Pankaj : When is Ravi expected back?

Rahul : In an hour or so.

Pankaj : Could you please give him a message?

Rahul : Most gladly.

Pankaj : My uncle, who is a journalist in Bombay, is here with us for a few hours. Ravi very keen to see him. My uncle says that he can meet him at 6 p.m. today at my place.

Rahul : Thank you for the message. I'll convey it to Ravi.

Pankaj : Please don't forget. Bye-bye.

Rahual : Bye-bye.

9. Read the following telephone conversation between Ram and Gopal. Gopal is about to leave home and will not be able to meet Ajit. He leaves a message for Ajit. Write this message, using not more than 50 words.

Ram : Hello! Could I speak to Ajit ?

Gopal : I am his brother Gopal. He has gone to see off someone at station.

Ram : When will he be back?

Gopal : Not before an hour or so ?

Ram : I am his friend Ram. Could you give him the message?

Gopal : Sure, with great pleasure.

Ram : We are going for a picnic to Badhkal Lake tomorrow in the morning. In case he can join us, tell him to ring me up today by 10 P.M.

Goapl : I'll inform him. Bye.

Ram : Bye.

10. Read the following telephone conversation between Manoj and Abhishek. Manoj is about to leave home and will not be able meet Atul. He leaves a message for Atul. Write the message, using not more than 50 words.

Manoj : Hello?

Abhishek : May I speak to Atul ?

Manoj : I'm afraid he is out Can I take your message?

Abhishek : Well, this is Abhishek here. I was wondering whether Atul will be free this evening. I am going to the new film at Rachna. I'd like him to come with me. When will he be back ?

Manoj : He won't be long. He's just gone to the Post Office. I don't think he's doing anything in the evening.

Abhishek : Well, it's 4. I'll be reaching Rachna at 5.30. Can you tell him to meet me there?

Manoj : Yes, I'll tell him. Good-bye!

Abhishek : Good bye! Thank you.

11. Read the following telephone conversation between Manav and Pinky. Manav would be leaving home as such he leaves message for his sister, Dolly. Write the message, using not more than 50 words.

Pinky : Hello! Could I speak to Dolly?

Manav : I'm sorry. She is not at home.

Pinky : When is she expected to come back ?

Manav : I think she will be back by 5 P.M.

Pinky : Could you please give her my message?

Manav : Why not?

Pinky : Well, tell her that our common friend Pinky has come from Calcutta. She is staying with me these days. She will be leaving for Calcutta tomorrow by the Hawrah Express.

Manav : I'll inform her.

Pinky : Thank you. Bye.

Manav : Bye.

12. Write a message to be left at the desk of Anu about a telephone call received for her when she was away. Write the message in about 50 words in your answer sheet.

Karan : Hello. Is it 3319167? Could I talk to Annu Malik who works in purchase section.

Receptionist : That's right. But I'm afraid Annu Malik has not yet arrived.

Karan : Could you convey to her that her mother is quite serious in Chandigarh and she should leave for Chandigarh immediately. She is very critical in the state of coma.

Receptionist : So sad. Anything else that I must convey.

Karan : Yes, that she should carry sufficient clothes. You never know about a patient in coma will you do this favour? Could you trace her?

Receptionist : I pray for her recovery. Bye.

Karan : Karan karan Bhatia, her next door neighbour in Chandigarh.

13. Read the following telephone conversation that took place when Rama answered the phone at Future Knowledge Encyclopaedias and Reference books. Write the message that Rama leaves for Mr. Debu using not more than 50 words.

Mr. Murli : Hello, This is Mr. Murli from Chennai. May I speak to Mr. Debu please ?

Rama : Mr. Debu is not in at the moment. May I take a message for him ?

Mr. Murli : Please convey my thanks to him. I have just received the encyclopaedia I ordered. The last payment would reach him tomorrow. I would also like some information on the latest reference books in Geography.

Rama : I'll make sure he gets that message Mr. Murli.

Mr. Murli : Thank you.

14. Read the following telephonic conversation between Kavita and Karan. Karan will not be able to meet Avik. He leaves a message for him. Write this message in your answer sheet using not more than 50 words.

Kavita : Heno! Hello! I am Kavita from Indore. Can I speak to Avik? I am his sister,

Karan : Hello! Kavita, I am Karan, Avik's colleague. Avik is on leave today. Can I take a message?

Kavita : Yes, Karan. I am coming to Mumbai tomorrow. Ask him to pick me up at the airport. I have an interview for the post of Scientist at NPL on the day after tomorrow.

Karan : Which flight are you coming on ?

Kavita : It is the Jetline flight which arrives there at 7-15 or so in the morning. I am bringing along with me that big box which contains his books. I hope it won't be any trouble for you.

Karan : Not at all. I will leave a message on his table. Okay, Kavita.

Kavita : Thank you, Karan. Bye.

❒

10

Writing of Telegrams

At some time or the other all of you may be called upon to send a telegram. To write a telegram one requires some skill as the meaning has to be made absolutely clear without the use of unnecessary words, since the cost of a telegram is based on the number of words used beyond a minimum fifteen words. This means that there is a standard fixed rate for any number of words under fifteen and each word over fifteen is charged extra.

1. **Economy in the use of words,** however, should not interfere with normal courtesy of expression. Even if the word costs a few paise extra, it is worth using it.

2. **Punctuation marks** are written and counted as individual words. Therefore, as far as possible their use is avoided unless there is a likelihood of the meaning being misunderstood.

In the following message a full-stop is unavoidable because the two names Pathak and Williams come one after the other and might cause confusion.

HAVE SENT GHOSH AND PATHAK STOP WILLIAMS UNSATISFACTORY

TANDON

In the message that follows the stop, could have been used where it is indicated in brackets but if it is left out, it would not harm the meaning.

ALL FLIGHTS CANCELLED (STOP) ARRIVING GOMTI EXPRESS SIXTEENTH MORNING

BHAKTAWAR

3. When a lot of information is to be given such as reasons, excuses etc. the thing to do is to send the absolutely urgent information by telegram and say letter follows. *e.g.* Meeting Postponed Cancel Hotel Reservations Letter Follows—Singh.

4. Remember to include the sender's name, otherwise the telegram might prove very misleading.

5. Reduce the address too as far as possible.

   e.g. Mr. Saurabh Sangekar
Sunder Sadan (Top floor)
Behind Kennaway House
63-A Rouse Avenue,
Madras

   Would become Saurabh Sangekar
63-A, Rouse Avenue
Madras

6. At each Telegraph Office there is a list of Standard Messages compiled by the Posts' and Telegraphs Department which are sent on special occasions such as 'Hearty Congratulations on your success in the examination.' or 'Id Mubarak'

Each of these have a code number which you send instead of a personal message and which is decoded at the other end: But be careful to give the correct code or else you may get your message mixed.

To practise writing-telegrams, write out the full message and then see which words you can delete without loss of meaning Occasionally you may have to change the word order a little for it to make sense.

Look at the following sentence. The 'bold-type 'Words are those which can be deleted without loss of meaning.

All flights have been cancelled due to bad weather. Train tickets are not available and the earliest booking have been able to get is on the K.K. Express which reaches Delhi on the sixteenth morning.

Yours in haste
Bani

Rewritten, the message would read:

All Flights Cancelled Arriving Delhi K.K. Express Sixteenth Morning

BANI

Familiarity with a simplified version of the telegram form supplied by the Posts and Telegraph Department would prove useful. In examinations, too, drawing a form and filling in the details would make your answer more effective.

1. Seema wrote the following letter to her father. But later on she decided to send a telegram instead of sending the letter. Write this telegram not more than 25 words.

Ajmer
March 3, 2007
Dear father

I had a comfortable journey but on arrival I found that I had forgotten my library notes on History along with the textbook. I think they were lying on the top of the bookshelf in my room. I need these urgently for my exams. Please send the notes through courier mail. I also need Rs. 400 to pay the fee for my coaching classes in Maths.

Regards and love

Seema

Receiver's Name : Receiver's Address :				
Sender's Name: (Not To Be Telegraphed) Sender's Address :				

Answer

B.N. Bose
33, Burman Street.
Burdwan

JOURNEY	COMFORTABLE	FORGOT	HISTORY	NOTES	AND
TEXTBOOK	PERHAPS	ON	BOOKSHELF	REQUIRED	FOR
EXAM.	ALSO	NEED	RS.	400	FOR
MATHS	COACHING	CLASSES	SEND	BY	COURIER

NATASHA

Seema
Room No. 36, Sarojini Girls' Hostel
Ajmer

2. Imagine you are going to Mumbai on an urgent work and shall stay there for three days. Write a telegram in not more than 25 words to Hotel Samrat, Marine Drive, Mumbai requesting reservation and confirmation of the same.

Answer

Hotel Samrat, Marine Drive, Mumbai

RESERVE SINGLE ROOM WITH BATH (STOP) ARRIVING 8 PM JANUARY 20 (STOP) STAYING 3 DAYS (STOP) CONFIRM

K.S. SHARMA

Sender's Address
(Not to be telegraphed)

Axel Gears Ltd.
265, Kashmere Gate
Delhi

3. Imagine that your annual examination is over but you are not going home after it as you have to attend a cricket coaching camp for ten days. Write a telegram to your father informing him of the same.

Answer

Satish Mahajan
23, Pandav Nagar
Agra

NOT COMING HOME AFTER EXAM (STOP) ATTENDING CRICKET COACHING CAMP FOR 10 DAYS.

DEEPAK.

Sender's Address
Not to be telegraphed

St. Columbus School
Dalhousie

4. Sudershan wrote the following letter to his father. Then he decided to send a telegram instead of the letter. Using relevant information from the letter, write this telegram in your answer sheet in about 25 words.

N/59, Nehru Vihar
New Delhi
26 July, 2007

Dear father

We received your letter yesterday in which you have expressed your concern and anxiety at Mummy's present state of health. I would, therefore, like to assure you that Mummy is feeling fine now. Her blood pressure has come down to normal and the doctor says that there is no need to worry. He has prescribed certain medicines for her and has also advised her complete bedrest. Myself and Suniti are taking special care of Mummy's health. Mummy also assures you to carry on with your work on the tour and not to hurry for home on her account.

All of us send you our love.

Yours affectionately

Sudershan

Answer

INDIAN POST AND TELEGRAPH

Mr. Ram Prakash
56, M.G. Road
Bangalore

MUMMY BITTER (.) DOCTOR ADVISED BEST-REST (.) PRESCRIBED, MEDICINES (.) LOOKED AFTER WELL (.) NO NEED TO RUSH HOME (.)

SUDERSHAN

Senders Address
(Not to be telegraphed)

N/59, Nehru Vihar
New Delhi

5. You are Ramganesh. Write a telegram to your uncle Vijayram informing him about your visit to Kolkata with five of your friends. You will spend a week in Kolkata and will require transport for sight-seeing. Also request him to book tickets for your return journey.

Answer

REACHING KOLKATA WITH FIVE FRIENDS FOR A WEEK (STOP) WILL REQUIRE TRANSPORT FOR SIGHT-SEEING (STOP) KINDLY BOOK TICKETS FOR RETURN JOURNEY (STOP).

RAMGANESH

6. Sudhir wrote the following letter to his friend. Then he decided to send a telegram instead of the letter. Using relevant information from the letter, write this telegram in not more than 25 words in your answer sheet.

115 Sector-D
Dombivilli, Mumbai

Oct. 23, 2007

Dear Verma

I shall now get an opportunity to see you. You will be glad to know that I have been called for an interview for the post of Regional Sales Manager by Bayer (India) Pharma, Patna. So I will be arriving in Patna by the Inter City Express on November 14 in the morning. Please book one room in a good hotel. Could you possibly meet me at the Railway Station ?

Yours sincerely,

Sudhir

Answer

Verma
Patna

ARRIVING PATNA NOV., 14 BY INTER CITY EXPRESS (STOP) INTERVIEW IN BAYER (INDIA) (STOP) BOOK ROOM IN GOOD HOTEL (STOP) MEET ME AT RAILWAY STATION (STOP).

SUDHIR

Sender's Address
(Not to be telegraphed)

115 Sector-D, Dombivilli
Mumbai

7. You are Lalit Kumar working in a private firm in Mumbai. You are to go home on leave on the 21st of April.

But you are unable to do so as you have some urgent work to do. You are not sure of the date of your arrival. Send a telegram to your parents in Kolkata using not more than 25 words.

Answer

INDIAN POST AND TELEGRAPH

AMIT GOEL
15 Kali Bari
Kolkata

REACHING HOME ON LEAVE POSSIBLY ON 21ST APRIL (.) SHALL WIRE EXACT DATE OF ARRIVAL (.)

LALIT

Senders Address
(Not to be telegraphed)

Lalit Kumar
15-Khar Road Extn.
Mumbai

8. You are Ram Mohan living at 13, Race Course, Surat. You are not in a position to attend the marriage of your friend Krishna Kumar at 27, Tilak Marg, Vadodara. Draft'a telegram to be sent to your friend using not more than 50 words in your answer sheet.

Answer

INDIAN POST AND TELEGRAPH

Address of the addressee

Name : Krishna Kumar
Address : 27, Tilak Marg
Telegraph Office : Vadodara

CONGRATULATIONS ON YOUR WEDDING. UNABLE TO ATTEND YOUR WEDDING. REGRET IT. MOTHER SERIOUS ILL.SHALL SEE YOU SOON. BEST WISHES TO ALL.

Sender's Name RAM MOHAN

Sender's Address
(Not to be telegraphed) 13, Race Course,
Surat

9. You are Vikram Vasantha of Class XI studying in Sun Residential School, Chennai, staying in the school hostel You wish to join a crash course in Computers. Draft a telegram in not more than 20 words to your father in Vishakhapatnam seeking his permission and requesting him to send you the registration fees of Rs. 100 immediately.

Answer

INDIAN POST AND TELEGRAPH

Address of the addressee — Name: P.K. Sanmugam
Address : 183, Haider Ali Road
Telegraph Office: Vishakhapatnam

MESSAGE

WILLING TO JOIN CRASH COURSE IN COMPUTERS (.) PERMIT (.) SEND RS. 100 FOR REGISTRATION

Sender's Name — Vikram/Vasantha

Address: (Not to be telegraphed) — Sun Residential School
Chennai

10. You are Vikram/Vasantha of Class XII studying in Sun Residential School, Chennai, staying in the school hostel. You are participating in an Inter School Drama Competition. You require money urgently for getting the necessary costume stitched and for paying the entrance fee. Draft a telegram in not more than 25 words to be sent to your parents in Trivendrum.

Answer

INDIAN POST AND TELEGRAPH

Address of the addressee	Name: P.K. Sanmugam Address : 10, M.G. Road Telegraph Office : Trivandrum

MESSAGE

SEND RS 1000 FOR COSTUMES & ENTRANCE FEE FOR PARTICIPATING IN INTER SCHOOL DRAMA COMPETITION

Sender's Name	VIKRAM
Sender's Name Address (Not to be telegraphed)	Vikram Sun Residential School Chennai

11. Write a telegraphic message to your friend at Allahabad informing him of your visit and asking him to receive you at the railway station. You are Rakesh Kumar of 13A/17 W.E.A. Karol Bagh, New Delhi.

B. Lall

23, Andrews Gunj, Allahabad

REACHING ALLAHABAD SANGAM EXPRESS ON TWENTIETH RECEIVE AT STATION

Rakesh Kumar

Address :
(Not to be Telegraphed)
13A/17 W.E.A. Karol Bagh,
New Delhi.

12. Send a telegram to your father informing him of your result in the Central Board Examination.

Mohan Rakesh,
34, The Mall,
Shimla.

PASSED EXAMINATION SECURING 83% MARKS

BHARAT BHUSHAN

Address :
(Not to be Telegraphed)
E-393, Ramesh Nagar,
New Delhi 110015.

13. You live in a hostel and plan to join a short trip to the hills with your class fellows. Draft a telegram for your father asking for necessary money.

U.R. Mediratta,
E-393, Ramesh Nagar,
New Delhi - 110015

JOINING TRIP TO HILLS WITH CLASS-FELLOWS SEND RS. 5000 URGENTLY

MANOJ

Address :
(Not to be Telegraphed)
Boys' Hostel,
Mrinalini Indian Public School,
Mussoorie.

14. Send a telegram to your father, Mr. Ram Singh 26, Big Street, Bombay expressing your inability to leave Madras as all trains have been cancelled for a week.

Mr. Ram Singh,
26, Big Street,
Bombay.

UNABLE TO LEAVE MADRAS ALL TRAINS CANCELLED FOR A WEEK

MANOJ

Address :
(Not to be Telegraphed)
56, Kautilya, Samajguda,
Madras.

15. Your younger brother has been selected as a member of the National Football team. Send him a telegram of congratulation.

Yogesh
40, M.K. Gandhi Road,
Ambala Cantt.

HEARTIEST CONGRATULATION ON SELECTION IN NATIONAL FOOTBALL TEAM

MANOJ

Address :
(Not to be Telegraphed)
E-393, Ramesh Nagar,
New Delhi 110015.

16. Your are XYZ, 6 M.K. Gandhi Road, ABC city. You and your friend went to Hyderabad to attend an interview and you were expected to return by A.P. Express starting on Friday. But you have postponed your return journey and planned to start on Sunday by the same train owing to the sudden illness of your friend. Father intimating the change in the return journey schedule and requesting him to inform the same to your friend's parents.

Shri Naval Kishore
6 M.K. Gandhi Road
ABC City.

STARTING SUNDAY AP EXPRESS FRIEND SUDDENLY ILL INFORM HIS PARENTS

XYZ

(Not to be telegraphed)
(Signature)
Sender's Address:

17. Send a telegram to your employer requesting extension of leave mentioning an unexpected emergency in the family as the reason.

Mr. Ushank Rai
Jiwan Publishing House,
New Delhi-110015.

EXTEND LEAVE THREE DAYS, FATHER SUDDENY ILL

XYZ

(Not to be telegraphed)
(Signature)
Sender's Address:

18. You need Rs. 100 urgently. Write a telegram requesting your father to send you the amount stating the purpose for which you need it.

Address : Colonel O.P. Sharma.
C/o 56 A. P.O., New Delhi

SEND RS. 100 URGENTLY FOR DEPOSITING EXAMINATION FEE

RAJIV SHARMA

Address :
(Not to be Telegraphed)
E-393, Ramesh Nagar,
New Delhi 110015

19. You have received a latter of appointment for a job you had applied for. Send a telegram to the Employer accepting the offer.

M/s Televista Electronic Ltd.,
East of Kailash,
New Delhi

THANKFULLY ACCEPT THE JOB OF SALESMAN JOINING 15TH INSTANT

RAJESH AHUJA

Address :
(Not to be Telegraphed)
24, Mayfair Garden,
New Delhi 110050.

20. You live in your school hostel. Sudenly you have had to cancel coming home for the winter vacation. Write out a suitable telegram for your parents.

M.M. Gupta
20, M.K. Gandhi Road,
New Delhi 110048

COACHING IN SCIENCE ARRANGED DURING WINTER VACATION COMING HOME CANCELLED

Address:
(Not to be Telegraphed)
Mahoj, Boys' Hostel, Maifair School,
Nagpur,

❒

11

Note Making and Abstraction

Note-making involves a regular practice at sorting out points from a passage. This being a very skilled work, it involves a lot of word knowledge and good vocabulary. While making notes, the following points should be kept in mind.

(a) Headings and sub-headings or titles and sub-titles are used for easy reference.

(b) Abbreviations are used wherever possible.

(c) The information is presented in points.

(d) Proper indentation should be used as it makes way for clarity.

(e) Thoughts are divided in the passage into the main points or phrases and sub-points in the following way:

1. Main points

2. Sub-points

3. Further sub-points.

Procedure:

(a) The passage should first be read quickly but carefully.

(b) The second reading should be slower and more thorough.

(c) Key-words should be located and main points should be underlined. Think of a possible title.

(d) Then the passage should be divided into chief divisions and sub-divisions. Titles and sub-titles should also be decided.

(e) Make a rough note of the main points and give them a logical sequence.

(f) Use one word substitution wherever possible.

(g) Dealing with the main points and sub-points, arrange your notes logically and systematically with abbreviations wherever possible by using a SHORTENED CONSTRUCTION.

ABBREVIATIONS

Abbreviations should be so selected or used as not to create confusion. They should be easily understood.

Examples:

Abbreviation	*Word*	*Abbreviation*	*Word*
A/c	account	N/A	not applicable
bk	book	org'zn	organization
cd	could	P.M.	Prime Minister
Capt.	Captain	pt.	point
Co	Company	retd.	retired
Col.	Colonel	relgn.	religion
CBSE	Central Board of	rec'd.	received
	Secondary Education	Sc.	science
cm.	centimetre	shd.	should
c/o	care of	soc.	society
dft	draft	std.	standard
dis.	discount	Sig.	signature
deptt.	department	Secy.	secretary
esp.	especially	tel.	telegram
estd.	established	tele.	telephone

fig.	figure	tech.	technical
ft.	foot, feet	univ.	university
Govt.	Government	wt.	weight
G.P.O.	General Post Office	WHO	World Health Oranisation
hon.	honourable		
ins.	inches	Yr.	year
kg.	kilogram	&	and
lab.	laboratory	∵	because
lib.	library	∴	therefore
Ltd.	Limited	100	hundred
m	metre	%	per cent

DIFFERENT WAYS OF USING ABBREVIATIONS/SYMBOLS

(a) Capitalisation of initial words *e.g.* U.K. for United Kingdom.

(b) Taking first few letters of the word *e.g.* Prac. for Practical and Com for Committee.

(c) Taking first & last letters of the words *e.g.* wrtg. for writing, Dte. for Directorate.

(d) Adding 's' to make plurals, *e.g.* fgrs. for figures.

(e) Contractions of words *e.g.* shan't for shall not, ain't for am not.

(f) Using universally recognized symbols *e.g.*

< for shorter than

> for greater than

WRITING IN POINTS

(i) Notes must be written in points, listed one under the other and numbered.

(ii) Complete sentences are not used.

(iii) Lifting of entire sentences from the original passage would be bad as marks would be deducted on this score.

(iv) Consistency must be maintained when numbering points *e.g.*, If (1) point is divided into (1), (2), (3)-etc., then II point should also be divided into (1), (2), (3) and Not as, (a), (b), (c).

INDENTATION

This implies that sub-points should be written under main points successively farther away from the margin.

Divide the thoughts contained in the passage into the main points and related sub-points in the following way:

(i) Main Point: 1, 2, 3, ...

(ii) Sub-points: a, b, c, ...

(iii) Further Sub-points: (i), (ii), (iii)

A Skeleton Outline:

1. Title:

(a) ....

(b) ....

(c) ....

2. ....

3. ....

(a) ....

(i) ....

(ii) ....

(iii) ....

(b) ....

2. Must come under 1

b must come under **a** and **c** under **b** and at equal distance from the margin.

(ii) must come under (i) and (iii) under (ii) and farther away from the margin, since they are parts of one point.

Points may also be listed using the decimal system:

e.g., 1. ....

1.1 ....

1.2 ....

2. ....

2.1 ....

2.1.1 ....

2.1.2 ....

2.1.3 ....

3. ....

3.1 ....

3.2 ....

3.3 ....

HOW TO WRITE A SUMMARY OR ABSTRACTION? DEVELOP NOTES INTO PARAGRAPH

While writing a summary remember that:

(a) You needn't construct a sentence for each point of the notes only. The main points of the notes are combined into one paragraph.

(b) Complete sentences are used.

(c) These sentences are logically and cohesively linked together with the help of suitable linkers.

(d) No abbreviations are used.

Given below is an acceptable format of preparing the notes:

Title: ....

NOTES

1. Sub-Title/Sub-Heading

(a) short points

(b) short points

(c) short points

(d) short points

2. Sub-Title

(a) short points

(b) short points

(c) short points

3. Sub-Title

(a) short points

(b) short points

(c) short points

(d) short points

In order to make it realistic, we should follow the above scheme and maintain the correct distance from the margin.

PREPARING SUMMARY OF THE PASSAGE

For developing a good habit of preparing a summary from the given notes or a paragraph, we should prepare our summary in a logical and systematic way. It requires a lot of mental ability and power of expression. A rich vocabulary always helps in writing a well defined summary. The summary should contain all the relevant and significant informations of the passage. Always use complete sentences without any use of abbreviated words. The sentences should show automatic flow duly interconnected with the other sentence.

ASSIGNING A SUITABLE TITLE OR HEADING

When we are selecting a title or a heading from a given passage, we should be careful enough to evolve such a short but impressive set of words so as to reflect the complete idea about the passage. Long sentences should be avoided otherwise it is a common saying or a maxim.

Following are given some examples of passages and answers for the students to know the topic properly.

PASSAGE-1

Read the passage given below and answer the questions that follow:

COMMERCIALISATION OF SPORTS

It is shameful enough that India should borrow money from the World Bank to finance primary education. More shocking is the news that the Indian Hockey Federation does not have adequate funds to provide uniforms and playing gear to our Olympic team and it has to depend on the multinational shoe company Reebok for the equipment. This bespeaks of the lamentable state of the game in the country in which it was world champions for decades. In this context, the decision of the new minister for human resource development, to frame a new sports policy has not come a day too soon.

Just as we are denying primary education to millions of our children through lopsided policies, we are also depriving our masses of sports facilities. India's huge investment in the expensive game of cricket has paid poor dividends. The India XI was recently humiliated even by the country team of Derbyshire. How ridiculous now seem those dives, in World Cup advertisement telecast, of Vinod Kambli and Sachin Tendulkar for a bottle of Pepsi, as if their lives depended on it?

More than sponsorship by multinationals, a mass involvement in athletics and physical fitness will lift the nation's sporting standards. Sponsorship can help only a few players, and like Tendulkar and Azaruddin enable them to become millionaries. Late Arthur Ashe, the black tennis star, correctly warned black youths years ago that their future lay in education, not sports. Only a few can make a prosperous career in sports. Others who cannot make it to the top in sports are condemned to swallow in penury and deprivation. Multinationals use, sports to promote themselves, of course. Coca Cola, Reebok and Macdonald will be dominating the coming Olympic Games in Atlanta. When it suited them, the vested interests in the West looked down upon making money in sports. In the early years of this century amateurism was promoted to keep commoners out of big, competitive sports. Jim Thorpe, the undisputed decathlon champion who excelled in athletic events, was to have played basketball for money in 1909. Although it was only a paltry sum, his name was struck off the Olympic records and he was stripped of all his medals. He died penniless in 1953. It was only after years of appeal that the International Olympic Committee restored Thorpe's honour and his medals to his family in 1983. Army officers were treated as amateurs but ordinary soldiers were not, and were kept out of competition. A Swedish cavalryman, Gehnall Persson, was promoted as a lieutenant through a royal decree so that he could ride in the equestrian events in the Olympics as an officer. After the event he was demoted again as an ordinary soldier.

Decathlon should be the ideal for sportspersons, not the brutally competitive modern games which have made a travesty of the Olympic ideal that participation, not winning, is important.

Sports author Frank Zarnowski points out that whoever wants to know the heart and mind of renaissance man had better learn decathlon. It reflects the ancient Greek ideal of all round balanced excellence in sports. The decathlon is a menu of event, which tests an individual's endurance, speed, skill and personality. Doherty, a former Olympic medalist, declared, "I have always rejected that sports which involves a violent struggle against antagonistic opponents". In the decathlon one sees other athletes as fellow competitors, helpful mediators, often good friends, never hostile. Whoever scores more points, wins. A very bandage, for years the president of the International Olympic Committee and a strong champion of amateurism, was himself a decathlon athlete of good standing.

Sports research scholars like Stanley Arnowitz question on various counts the cut-throat competition in modern sports. Sports has ceased to be fun, as famous cricket umpire Dicky Bird said on his retirement recently in America, even children's sports have lost their innocence. Children are subjected to extreme pressures by parents and coaches to win. As a result, some children "retire" from sports very young and violence mars children's matches.

Q. 1. On the basis of your reading of the above passage, make notes on it, using to recognizable abbreviations wherever necessary. Assign a suitable title to the passage.

Ans. Title. Cut-throat Competition in Sports.

NOTES

(a) Borrowing money—a shame

(i) money for primary education

(ii) Indian hockey federation lacking funds

(iii) dependence on multinational company.

(b) Need for mass involvement

(i) lifting sports standard

(ii) sponsorship and help

(iii) interest of multinationals

(iv) commoners remain behind.

(c) Decathlon and sportsman

(i) an ideal for sports

(ii) a testing signal

(iii) athletes as competitors

(iv) cut-throat competition.

Q. 2. Write a summary of the above passage in about 80 words.

Ans. SUMMARY

There is a great cut-throat competition in sports and they have become commercialised. It is shame for us to borrow money for primary education. We are unable to provide uniforms to our hockey olympic team. There is dependence on multinational companies like Reebok etc. In order to raise sporting standard, mass involvement is needed. Multinationals have their own interest and provide sponsership ,but the commoners lag behind Jim Thorpe, died penniless; Decalthlon should be the ideal for sports persons as it is an ideal for sports. It provides a testing signal for the athletes and they can see others on competitors.

PASSAGE-2

Read the given passage very carefully:

POLLUTION THROUGH NOISE

Noise is defined as 'sound without value' or any sound that is undesired by the recipient. Noise can be measured by a sound meter arid is expressed in a unit called the decibel (DB). High intensity or noise pollution is caused by many machines man has invented during his technological advancement. While the modern household gadgets such as mixture-cum-grinder, vacuum cleaner, washing machine, coolers and air conditioners greatly enhance the levels of sounds and are potentially harmful to health, loudspeakers disturb the students in their studies and the peace of the locality. Similarly loudly played radios, stereos, televisions, telephones and pressure horns are other major sources of noise pollution. Printing presses, small scale industries, trucks, buses, rails, autos, motorcycles, aeroplanes, ships, social and political gatherings, all contribute to the noise problems in almost all the larger cities of India.

Noise causes disturbances in the atmosphere which in turn interferes with the systems of communication. They affect our peace of mind, health and behavour. Sudden loud note can cause acute damage to the ear drum and the tiny hair cells in the internal ear, whereas prolonged noise results in temporary loss of heaving or even permanent impairment. It causes headache, irritability and impairs focussing. It is known to flame the skin, construct stomach muscles and produce ulcers, heart disease, high blood pressure, nervousness and other defects in sensory and nervous systems. It is almost difficult to completely get rid of the malady of noise pollution in the current electronic age. However we can adopt certain measures to minimise the intensity of noise pollution. Legislation and public awareness are essential. Nobody should be permitted to create noise in silent zones or during night. Noise producing traffic vehicles should be prevented from plying on the roads and their use of pressure horns should be entirely checked.

Here the horticulturists can help a lot. They can suggest adequate varieties of vegetation which can be planted around factories, hospitals, educational institutions, public libraries and houses which may reduce sound pollution and also may minimize dust pollution. But a lot of hue and cry due to pollution is caused by pesticides that has been prevailing among the residents living in the industrial areas and their son outings and other inhabited parts for a long time. The genesis is that when the bad smell and the noise and other of machines in the manufacturing process become inevitable, the workers have to suffer a lot. Pesticides do kill the harmful insects, rodents but plants are adversely affected. These plants are rather.helpful to absorb the extra noise prevalent in the atmosphere. It is our moral duty to preserve the atmosphere from noise so as to keep ourselves away from many harmful effects of noise pollution. In reality man is responsible for his degradation.

Q. 1. On the basis of your reading of the above passage, make notes on the contents of the passage in points only, using the recognizable abbreviations wherever necessary in a suitable format.

Assign a suitable title to the passage.

Ans. Title. Noise Pollution

NOTES

(1) Definition of noise

(a) sound without value

(b) measurement and its unit

(c) high pitch harmful

(d) industries, vehicles, domestic appliances.

(2) Effects

(i) disturbance in atmosphere

(ii) harmful to health

(iii) defects in nervous and sensory system.

(3) Remedies

(i) creation of silent zones

(ii) growing vegetations

(iii) preserving the atmosphere.

Q. 2. Write a summary of the above passage in about 80 words.

Ans. **SUMMARY**

Any undesired sound is called a noise. It is expressed in unit called decibel. High intensity of noise is always harmful to all. Industries, vechicles and domestic appliances contribute to noise pollution which creates disturbance in the atmosphere. It is very harmful to our health and brings defects in our nervous and sensory system. It is difficult to get rid of this malady but we can suggest measures. Silent zones should be created and vegetations should be grown in the nearby surroundings. We should try to preserve the atmosphere.

PASSAGE-3

Read the passage given below and answer the questions that follow:

AN AFRICAN SAFARI

If an African safari conjures up visions of an adventurous drive through the grasslands, almost fraternising with animals in their natural habitat, then come to Masai Mara, Kenya.

Kenya, a land of diverse beauty, has a special appeal in its rich and varied wildlife. And the country offers the wildlife lover that magic called 'safari'. The word 'safari' is derived from Swahili—the main language spoken in Kenya—which literally means 'voyage'. In a wider perspective, an African safari is in fact a voyage into Africa. For the visitor or tourist who wants an insight into this exotic land, Kenya offers a breathtaking and' spectacular variety of holiday destinations ranging from wide, undulating plains and bushes to the snow-capped mountains, large lakes and exotic beaches. While game viewing is the biggest attraction for the tourist and the biggest moneyspinner for the nation, Kenya lays great emphasis on the protection and preservation of its wildlife and environment. There are some 45-odd conservation areas in Kenya, and Masai Mara, the leading game reserve which covers more than 15 per cent of the nation's land area, is situated at an attitude of 1,800 m. Widely acclaimed as the 'Jewel of Kenya', Masai Mara is a feast for the eyes especially for 'The Big Five'—lion, leopard, buffalo, rhino, and elephant. This is apart from some beautiful birdlife. A four-and-a-half hour drive west of Nairobi brings you to Masai Mara which shares its south-western boundary with Tanzania's famous Serengeti National Park.

One can get to the park by air and road with the latter reaching right upto the camps, while airstrips are within the reserve area. There are about 10 lodges and camps located at different spots inside the reserve, and accommodation is normally of the very best standard.

Our drive from Nairobi through the famous Rift Valley and other breathtaking places on route took us to our destination—the Fig Tree Camp. Smiling Kenyan porters came forward and greeted us with a loud Jambo'—in Swahili the word means hello. The passage to our camp was *via* a log bridge over the rivet Talek. Scores of beautifully furnished log cabins and tents greeted us. We chose to stay in the cabins.

On arrival we were promptly handed a glass of passion juice at the reception. The accommodation was comfortable, with cosy beds, a clean and smart interior with a toilet and shower. There is also a swimming pool and a shopping arcade. We then left for our first safari in an open-topped van.

Our driver Alex was a friendly chap and knew how to navigate his van over rugged terrain at breakneck speed. However, it did take some time for novices like us, to get accustomed to the bumpy ride. Each time, we braced ourselves following a big bump, Alex would smile and say 'hakuna matata'- meaning don't worry, and continue to drive on. But if you think, this drive in the heart of Africa was hot, think again, the bush was lush green and the air cool.

There was silence everywhere except for the chirping of birds and the wind whispering in our ears. In some places, the distant blue hills lent an eternal touch to the atmosphere. We got out our cameras to capture the serenity of the countryside, but at a signal from Alex we began to eagerly scan the area around us for the big game.

The driver gingerly cruised towards a group of gentle gazelles who skipped away quickly; from there, he drove to a pack of hyenas who eyed us belligerently and we didn't like them either. Next came various species of the deer family, particularly the impalas and antelopes. A lone eagle sat atop an acacia tree watching warthogs hopping around quietly in the grass. Giraffes seemed to be hanging from tall bushes munching tender leaves oblivious of our van, whilst a rhino family stood aloof.

Q. 1. On the basis of your reading of the above passage, make notes on it, using the recognizable abbrivations wherever necessary. Suggest a suitable title to the passage.

Ans. Title. Kenye—a land of diverse beauty

NOTES

(a) An adventurous African safari

(i) animals in natural habitat.

(ii) rich and varied wild life.

(iii) a spectacular variety.

(iv) stress on protection of wild life.

(b) Big Five and Jewel of Kenya

(i) Lion, rhino, leopard, buffalo and elephant.

(ii) best standard accommodation.

(iii) greeting by porters.

(c) Driving and Hakuna Matata

(i) a bumpy ride.

(ii) nothing new.

(iii) serenity everywhere.

(iv) sighting wild life.

Q. 2. Write a summary of the above passage in about 80 words.

Ans. SUMMARY

An African Safari means a voyage which is an adventurous drive to see the animals in their natural habitat. The wild life is rich and varied. It provides a spectacular variety of birds' and animals. Kenya is a land of diverse beauty and a great emphasis is laid on protecting wild life. Masai Mara is a games resort where big five—*i.e.* rhino, elephant, buffalo, lion and leopards are avalable. There one can get best standard accommodation. Similing Kenyan poters greet the tourists. The driving is very fast and nothing is new. There is serenity everywhere an our driver spoke Hakuna Matata which means do not worry. The sighting of wild life is enjoyable.

PASSAGE-4

Read the given passage carefully:

THE GREAT WALL OF CHINA

The Great Wall of China is said to be one structure built by man on earth which would be visible to observers on the moon. It covers a distance of 1,500 miles as the crow flies. From the Liaotung Peninsula westward to the last fortress in Central Asia, it crosses the northern province of China.

In the eastern section its height varies from 15-30 feet, and its width from about 25 feet at the bottom to 15 feet at top, where there is a pathway wide enough for six horsemen to ride side by side protected by parapets. When the Wall was first built it had about 25,000 towers each 40 feet square and 40 feet high projecting from it every few hundred yards, with holes from which the defenders could shoot at attackers. There are also many watch-towers on the enemy side, outside the Wall on hilltops or passes. These and the towers of the Wall were used for signalling with smoke or flags by day and with fire by night.

The great Emperor Shih Huang Ti joined three earlier frontier walls to form a great wall to act as a boundary between China and the north and keep out the feared nomads of the Mongolian Steppes. The Wall was designed to strengthen the nation's defences. Later it became in Ming times a substitute for a strong army and state. Construction was started in about 221 B.C. and the structure was practically complete when Shih Huang Ti died in 210 B.C. The man who did most in carrying out the Emperor's plans was General Meng Tien, who in 221 B.C. led an expedition against Tartars and drove them back from the Yellow River into the Steppes, and set his men to work on building the Wall. They were later joined by thousands of convicts. Year in year out, in icy winds and snowstorms in winter, and in duststorms in summer, the work went on, and so many men died that the Wall was sometimes, called the longest cemetery in the world. The core of the Wall is earth and stone, faced with brick, and set in a stone foundation. In hilly places the design was altered; two parallel ditches were dug out of the rock, 25 feet apart, and great blocks of stone were laid in the trenches to a height of several feet. Along each side of these stones, baked bricks about two feet long were laid at right angles to the face of the Wall, joined together with a white mortar so hard that no nail could be driven into it.

Emperor Wu Ti (140-86 B.C.) resumed work on the Wall and extended it to its greatest length. The Emperors of Ming Dynasty (A.D. 1386-1644) carried out more work on the Wall repairing its whole length and established new walls west of the Yellow River. The Wall which now exists mostly dates back to the Ming Dynasty, but many of the foundations are nearly 2000 years old.

Q. 1. On the basis of your reading of the above passage make notes on it, using headings and sub-headings. Also use recognizable abbreviations, wherever necessary (minimum 4). Use a format you consider suitable. Supply an appropriate title to it.

Ans. Title. The Great Wall of China.

NOTES

(a) Dimensions of the long wall

(i) 150 miles long to last fortress in C. Asia

(ii) height & width vary

(iii) 25000 towers with holes

(iv) watch towers.

(b) Work by Emp. Shih Huang Ti

(i) Three frontier walls-boundary

(ii) Keeping the nomads out

(iii) Strengthen'g nation's defence.

(c) Further Completion

(i) General Meng Tien's men set to work

(ii) natural hurdles-work continued

(iii) resumption of work by Wu Ti

(iv) work by Ming dynasty.

Q. 2. Write a summary of the above passage in about 80 words.

Ans. SUMMARY

The 1500 miles long Great wall of China is a massive structure with varying heights from 15 to 30 feet. In the beginning there were 2500 towers to be used for signalling. Three earlier frontier walls were to act as a boundary between China and the north to keep out the nomads. Empire Shih Huang Ti joined the structure work and his plans were carried out by Ming Dynasty. There came natural hurdles but the work was completed. Emperor Wu Ti extended the wall to its greatest length. Then the new wall on west as the Yellow river was established.

PASSAGE-5

Read the following passage carefully and answer the questions that follow:

NORMAL LIVING

Occasional self-medication has always been part of normal living. The making and selling of drugs has a long history and is closely linked, like medical practice itself, with belief in magic. Only during the last hundred years or so has the development of scientific techniques made it possible for some of the causes of symptoms to be understood, so that more accurate diagnosis has become possible. The doctor is now able to follow up the correct diagnosis of many illnesses with specific treatment of their causes. In many other illnesses of which the causes remain unknown, he is still limited, like the unqualified prescriber, to the treatment of symptoms. The doctor is trained to decide when to treat symptoms only and when to attack the cause. This is the essential difference between medical prescribing and self-medication.

The advance of technology has brought about much progress in some fields of medicine, including the development of scientific drug therapy. In many countries public health organisation is improving and people's nutritional standards have risen. Parallel with such, beneficial trends are two which have an adverse effect. One is the use of high pressure advertising by the pharmaceutical industry which has tended to influence both patients and doctors and has led to the overuse of drugs generally. The other is the emergence of the sedentary society with its faulty ways of life: lack of exercise, over-eating, unsuitable eating, insufficient sleep, excessive smoking and drinking. People with disorders arising from faulty habits such as these, as well as from unhappy human relationships, often resort to self-medication and so add the taking of pharmaceuticals of the list. Advertisers go to great lengths to catch this market.

Clever advertising aimed at chronic sufferers who will try anything because doctors have not been able to cure them, can induce such faith in a preparation, particularly if steeply priced, that it will produce by suggestion a very real effect in some people. Advertisements are also aimed at people suffering from mild complaints such as simple colds and coughs which clear up by themselves within a short time.

These are the main reasons, why laxatives, indigestion-remedies, pain-killers, cough-mixtures, tonics, vitamin and iron tablets, nose drops, ointments and many other preparations are found in quantity in many households. It is doubtful whether taking these things ever improves a person's health, it may even make it worse. Worse, because the preparation may contain unsuitable ingredients; worse because the taker may become dependent on them; worse because they might be taken in excess; worse because they may cause poisoning and worst of all because symptoms of some serious underlying cause may be asked and therefore medical help may not be sought. Self-diagnosis is a greater danger than self-medication.

Q. 1. On the basis of your reading of the above passage, make notes on it, in points only, using headings

and sub-headings. Also use recognizable abbreviations, wherever necessary (minimum 4). Use a format you consider suitable. Supply an appropriate title to it.

Ans. Title. Self-medication

NOTES

(a) Self-medication a part of normal living

(i) long history making and selling drugs.

(ii) accurate diagnosis through scientific research

(iii) still limitations

(b) Technology and development of scientific drug therapy

(i) improvement in people's nutritional standards

(ii) influence of advts

(iii) emergency of sedentary society

(iv) faulty ways of life and unhappy human relationships.

(c) Effect of advts

(i) faith by chronic sufferers

(ii) availability of more medicines in houses

(iii) self-diagnosis a greater danger.

Q. 2. Write a summary of the above passage in about 80 words.

Ans. **SUMMARY**

Self-medication is becoming a part of normal living. Drug preparation and its sale has a long history. The scientific research has provided accurate diagnosis but there are still limitations when the causes remain unknown. Advanced technology has brought changes in scientific drug therapy and thereby people's nutritional standards have improved. High pressure of advertising has influenced the doctors, the patients and thereby a sedentary society has emerged up with faulty ways of life habits. All this has led to self-medication mostly by chronic sufferers. As a result of this, one can see medicines in quantities in many households. This may have even worse effects as self-diagnosis is a greater danger than self-medication.

PASSAGE-6

Read the given passage carefully:

GETTING HAPPINESS

Whether work should be placed among the causes of happiness or among the causes of unhappiness may perhaps be regarded as a doubtful question. There is certainly much work which is exceedingly irksome, and an excess of work is always very painful. However, work is not to most people less painful than idleness. There are in work all grades, from mere relief of tedium upto the profoundest delights, according to the nature of the work and the abilities of the worker. Most of the work that most people have to do is not in itself interesting, but even such work has certain great advantages. To begin with, it fills a good many hours of the day without the need of deciding what one shall do. Most people, when they are left free to fill their own time according to their own choice are at a loss to think of anything sufficiently pleasant to be worth-doing. And whatever. they decide on, they are troubled by the feeling that something else would have been pleasantry. To be able to fill leisure intelligently is the last product of civilization and at present very few people have reached this level. Moreover the exercise of choice is in itself tiresome. Except to people with unusual initiative it is positively agreeable to be told what to do at each hour of the day, provided the orders are not unpleasant. Most of the idle rich suffer unspeakable boredom as the price of their freedom from drudgery. At times, they may find relief by hunting big game in Africa or by flying round the world, but the number of such sensations is limited especially after youth is past. Accordingly, the more intelligent rich men work nearly as hard as if they were poor. Work, therefore is desirable, first and foremost as a preventive of boredom, for the boredom that a man feels when he is doing something out of compulsion; though uninteresting work is as boring as having nothing to do. With this advantage, of work another is associated, namely that it makes holiday much more delicious when they come. Provided a man does not have to work so hard as to impair his vigour, he is likely to find far more zest in his free time than an idle man could possibly find.

The second advantage of most paid work and some of unpaid work is that it gives chances of success and opportunities for ambition. In most work, success is measured by income and while our capitalistic society continues, this is inevitable. However dull work may becomes bearable, if it is a means of building up a reputation. Continuity of purpose is one of the most essential ingredients of happiness and that comes chiefly through their work.

Q. 1. On the basis of your reading of the above passage, make notes on it, in points only, using headings and sub-headings. Also use recognizable abbreviations, wherever necessary (minimum 4). Supply an appropriate title to it. Use a suitable format.

Ans. Title. Happiness through Work

NOTES

(a) Work as a source of happiness or unhappiness

(i) a doubtful question

(ii) excess work painful

(iii) work in grades granting relief to pain.

(b) Facts about work

(i) keeping busy for many hrs.

(ii) last product of civilization

(iii) idle suffer unspeakable boredom

(c) Work as preventive of boredom

(i) making holidays delicious

(ii) finding more zest in free times

(iii) providing chances of success

(iv) opportunities for ambition

(v) building reputation and continuity.

Q. 2. Write a summary of the above passage in about 80 words.

Ans. **SUMMARY**

People have doubtful question if the work causes happiness or unhappiness. Though an excess of work is always painful. We have work in different grades granting relief to boredom but even an interesting work has advantages as it keeps one busy for many hours. Keeping busy is the last product of civilization and very few people do this while idle rich suffer unspeakable boredom and get relief by doing some hard work. In reality, work is the best method of removing boredom and makes our leisure delicious which may lead to vigour and zest in our life. Side by side it gives chances of success, continuity, income, building reputation, ultimately happiness.

PASSAGE-7

Read the given passage carefully:

MOTHER AND THE MINOR

After the rejoicing and reckoning, there is jubiliation among the Indian women over the recent Supreme Court ruling that the mother is also the natural guardian of a minor. This means that the children of unwedded mothers and bigamous marriages will no longer be called illegitimate. He can take his mother's name. There is no simple answer to it since Indian women continue to be governed by a forceful feudalistic society that traps them in the maze of the personal laws of assorted religion. And is there any religion which, at its crux and very care, permits women to breathe fully and freely as individuals? In 1856 our politicians decided that women cannot win against pseudo-political religiosity. The collective fate of crores of Hindu women was sealed that day. But today the Supreme Court says that a mother is a natural guardian. Our Hindu Minority and Guardianship Act, 1956 provides that the natural guardians of a Hindu minor for person and property in the case of a boy or an unmarried girl is the father, and after him, the mother.

Here we hold that in all situations where the father is not the actual in charge of the affairs of the minor either because of his indifference or because of an agreement between him and the mother of the minor and the minor is in the exclusive care and custody of the mother or the father or any person is unable to take care of the minor because of his physical or mental incapacity, the mother can act as natural guardian of the minor and all her actions would be valid even during the life time of the father. Who would be deemed to be 'absent' for the purposes of the section 6 (a) of HMC Act and Section 19 (b) of CW Act. The court has now decided that there cannot be an illegitimate human being, only society makes for bastards, illegitimate offspring are also covered under inheritance and succession, rights unless specially willed out. According to Hindu Adoption Law, an unmarried woman can adopt a child but a married Hindu woman cannot. Her husband has to do it and she can only give consent.

Once the child is adopted, she is an equal guardian. The legal experts says that the ruling of the Supreme Court does not change the face of family law in any way as the courts always look towards the best interest of the minor and in most cases the mother is understood to be the natural guardian. It was also argued when the financial settlements are made in court the fathers tend to insist that the minor maintenance will be kept in instruments like fixed deposits until they turn 18 because the mother is always viewed as incapable. Incidentally prominent legal activists say that the ruling is narrow. They point out that if the mother changes her religion, she ceases to be the child's natural guardian but the others point out that the onus of proving that factually the father is absent, the mother will be the natural guardian. The ruling of the Supreme Court is just a feel good factor.

Q. 1. On the basis of your reading of the above passage, make notes on the content of the passage in points only by using minimum four abbreviations. Also suggest a suitable title to the passage.

Ans. Title. Mother as a Natural Guardian

NOTES

1.1 Guardianship of Mother

(a) natural guardian of a minor

(b) no illegitimacy

(c) governance through feudalistic society

(d) natural guardian - father, mother

1.2 Hindu Minority Act

(a) father's indifference

(b) no take care of minor

(c) no illegitimate human being

1.3 Ruling by Supreme Court

(a) views of legal experts

(b) need for best interest of minor

(c) mother as a natural guardian.

Q. 2. Write a summary of the above passage in about 80 words.

Ans. SUMMARY

Indian women are elated over the ruling of Supreme Court that the mother is now a natural guardian of a minor. There will be no illegitimacy. But our women live and have the governance of a feudalistic society which entraps them fully. Our Hindu Minority and Guardianship Act provides that father is a natural guardian of a minor and after him the mother. In case father is absent or unable to take care or in other in valid situations, the mother can act as natural guardian of a minor. Now there will be no illegitimate human being. The legal experts say that the ruling is narrow. In all probability court has to see the best interest of the minor so the ruling is good.

PASSAGE-8

ıd the following passage and answer the questions that follo

NATURE AND MAN

So often these days we hear and speak of the conquest of nature, 'the taming of a river', 'the war against insects' and so on. Often these phrases are used without consciously attaching any values to them, but they have underlying in them an attitude of hostility towards Nature and Nature's creatures, a view point which seems to assume Nature as an enemy that needs to be vanquished. Alternatively, Nature sees merely as a 'resource' to be 'exploited' takes the maximum out of it, regardless of what this does to natural processes and to other creatures which depend on these processes. It is this attitude which sees fellow humans too as a resource to be exploited, or other human communities as enemies to be conquered.

There is a growing lack of sensitivity and respect for our fellow creatures. This attitude is being drilled into a child by social forces, which can only be countered by environmental education. Yet, sadly, in most cases this is not done. What is done is talk about the food, web and energy cycles and ecological balance and how removal of any element disrupts the whole system, and how this can affect human beings too. What this approach lacks is the essential interaction with Nature and with other humans. Indeed in many environmental activities the opposite takes place. A clssic example of this is making of a herbarium, of even worse, and insect collection, as common in both formal and non formal education in India. A child is often encouraged to pluck leaves and flowers and run after butterflies with a net, and is part of a large group of children similarly, marauding a patch of nature within it. Such a child is not likely to develop any strong feeling of respect for nature, or for the individual "specimens" pressed in the plant file or trapped in a jar. It is even worse when the activity is also competitive *i.e.* who collects the maximum. A lot of knowledge may be gained, but it is gained in a value system which emphasises exploitation and conquest, not sensitivity and respect. Learning under a tree, (Santivana) rather than in a classroom, is indeed the Indian tradition, is far more effective and long lasting.

The alternative is to take up activities where ecobalances, ecological diversities animal behaviour, human plurality and other such concepts and systems are introduced with the stress on their intrinsic worth. Materials, processes, living beings do not exist only for human use, but more importantly they are worth where in themselves.

A frog is as much in love with its life as the human child is with its; the feelings of the frog must be respected. The final thrust of environmental education seems to be embodied in the vital question: 'Am I doing something which disrespect or violates some other creature's right to live and live freely? If I am, what can I do to minimise the damage I am causing?

Once again, the Indian tradition of ahimsa comes out as infinitely more relevant then much of what we learn in modern education.

Q. 1. On the basis of your reading of the passage make notes on it, using recognizable abbreviations wherever necessary. Use a format you consider suitable. Supply a suitable title.

Ans. Title. Interaction between Nature and Human Being.

NOTES

(a) Need for removing hostility

(i) nature as an enemy

(ii) human community as an enemy

(iii) lack of sensitivity.

(b) Environmental Education and its recognition

(i) maintenance of ecological balance

(ii) respecting and recognising nature

(iii) evaluating fellow creatures.

(c) Need for interaction with nature

(i) human personality and animal behaviour

(ii) respect for natural entities

(iii) following the tradition of ahimsa.

Q. 2. Make a summary of the above passage in about 80 words.

Ans. **SUMMARY**

All of us speak our triumph over nature, still we have a great hostility for nature and its creatures. There is a great need to leave this attitude as nature and human community are not the enemies. It is our lack of sensitivity for having such a view. We can get maximum out of nature. We exploit nature and fail to recognise and respect it. There is a need for maintaining the ecological balance and evaluating its fellow creatures. We can get a lot of knowledge from the nature. Hence there is a great need for having interaction between nature and human beings. We should pay proper respect to nature and its entities. Following the tradition of ahimsa is relevant in our modern education.

PASSAGE-9

Read the given passage carefully:

A MAN DRIVES AS HE LIKES

Before we can develop a really effective programme to prevent auto accidents, we will have to learn for more than we know about why such accidents happen. The National Safety Council, while pointing out that most accidents result from a combination of causes and that "few accidents are investigated carefully enough to determine exactly what their underlying causes were," estimates that in about 80% accidents, the most important single factor is the driver himself. But whether, poor road accidents, and defects in case do cause some accidents, but, generally speaking, such circumstances appear to be of minor significance compared with the mental and physical condition of the driver. And recent research indicates that driver's physical condition is of less importance than his personality and his emotional state. Many, if not most accidents, this research suggests are the result of wayward impulses and motivations of faulty judgements and attitudes, of poorly controlled aggressiveness and competitiveness. Nearly two thirds of the drivers involved in fatal accidents were speeding driving while under the influence of alcohol, disregarding stop lights or signs, or otherwise, violating the law, according to the safety council. The pertinent question is why do people drive so fast, drive after drinking, take risks in passing or in general commit dangerous, careless, illegal, impulsive or unfriendly acts when they get behind the wheel?

A small beginning has been made forward finding answers to this question. Several studies comprehensively described by Dr. Ross Mc Farland and his associates at Howard's School of

Public Health have probed the personality and emotional characteristics of so called accident prone drivers and discovered such traits as emotional instability, impulsiveness, suggestibility, excitability, lack of proper sense of social responsibility, aggressiveness and intolerance of authority. Although fault may be found with the quality of this research in terms of controls and other safeguards, it may prove provocative enough to lead to sounder efforts. "A man drives as he lives," Say Dr. Tillman and Hobbes in an article in the American Journal of Psychiatry. "If his personal life is marked by caution, tolerance, foresights, consideration for others, then he will drive in the same way. If his personal life is devoid of these desirable characteristics, then his driving will be characterized by aggressiveness and over a long period of time, he will have a higher accident rate than his more stable companions." The trouble with the first part of these statement is that no human being is, at all times cautious, tolerant, foresighted and considerate of others. Even though we may be exemplary persons, most of the time, there are certain moments, or longer periods, in the lives of all of us when we become temporarily impulsive, aggressive or otherwise emotionally off balance. If we happen to be driving during one of these episodes —and if external circumstances favour an accident—then an accident is likely to occur.

Q. 1. On the basis of your reading of the above passage, make notes on it in points only, using headings and sub-headings. Also use recognizable abbreviations, wherever necessary (minimum 4). Supply a suitable title to it.

Ans. Title. Causes and Prevention of Accidents

NOTES

1.1. Causes

(i) driver and weather condition

(ii) Condition of road

(iii) Defects in car.

1.2. Driver and his condition.

(i) Physical state.

(ii) emotion'l state.

(iii) faulty judgem't

(iv) influence of alcohol.

1.3. Personality and emotional characteristics of Driver

(i) Emotional instability

(ii) Lack of proper social responsibility.

(iii) Aggressiveness

(iv) Intolerance of authority

(v) Personal life of a driver.

Q. 2. Write a summary of the above passage in about 80 words:

Ans. **SUMMARY**

Accidents are caused more often due to lack of driving sense of the driver, bad weather, poor road conditions and defects in the car. Major causes of the accidents are the physical condition of the driver, his personality and emotional state. Emotional instability, impulsiveness, suggestibility, excitability, lack of proper sense of social responsibility, aggressiveness and intolerance of authority are the major personality and emotional characteristics of the driver. If the driver's personal life is marked with caution, tolerance, foresight, consideration for others then he will drive in the same way.

PASSAGE-10

Read the given passage very carefully:

THE IMPACT OF TOURISM

Governments have seized on tourism as a way of creating employment and bringing income—preferably foreign exchang into troubled economies. For years tourism's capacity to filter wealth through communities has been a major argument in its favour. The tourist spends money on accommodation, food and souvenirs, bringing income lie to the suppliers of these goods and service whose money will in turn circulate through the economy. But if the hotels are foreign-owned, local people have little to gain. Nor are they better off if tourists stay among them but come prepared to be self-sufficient. In both cases tourists are often strongly resented by locals, who see huge increases in prices as the only tangible result of tourism's economic impact.

Job creation is another common spin off from tourism. Government subsides tourism projects in the expectation of increasing employment opportunities in the new hotels and restaurants. But such work is frequently poorly paid and is reasonable. Local people may be neither willing to do demeaning unskilled jobs, nor highly trained enough to be managers and entrepreneurs, they stand on the sidelines while expatriate staff and migrants fill the vacancies. Social tensions surface all too easily in such situations.

Any kind of change brings tensions, and economic development tends to exaggerate the generation gap as the young master knew skills and the older generation finds its traditions devalued or rejected. Tourists bring with them very different cultures and ideas, demonstrated by the way they dress and behave, and these way be very attractive to the younger generation. On the beaches and bar strips of Asia, Africa and the Pacific you can see how readily young people have been lured from their villages by the promise of bright lights and money.

A country's culture is often a major attraction, particularly when it can be combined with sun, sea and sand. In Thailand, as in many countries with a rich heritage, tourists' demands have given a much needed boost to local arts and crafts, after all, a local economy can only stand many baskets, pots and carvings.

The phenomenal growth in Arts Festivals, from Edinburgh to Hong Kong has brought tourists in festival towns and given some of their inhabitants access to global culture. But tourists spoil environment.

Q. 1. On the basis of your reading of the above passage, make notes on the contents of the passage in points only, using recognizable abbreviations wherever necessary in a suitable format.

Assign a suitable title to the passage.

Ans. Title. Importance of Tourism

NOTES

(1) Tourism-a way to income

(i) creating employment

(ii) earning foreign exchange

(iii) economic impact.

(2) Means of job-creation

(i) hotels, restaurants and jobs

(ii) vacancy filling by migrants

(iii) locals are side lined

(iv) tension in social sphere.

(3) Exchange of culture

(i) dress, culture and ideas

(ii) demand of local crafts

(iii) access to global culture

(iv) spoiling the environment.

Q. 2. Write a summary of the above passage in about 80 words.

Ans. **SUMMARY**

Tourism is a way of creating employmept and earning foreign exchange because the tourists spend money on food, lodging and souvenirs. It the hotels and foreign owned, the locals resent and raise their prices which result in tourism's economy. Being a means of job-creations, vacancies occur for varieties of posts. Generally these are filled through migrants and the locals are sidelined that again creates social tension. Through tourism, there is an exchange of culture, dress, and ideas. The tourists purchase things and the local crafts develop and get demand. Tourism is an access to global culture though it spoils the environment.

PASSAGE-11

Read the given passage and answer the questions that follow:

CHILD-CARE EFFORTS

Wide disparities in the achievement levels of various states in child-care programmes are vividly brought out in a special report, "The progress of Indian States", prepared by the United Nations International Children's Educational Fund (UNICEF).

While the country's overall averages have shown distinct improvements over the years, the condition of children varies enormously across the country, says the report. In fact, a persistent feature of child survival in India is the disparities existing between and within the states, rural and urban areas and communities, the report adds. The report shows that saving children does not exacerbate population growth. Kerala and Goa with underfive mortality rates of 32 and 39 are also the two states with the lowest fertility rates in the country. The report demonstrates that the reasons for low infant mortality levels can be due to a variety of reasons, varying from region to region. Kerala and Manipur are known for their low infant mortality rates. Yet the female literacy level in the northeastern state is 48 per cent while in Kerala it is 86 per cent. But women in Manipur are not discriminated against and are valued for their economic contribution, being seen as assets to society. The female work participation rate in Manipur is 23 per cent while it is only percent in Kerala. Kerala's infant mortality rate is 13 in 1,000 live births; Orissa's is 110. Again, the life expectancy of a girl born in Kerala today is around 74 years, about 20 years more than a girl born in Uttar Perdesh. Education datas are similarly diverse : in Rajasthan, only 17 women out of 100 could read and write, while in Karala as many as 75 women can.

The performance of the four Hindi-heartland states of Uttar Pradesh, Madhya Pradesh, Rajasthan and Bihar have been fairly dismal, confirms the report. It notes these four states accont for nearly half the children born and for more than half of infant deaths in India. Nearly two million children die every year before reaching the age of one, almost the same number as in 1961. ''Were all Indian states to have Kerala's birth and Child death-rates, there would be 10 million fewer births and 1.5 million fewer infant deaths in India, every year", the report observes. India has nearly 75 million malnourished children, the largest number in the world. Only Bangladesh and Nepal have a higher proportion of malnourished Children, says the report. It adds, the rate of malnutrition among children below five years—63 per cent—is more than double the average in sub Saharan Africa. Poverty or lack of purchasing power has no relation with prevailing rates of malnutrition, shows the report. It notes the per capita income of Maharashtra is more than one-and-a-halftimes that of Madhya Pradesh, but both states have the same level of Child malnutrition, 55 per cent. Agen, Gujarat and Kerala have the same proportion of population below the poverty line, 17-18 per cent. But the level of Child malnutrition is 59 per cent in Gujarat and 35 per cent in Kerala. Say Dr. Shanti Ghosh, pediatrician : "Malnutrition has nothing to do with economic levels of families. It is generally due to the ignorance of the mother. Or the fact that a child is often left to the care of young siblings".

Kerala, Tamil Nadu and Andhra Pradesh, says the report, have the lowest levels of child malnutrition, despite relatively low per capita incomes. Mrs. Sarla Gopalan, Secretary, women and child department, says some gains have been made but much remains to be done. "We have come a long way in dealing with infant mortality but this important document shows us which states are pulling down the national averages".

Q. 1. On the basis of reading the above passage, make notes on the contents of the passage in points only using the abbreviations wherever necessary. Supply a suitable title to the passage.

Ans. Title. Caring the child.

NOTES

(a) Child-care programmes and improvement

(i) Child survival for states

(ii) lowest fertility in Kerala and Goa

(iii) female literacy

(b) Other factors

(i) economic contribution of ladies in Manipur;

(ii) climatic and environmental factors

(iii) purchasing power.

(c) Dismal performance in Hindi heartland states

(i) 2 million children die every year

(ii) 75 million malnourished Indian children

(iii) poverty no consideration

(iv) ignorance of mother

(v) improving infant mortality.

Q. 2. Make a summary of the passage in about 80 words.

Ans. **SUMMARY**

Child care is of utmost importance. For this child care programmes have been started. But there is a great disparity of child survival in India in rural and urban areas. In Kerala and Goa there is the lowest fertility rate and female literacy is higher. In Manipur, ladies contribute towards economic distribution. Even the climatic and environmental factors work. In Hindi heartland states there is dismal performance in mortality rates. Nearly 2 million children die every year. It can be due to ignorance of mother. We must improve infant mortality and remove malnutrition. It is need of the hour to work enthusiastically.

PASSAGE-12

Read the given passage carefully:

DIVERSITY IN UNITY

There are two problems which cause great worry to our educationists. The problems of religious and moral instruction in a land of many faiths and the problems arising out of a large variety of languages. Taking up the education of children, we see that they should be trained to love one another, to be kind and helpful to all, to be tender to the lower animals, and to acquire skills to write, count and calculate. It should however, not make us lose sight of the primary aim of moudling personality in the right way. For this it is necessary to call into aid culture, tradition and religion. But in our country we have, in the same school, to look after boys and girls born in different faiths and families with diverse ways of life as ordained in their respective religions. It will not do to tread the easy path of evading the difficulty by attending solely to physical culture and intellectual education. We have to evolve a suitable technique and method for serving the spiritual needs of school children professing different faiths. We would thereby promote an atmosphere of mutual respect, a fuller understanding and helpful co-operation among the different communities in our society. Again, we must remain one people and we have, therefore to give basic training to our schools to speak and understand more languages than one and to appreciate and respect the different religions prevailing in India. It is not right for us in India to be dissuaded from this by consideration as to overtaking the young mind. What is necessary must be done. And it is not in fact too great a burden.

Any attempt to do away with or steam roll the differences through governmental coercion indirect pressure would be as futile as it would be universal. Any imposition of a single way of life and form of worship on all children, or neglect of a section of the pupils in this respect, or barren secularization, will lead to a conflict between school and home life, which is harmful. On the other hand, if we give due recognition to the different prevailing faith in the educational institution by organising suitable facilities for religious teaching for boys and girls of all communities, this may itself serve as a broadening influence of great national value.

Q. 1. On the basis of your reading of the above passage make notes on it, in points only, using abbreviations (minimum 4) wherever necessary supply an appropriate title to it.

Ans. Title. Varied Religious Faiths and Languages:

NOTES

1.1 Mess of the Educationists

(i) two problems for the educationists.

(ii) religious and moral instructions.

(iii) Varied faiths

(iv) variety of languages.

1.2 Moulding the Personality.

(i) Training to love one another.

(ii) Kind and helpful

(iii) Tender to lower animals.

(iv) Acquiring skills.

1.3 Serving Spiritual Needs of Children.

(i) teach mutual respect.

(ii) understanding and co-operation.

(iii) respecting all the religions.

(iv) organising religious teachings for all.

Q. 2. Write a summary of the above passage in about 80 words:

Ans. **SUMMARY**

Our educationists are troubled with two major problems. In India, we have different religions and moral instructions are given in a land of many faiths as we have large variety of school children. Inspite of all this, our main aim should be to mould right personality in the school children by giving love to another, being helpful, and tender to lower animals. Suitable techniques have been found to achieve different spiritual needs by understanding more than one language, respect different religions and organising different religious teachings for all boys and girls of varied communities.

PASSAGE-13

Read the passages given below and answer the questions that follow:

HEADACHE

It's headache having a headache. Almost all of us have suffered from a headache at some time or the other. For some a headache is a constant companion and life can be a painful hell of wasted time.

The most important step to cope with headaches is to identify the type of headache one is suffering from. In tension headaches (two hand headache); a feeling of a tight band around the head exists along with pain in the neck and shoulders. It usually follows activities such as long stretches of driving, typing or sitting on the desk. They are usually short-lived but can also last for days or weeks.

A headache is usually caused due to spinal misalignment of the head, due to poor posture. Sleeping on the stomach with the head turned to one side and bending over positions for a long time make it worse.

In migraine headaches (one handed headaches), the pain is usually on one side of the head and may be accompanied by nausea, vomiting, irritability any bright spots of flashes of light. This headache is made worse by activity, especially bending. The throbbing pain in the head gets worse by noise and light. Certain triggers for migraines may be chocolate caffeine, smoking or MSU in certain food items. The pain may last from eight to 24 hours and there may be a hangover for two-three days.

Migraines are often preceded by an "aura" changes in sight and sensation. There is usually a family history of migraine.

In a headache the pain originates not from the brain but from irritated nerves of muscles, blood vessels and bones. These send pain signals to the brain which then judges the degree of distress and relays if at appropriate sites. The pain may sometimes be referred to sites other than the problem areas. This is known as referred pain and occurs due to sensation overload. Thus, though most headaches start at the base of the skull the referred pain is felt typically behind the eyes.

Factors causing headaches are not fully understood but it is known that a shift in the level of body hormones and chemicals, certain food and drinks and environmental stress can trigger them.

If headaches trouble you often, visit the doctor, who will take a full health history relating to diet, lifestyle stresses, the type of headache, triggering factors and relief measures. You may be asked to keep a "headache diary" which tells you to list—the time the headache started, when it ended, emotional, environmental and food and drink factors which may have contributed to it. The type and severity of pain and the medications used which provided most relief, are also to be listed.

This helps the doctor in determining the exact cause and type of headache and the type of drugs to use. Apart from this a physial examination is done to rule out any serious underlying cause. The blood pressure is recorded, vision tested and muscle corrdination of the eyes is checked to rule out these as causes. Blood tests may be done to rule out anaemia, diabetes and thyroid disease. If any of the above is abnormal or otherwise a CT Scan or MRI may be done to see tissues and structures around the brain. These will role out causes such as tumors, haemorrhage and infection of the brain. This examination gives a clear picture of the problem to the doctor.

Immediate relief can be had if certain medications and few simple self-care techniques are used. Using ice against the pain 'site', covering eyes with dark glasses, drinking plenty of fluids and lying down in a dark and quiet room, provide relief in a migraine attack. Pain killers like aspirin, ibuprofen (brufen) and crocin can be taken and provide relief in different proportions. These should be used with caution and under medical supervision if used for long periods and large quantities as all of them can cause many side effects. An antiemetic like perionorm can help the nausea associated with a migraine.

Q. 1. On the basis of your reading of the passage make nots on it, using recognizable abbreviations wherever necessary. Use a format you consider suitable. Supply a suitable title.

Ans. Title. Headache and its treatment.

NOTES

(a) Different kinds of headache

(i) tension headache

(ii) headache caused by bodily posture

(iii) migraine headache.

(b) Reasons for headache

(i) shift in level of body hormones

(ii) eating habits

(iii) environmental factors.

(c) Suggestions

(i) physical examination

(ii) testing of B.P. and eyes etc.

(iii) ailments like diabets

(iv) self-care

(v) using pain-killers and consultancy of a doctor.

Q. 2. Write a summary of the above passage in about 80 words.

Ans. **SUMMARY**

Almost all of us are the victims of headache. It has different kinds. Tension headache is short-lived. The headache caused due to bodily postures troubles us more. The migraine headache has symptoms of nausea, vomiting: and irritability. Generally the headache pain starts from the irritated nerves of muscles, blood vessels and bones. Certain other factors like food, environment and body postures do cause headache. It must be cured by consulting a doctor. Side by side diseases like B.P. and diabetes should also be considered. Self-care is the best treatment for headache.

PASSAGE-14

Read the following passage and answer the questions that follow:

BIRD'S HOSPITAL

It is an unpreretentious structure tucked in a corner of Chandni Chowk. It could be missed by a passer-by but for the chirping which gives away its unique mission. The Charity Birds Hospital is the only one of its kind in the country. Many people arrive here daily with injured birds which they may have found lying by the roadside. After a quick inspection, attendant makes a simple entry in the register, name of the person, kind of bird and date and "admit the patient" for treatment free of cost. The bird then becomes the sole responsibility of the hospital.

The ailing bird is administered first aid and then kept in an isolated cage. Offer medication and proper care is all that is needed. After the wound heals, the bird is moved to a common section with other birds of its kind. Soon it will be healthy enough to flyaway, many keep visiting the terrace for food and water. The work began way back in 1929 in a small one-room structure. One Lala Lachumal Jain, along with others decided to start a medical facility for birds, later it became increasingly difficult to treat the large number of birds being brought. In 1957 the present building was inaugurated.

The progress of the hospital has been slow but steady. Till 1968 only ayurvedic treatment was being administered. Allopathy was adopted that year and it was as recently as in 1992 that a laboratory was set up to conduct pathological tests. Though surgery is conducted at times and doctors try their best to save the bird's life, it is often too late. The mortality rate is quite high around five to six birds die everyday.

The hospital survives only on charity. The trustees proudly claim that there is a steady flow of donations. Rich businessmen, visitors and even tourists donate generously. Till date they have never approached the government for funds.

However, the hospital has drawbacks. It does not accept carnivorous birds and does not admit pet birds. Moreover, the bird is subjected to a lot of stress as, being in old Delhi, the place is not easily accessible. Since it survives on charity, it is unable to take up research work.

But work goes on. The staff says, they have received as many as 50-60 cases a day. The hospital has an emergency ward and stays open round the clock. It spends approximately Rs. 6 lakh to Rs. 7 lakh annually and at any given time looks after 4000 to 5000 birds.

Q. 1. On the basis of your reading of the passage make notes on it, using recognizable abbreviations wherever necessary. Use a format you consider suitable. Supply a suitable title.

Ans. Title. Birds Hospital in Chandni Chowk.

NOTES

(a) **An Unpretentious Structure**

(i) chirping of birds

(ii) wounded and injured type

(iii) free treatment

(iv) medical-aid.

(b) **Functioning of the Hospital**

(i) a small structured room in the beginning

(ii) building and its inauguration

(iii) different deptts.

(i) allopathetic

(ii) ayurvedic

(iii) testing labs.

(c) Financing of the hospital

(i) through donations

(ii) charity through businessmen etc.

(iii) no treatment for carnivorous birds

(iv) working round the clock.

Q. 2. Write a summary of the above passage in about 80 words.

Ans. **SUMMARY**

In Chandni Chowk there is a Charity Birds Hospital where the birds are treated free of cost. In the beginning it was housed in a small room. With the efforts of Lala Lachumal Jain, its big building was inaugurated in 1957. This hospital is the only one of its kind in the country. It has different departments namely ayurvedic and allopathetic. There is a pathological laboratory for testing purposes. It is run on charitable basis. People and foreigners donate to meet out its expenses.

PASSAGE-15

Read the given passage carefully:

IMPORTANCE OF PRAISE

Real praise, the sincere compliment is probably the most useful social tool of all. It is the valued gold coin of our conversation. Yet today, it is in danger of losing its brightness. For it is greatly misused and not properly exchanged.

What is a true compliment? It's one that benefits both giver and receiver. Once a painter and his young assistant were painting our house. The older man was wearing shiny new shoes. As the man started skilfully painting, my father-in-law said to the boy, "Son, when you can show up on the job to paint a house, wearing new shoes, you will be the master of your trade." The painter smiled and did the best job.

We all like to have our sense of personal worth built up or pointed out. And when one expert adds to another's sense of dignity and speaks favourably of his skill, he is offering a compliment of the highest and rarest kind.

A compliment differs from flattery. It is objective and given without thought of gain. Flattery is often merely lip service or excessive praise given for motives other than expressed. The greatest efforts of the human race have always resulted from the love of praise. This should be inspired in childhood. The wise parent makes it a point to compliment a child who deserves it. A woman I know has a 12 year old son who considers washing dishes for his mother a great honour. One night, while washing a large dish, it slipped and crashed on the floor. Then his mother said, "You know, Robert, of all the times you have washed the dishes for me, this is the first time you dropped one." Anxiety left the boy's face and he smiled. As one psychologist advises, "Praise virtue and you will find few vices to criticise."

There is an art in this giving of compliments. Thus the good compliment is always to the point and timing is important. Don't wait too long to tell a person what a good talk he gave or how well he cut your grass. But don't do it immediately when he is expecting it either. Wait then when he thinks you may have forgotten, pass the praise.

Confidence, it has been said, is the greatest gift that one human can give to another. But that does not mean we should be wasteful with our compliments. Rather we should count them carefully remembering that a good compliment has greater purchasing power than money, that no one is too busy or successful to receive a word of praise. (About 450 words)

Q. 1. On the basis of your reading of the above passage, make notes on it in points only, using headings, sub-headings and abbreviations (minimum 4), wherever necessary. Supply a suitable title to it.

Ans. Title. Sincere Compliment

NOTES

1. Praise and true compliment

1.1. useful soc'l tool.

1.2. benefit'g receiver & giver

1.3. helpful in doing the best jobs

2. A rarest kind of compliment

2.1. pointing out personal worth

2.2. flattery- a lip service

2.3. love of praise

2.4. praising virtue

3. Compliment is an art

3.1. timely & to the point complem't

3.2. confidence—greatest gift

3.3. more powerful than money.

Q. 2. Write a summary of the notes in about 80 words.

Ans. **SUMMARY**

Sincere compliment or the real praise is the most useful social tool of all. A true compliment benefits both the receiver and the giver. By praising a man, we can get the work done skilfully. Being rarest in nature we should point out the personal worth and his skill. There is a difference in compliment and flattery as the later shows only a lip service. We should rather inspire the love of praise as it is the best compliment. There is an art in giving of compliments. It should be timely and to the point. It needs not be prolonged. Confidence is the greatest gift but a good compliment has greater purchasing power than money.

PASSAGE-16

Read the given passage and answer the questions that follow:

ALLERGY OF FALSE ALARM ?

Some time ago a minor pop-star died of anaphylactic shock after eating just a mouthful of food that he was allergic to. Within a few minutes of eating, he had difficulty in breathing, his blood pressure fell, his throat swelled and he lost consciousness.

The news puzzled and frightened some people. After all, so many people fall prey to temptation or error and eat foods that don't agree with them. Why is it that most people only suffer an upset stomach while a rare few go into severe allergic reactions?

That is because true food allergies are less common than we think. Most often, what we consider an allergy is actually a food intolerance. Intolerance to a particular food is quite common, say allergists, while genuine food allergies affect only a small per cent of the population. The difference is not only in name, but the dividing line as not always clear. True allergies occur when the immune system, which guards the body against "enemy invasion", identifies an ordinary food as a foreign invader. It produces antibodies to counter-attack the enemy. Signs of this inner battle appear as itching, rash, sneezing or swelling somewhere on the body. It could also show up as breathing difficulty, wheezing, vomiting or cramps in the stomach. The reactions to be taken most seriously are swelling of the tongue or throat. The faster the reaction appears after eating, the more severe the allergy.

An intolerance is less serious simply a difficulty in digesting a food because the body does not make the right chemicals needed for the job. It is not an immune system response, so the discomfort is usually limited to tummy ache, gases, cramps and diarrhoea. Milk, beans and nuts are common foods any people cannot tolerate. Luckily, discomfort can be controlled by eating the food in small amounts and it is possible to gradually teach the body to tolerate it. Childhood intolerances, however, seem to return in old age. The body is more stubborn about allergies, so it is safer not to try and teach it to accept the food.

If there are foods which make you sick, it is better to know as if, it is an allergy or intolerance. If tummy discomfort is accompanied by itching or sneezing, it is probably an allergy. People who already suffer from asthma or skin allergies are likelier to be allergic rather than intolerant. Digestive problems which show up several hours after eating are probably an intolerance. The time of eating, the amount of food, the type and timing of the reaction may reveal whether your body considers' the food life-threatening or simply difficult to digest.

Q. 1. On the basis of your reading of the above passage, make notes on it, using recognizable abbreviations wherever necessary. Also suggest a suitable title to it.

Ans. Title. Allergic Reactions

NOTES

(a) Effects of Allergy

(i) breathing difficulty

(ii) only a few suffer reactions

(iii) allergy—a food intolerance.

(b) Occurrence of true allergy

(i) disturbance of immune system

(ii) symptoms of itching and swelling ete.

(iii) taking the reactions seriously.

(c) Body unable to make right chemical

(i) cramps and diarrhoea

(ii) food control

(iii) other factors like food, time and reaction etc.

Q. 2. Write a summary of the above passage in about 80 words.

Ans. **SUMMARY**

Once a pop star died of anaphylactic shock after eating a mouthful of food that he was allergic to. He got breathing difficulty, other reactions and then died. Actually an allergy is a food intolerance. Here our immune system fails to guard us against the enemy. Then there appears signs of inner battle like itching, swelling etc. We must take these reactions seriously. An intolerance is less serious and the discomforts caused like gases, diarrhoea etc. can be controlled by avoiding the food that creates allergy. Even food, time and its reaction can stimulate to the effect of allergy.

PASSAGE-17

Read the following passage carefully and answer the questions that follow:

WIDESPREAD POLLUTION OF WATER

The seasonal problem of water taps running dry is plaguing most of our major cities. With the bigger rivers flowing in trickles and ponds and wells reduced to clay-pits, village women in remote areas have to fetch every drop of water for drinking, cooking, washing and so on, across large distances. This has only worsened a perennial problem, that of widespread pollution of water, rendering it unfit for human consumption. The monsoons—and the attendant floods will not solve this problem. The Delhi Administration is seriously worried about the threat to civic health posed by the polluted waters of the Jamuna. Two new tanks are to be set up to treat sewage. At present, only 60 per cent of the 200 million gallons of the city's sewage receives any kind of treatment before it is dumped into the river which supplies water not only to this city but to innumerable towns and villages downstream. The Ganga, the Jamuna, the Cauvery, in fact all our important rivers, serving many urban conglomerations are fast becoming a major source of disease.

A comprehensive bill, introduced in Parliament recently, envisages the setting up of Central and State boards for the prevention and control of water pollution. But it will obviously take some time before legislation is passed and effectively implemented. Meanwhile the problem continues to swell.

According to a survey of eight dwelling countries conducted a couple of years ago, 90 per cent of all child deaths were due to water borne diseases. It is the same unchanged story today. In a country like India, a burgeoning population continuing to use the open countryside as a lavatory means that with every dust storm and rain, human excreta laden with germs and parasite spares find their way to ponds, shallow wells and even the streams and rivers. Only 18 per cent of the rural folk have access to portable water.

A new threat that has already assumed alarming proportions is from industrial waste which is generally dumped, untreated, into the nearest river. For instance, for every kilogram of process hide, 30-40 litres of foul smelling, waste water has to be disposed of. There are at least 900 licensed tanneries in the organised sector. Putrefied paper and Jute waste, metallic waste from straw board and textile mills, sulphur, ammonia, urea, metallic salts and corrosive acids—all find their way to the rivers of India.

It is important not only to make new laws to ensure the purity of water, but also to realise the urgency of implementing them ruthlessly, if we are to avoid a national health disaster cutting across the barrier between towns and the countryside.

Q. 1. On the basis of your reading of the above passage make notes on it, in points only, using abbreviations (minimum 4) wherever possible. Supply a suitable title to the above passage.

Ans. Title. Water and its Hazards

NOTES

1.1. Seasonal problem of water

(i) Water taps dry

(ii) Bigger rivers flowing in trickles

(iii) Ponds and wells to clay pits.

1.2. Worry of Delhi Admin.

(i) health hazards by polluted Jamuna water

(ii) Rivers as major source of disease

(iii) 90 percent child death due to water-borne disease.

1.3. Dumping of industrial water

(i) dumping of untreated wastes

(ii) Licensed tanneries

(iii) Putrefied paper, and metallic waste into the river

(iv) laws for purity of water.

Q. 2. Write a summary of the above passage in about 80 words:

Ans. **SUMMARY**

Most of our major cities are plagued due to running of water taps dry. Even the bigger rivers flow in trickles and ponds as well as wells are reduced to day-pits which impose a major threat to human life. The polluted water of Ganga, Jamuna and

Cauvery are the major source of disease. Industrial waste like putrefied paper and jute waste alongwith the metallic waste soul of, are the major threats to civic health. For the prevention and control of water pollution a comprehensive bills has been introduced in Parliament which envisages the setting up of control and state boards for the prevention and control of water pollution.

PASSAGE-18

Read the given passage and answer the questions that follow it:

SOURCES OF HAPPINESS

There are many sources of happiness as there are men. Each man has his own ideas of happiness, and it differs in many details from his neighbour's. Napoleon and Dante could not have been happy in the same environment. Carlyle points out that it is difficult to imagine any environment in which Dante could have been happy.

A satisfactory sexual life may not be necessary for a man's existence, but it is necessary for his happiness. There are other men, more rare, whose happiness lies in the satisfaction of their hunger for truth or in their ambition. But men often confuse pleasure with happiness. Pleasure is brief and leads to envies, ignorance and frivolity. Those who seek pleasure spend much time and energy in gossip, indoor games, whist, bridge, novel reading, cheap tobacco and the cinema, flirtations and sex-stimulation. They are disinclined to exert themselves strenuously in any way except for the necessary task of earning their livelihood. They wish to get as many pleasant sensations and thrills' as they can manage to get. Pleasure follows the law of diminishing returns known to student of economics. More and more stimulation is required as time passes, and at last even the maximum of stimulations fails to produce the minimum of nervous and sensuous response. Happiness, on the other hand, consists in the harmonious development of all one's faculties—it is a balance between reason and emotion. If we concentrate on selfdevelopment of the whole of our personality, happiness will automatically follow. Happiness is in us, it is a part of our life, our very ego. It is always carried on our person, like the beauty of the belle, of the voice of the singer. It consists in our personality as completely stripped of all adventitious and accidental adjuncts as odysseus was when he stood before Nausicaa, or St. Francis in the presence of Bishop Guido of Assisi. It was to have this imperishable wealth, then everything that we do will add to our true treasury of happiness as touch of Midas turned everything to gold. Those who do not seek this development, do not get any lasting happiness and are unaware of what they have missed, as a man born blind cannot measure his loss. They are lazy and deprive themselves of science and literature and so many other precious things in life.

Even in grief one can be serene. One must realize that all suffering is in ultimate analysis self-inflicted and be grateful to the law in the universe, which tries to grow on one's dark soil of pain the white flowers of virtue and strength. A time comes when the body wears away and the senses are blunted and the business of living slackens. Even then one must not grieve.

Read the passage carefully and prepare notes on the contents of the passage in points only. You can use the abbreviations wherever necessary:

Q. 1. Write a suitable title to the passage.

Ans. Title. Happiness

NOTES

(a) Sources of Happiness

(i) Different views

(ii) Pleasure and thrill

(iii) Stimulation

(b) Harmonious development

(i) Balance in reason and emotion.

(ii) Happiness—a part of life.

(iii) Suffering and its analysis

(iv) No grieving.

(c) Need for self development

(i) Following of happiness

(ii) Serene in grief

(iii) Suffers self inflicted.

Q. 2. Make a summary of the passage in about 80 words.

Ans. **SUMMARY**

Sources of happiness differ from person to person. People have given different viewpoints on this. Some think that a satisfactory sexuals life is necessary for happiness. Others view that pleasure is brief and leads to ignorance and frivolity. Some try to get as many pleasant sensations and thrills as they can manage to get. There is a great need for self development. Though happiness consists in the harmonious development of one's all faculties. It is a balance between reason and emotion. Happiness is a part of life, our very ego. Even in grief one can be serene as sufferings bring white flowers of virtue and strength in turn.

PASSAGE-19

Read the passage given below and answer the questions that follow:

EASING OF PAIN

Pain is always real, and each person experiences it differently. For children as well as adults, physical, emotional, cultural and social factors influence how pain is experienced and how they respond to diferent methods of pain control.

Mary Kachoyeanos and Margaret Friedoff, nurses who specialise in the management of pain at Children's Hospital of Wisconsin, USA, have found that helping children to cope with pain gives them a sense of mastery and self-control that they can apply to other stressful situations as well as to future painful health problem. Experts in controlling pain in children, condemn the common practice of restraining children who resist painful treatments. Restraint, they say, only' increases a child's anxiety and fear, which can complicate and delay recovery. While most people think first of drugs to curb or prevent the perception of pain, children are often highly responsive to pain-control strategies that involve their imaginations and sense of play. The nurses, who summarised behavioural and cognitive strategies for reducing children's pain in the journal *Maternal-Child* Nursing, point out that not only are these methods completely safe and effective, but they also "cost nothing to implement and actually save staff time." Behavioural and cognitive methods can also be used as supplements to drugs, reducing the amount of pain medication needed to comfort the child. Many of the techniques the nurses describe can also be applied by parents both in medical settings with the aid of health professionals and on their own at home.

Some of the most effective methods for minimising children's pain capitalise on a child's natural imaginative skills and high degree of suggestibility. These approaches usually work with children of three years and older. The simplest technique, and probably the one most often used instinctively by parents, is to distract the child from the pain by telling a story, either with the child or to the child. A young child can often defuse momentary pain, like that associated with an injection or removal of a wound dressing, by turning off an imagined "pain switch" just as the child might turn off a light switch. Another method for calming a child who faces a painful experience is controlled breathing ; The child is taught to take slow deep breaths through the nose and then to let the breath out slowly, through pursed lips. Children are very susceptible to the power of suggestion, which makes the "magic glove" technique especially effective. An imaginary glove is placed on the child's hand, finger by finger. Then the child is told that the golve can help to lessen the discomfort of a medical procedure. If pain is widespread, a "magic blanket" might be used to cover the painful area. A related techriique, tactile transference, is already likely to be used in its most basic form by most parents, who would naturally try to comfort a child by touching or stroking him.

In a more sophisticated form, the child's hand is stroked at the same time as the parent or health professional strokes the area where pain will be inflicted, for example, where a needle is about to be inserted. The child is told when the needle goes in. After some regular practice, the pain ceases and the patient is recovered completely.

Q. 1. On the basis of reading the above passage, make-notes on the contents in points only using the abbreviations wherever necessary. Supply a suitable title to the passage.

Ans. Title. Getting Relief from Pain

NOTES

(a) Factors influencing pain

(i) experiencing the pain.

(ii) research and self-control.

(iii) fear and auxiety by restraint.

(b) Behavioural and cognitive methods

(i) effectiveness and no cost.

(ii) suggestibility, and imaginative skills.

(iii) distraction.

(c) Other techniques

(i) controlled breathing.

(ii) using magic blanket.

(iii) stroking method.

Q. 2. Make a summary of the passage in about 80 words.

Ans. SUMMARY

There are many factors that influence the adult and the child to experience pain but all respond it differently. It can be due to fear and anxiety which may even delays the recovery of pain. The nurses have summarised behavioural and cognitive strategies for reducing children's pain. These are effective methods and cost nothing. These are to distract the child from pain and to have controlled breathing. Use of the magic glove is an effective technique. Even the stroking method has been of great success in pain. It is done through 'needles. The child is told that when the needle goes in. The patient recovers very soon after its regular practice.

PASSAGE-20

Read the passage given below and answer the questions that follow:

PAIN-A DIFFICULTY FOR ALL

Pain may be indispensable providing information about tissue damaging stimuli, enabling us to protect ourselves from greater damage, initiating the search for medical assistance and helping to pinpoint the underlying cause of disease. But modern research proves that there's no reason on earth and certainly no wisdom in the old dictum, grim and bear it. Effective pain management means a faster recovery and fewer complications. It is now recognised that pain needs treatment because it can be damaging to the body. It directly affects the heart rate, respiration, blood pressure and urine production. The stress of pain also appears to inhibit immunological defences. And yet people tend to wait till the suffering becomes unbearable. In a study of the effects of surgery-related pain on laboratory rats with lung cancer, it was found that tumours developed two to three times as fast in rats that received no pain-killers as in those that were given morphine. While doctors earlier restricted the use of pain-killers, fearing that patients would get addicted to them, a study of 12,000 hospital patients who were on narcotic pain-killers in Boston, USA, found that only four became addicted to the drugs they received. Other studies reveal that the longer the pain goes untreated, the more the pain-killers that are required to make it subside. Repetition of impulses through nerve fibres cause the nerves to become more sensitive and feel more pain. Pain sensations may be controlled by interrupting the pain impulse between the receptors and the interpretation centres of the brain. Most pain sensations respond to pain-reducing drugs, which act to inhibit nerve inpulses. Pain can also be controlled by surgery that interrupts that pain impulses by severing the sensory nerve or certain tracts in the spinal cord or brain. It has been established that sensory pain fibres release chemical, a neuro transmitter called Substance P, which is used by neurons to produce sensations of pain.

Other neurons in the pain pathway release a chemical known as enkephalin, which blocks the release of Substance P and thus inhibits the transmission of pain to the brain. There has been better use of existing analgesics in recent years. Drugs originally used for other purposes have been found to be effective against pain. Tricyclic anti depressants are now recognised as highly effective for acute pain caused by damaged nerves as in herpes zoster and diabetes. Clonidine, a medication traditionally used for treating hypertension, is also used against pain. It is given to patients before surgery. Postoperative pain often goes untreated, quite needlessly. The latest concept in acute pain management, such as postoperative pain or cancers, is PCA (Patient Controlled Analgesis), based on the realisation that the patient is the best judge of how much pain he or she feels and is therefore in the best position to decide the appropriate dosage of an analgesic. PCAs use a digital pump that is connected to a catheter. Doctors set a ceiling on the amount of the drug that can enter the body continuously but the precise dosage is controlled by the patient himself. The individual no longer waits for hours between injections of pain-killers and ends up suffering less pain while using smaller quantities of pain-killers. The PCA consists of a small pump which hangs from a shoulder strap, feeds a tube leading under the skin or into a vein. Cancer patients can use PCAs even at home. And children as young as five can learn to use PCAs for acute pain.

Q. 1. On the basis of reading the above passage, make notes on the contents of the passage in points only, using the abbrevations wherever necessary. Supply a suitable title to the passage.

Ans. Title. Experiences of Pain.

NOTES

(a) Pain - a help to pinpoint disease

(i) direct effect on heart rate

(ii) respiration, B.P. and urine production

(iii) restrict use of pain killers.

(b) Control of Pain

(i) interrupting the pain impulse

(ii) through surgery

(iii) using anti-depressant medicines

(iv) a precise dosage.

(c) Better use of analgescis

(i) use of drugs

(ii) use of clonidine in hypertension

(iii) acute pain management

(iv) use of PCA.

Q. 2. Make a summary of the above passage in about 80 words.

Ans. **SUMMARY**

Pain is a tissue damaging stimulii that enables us to protect from 'greater damage. Modern research proves that there is no wisdom to bear it. It directly affects the heart-rate, respiration, blood pressure and urine production. For this we should immediately consult a doctor for treatment. We should use the pain-killer in a restricted sense. Pain sensations may be controlled by interrupting the pain impulse through surgery and drugs. These can be better use of analgescis to avoid pain. Clonidine treats hypertension. In acute pain tricyclin and anti-depressants are generally recognised. Even the patient can be told the use of precise dosage. For acute pain PCA is beneficial and even small children can learn its use.

PASSAGE-21

NEED FOR RESISTANCE

1. In the democratic countries, intelligence is still free to ask whatever question it chooses. This freedom, it is almost certain, will not survive another war. Educationists should, therefore, do all they can, while there is yet time to build up, the men and women of the next generation will be at the mercy of that skilful propagandist who contrives to seize the instruments of information and persuasion. Resistance to suggestion can be built up in two ways. First, children can be taught to rely on their own internal resources and not to depend on incessant stimulation from without. This is doubly important. Reliance on external stimulation is bad for the character. Moreover, such stimulation is the stuff with

which propagandists bait their books, the jam in which dictators conceal their ideological pills. An individual who relies on external stimulations thereby exposes himself to the full force of whatever propaganda is being made in his neighbourhood. For a majority of people in the West, purposeless reading, purposeless listening in, purposeless listening to radios, purposeless looking at films have become addictions, psychological equivalents of alcoholism and morphinism. Things have come to such a pitch that there are many millions of men and women who suffer real distress if they are cut off for a few days or even a few hours from newspaper, radio, music or moving pictures. Like the addict to a drug, they have to indulge their vice, not because the indulgence gives them any real pleasure, but because, unless they indulge, they feel painfully subnormal and incomplete. Even by intelligent people, it is now taken for granted that such psychological addictions are inevitable and even desirable, that there is nothing to be alarmed at in that fact that the majority of civilized men and women are now incapable of living on their own spiritual resources, but have become abjectly dependent on incessant stimulation from without.

2. How can children be taught to rely upon their own spiritual resources and resist the temptation to become reading addicts, hearing addicts, seeing addicts? First of all, they can be taught how to entertain themselves by making things, by playing musical instruments, by purposeful study, by scientific observation, by the practice of some art, and so on. But such education of the hand and the intellect is not enough. Psychology has its Gresham's Law, it is bad money that drives out the good. Most people tend to perform the actions that require least effort, to think the thoughts that are easiest to feel, the emotions that are most vulgarly commonplace, to give rein to the desires that are most nearly animal. And they will tend to do this even if they possess the knowledge and skill to do otherwise. Along with the necessary knowledge and skill must be given the will to use them even under the pressure of incessant temptation to take the line of least resistance and become an addict to psychological drugs. Most people will not wish to resist these temptations unless they

have a coherent philosophy of life, which makes it reasonable and right for them to do so. The other method of heightening resistance to suggestion is purely intellectual and consists in training young people to subject the diverse devices of the propagandists to critical analysis. The first thing that educators must do is to analyze the words currently used in newspapers, on platforms by preachers and broadcasters. Their critical analysis and constructive criticism should reach out to the children and the youth with such a clarity that they learn to react to forceful suggestions the right way at the right time.

Q. 1. On the basis of your reading of the above passage, make notes on it using headings and sub-headings. Use recognizeable abbreviations wherever necessary.

Ans. Title. Developing Resistance to Suggestion

NOTES

1. Two ways to built upon resistance

1.1 childr. rely on themselves

1.2 Avoiding external stimulation

1.3 internal resources

2. Its effect.

2.1 bad for character

2.2 propagandists & dictators use it

2.3 getting addicts

2.4 spiritual help

3. Teaching school children to rely on themselves

3.1 self entertainment

3.2 musical instruments

3.3 scientific observation

4. Education not to take the line of least defence

4.1 critical analyse

4.2 react to suggestions right way—right time

4.3 help of educations

Q. 2. Write a summary of the above passage in 80 words.

Ans. **SUMMARY**

In democratic countries, resistance to suggestion can be built up in two ways. Here the children can be taught to rely on their own internal resources and not on incessant stimulation from without. Reliance on external stimulation is bad for character. Such things are used by the propagandists and dictators. People get addicted to purposeless reading, listening and watching films etc. Thus they feel themselves incomplete. It is necessary that the children be taught to rely upon their own spiritual resources. They can be taught to entertain themselves by using musical instruments, scientific observations. The education need not to take the line of least defence. The educators can analyse things critically and the constructive criticism should reach out to the children with classification so that they can react to the suggestions well in time.

PASSAGE-22

Read the given passage and answer the questions that follow it:

SELF-RELIANCE

Self-reliance is a sure key to success and happiness. A self-reliant person always depends upon his own energy, capacity to work, prudence and the resources. Therefore, a self reliant person is master of himself and the circumstances as he does not depend on others. Such a person is always calm, sure, confident and self-possessed. He is firm, prompt in action and even ready to face any challenge, and fertile of resources. While others who are not independent are surely much handicapped. It is really a slavery to depend on others for help, guidance and aid or resources. And a slave is always at a great disadvantage. A person is most happy and satisfied when he relies upon his own strength, power and resources. Fe ever walks without crutches or outside support. Self-reliant people have always been found sure, self-assured, decisive, optimistic, free, independent and bold. They do not suffer from indecision or delay. They are rich in expediency, quick in action, and steadfast in decision. Their will-power is ever strong and their resolutions unfailing. They are the makers and masters of their destiny. They never blame fate, circumstances or the tools for they make their own tools and use them with greatest skill and concentration which is at their command. Their work, their creations and achievements bear the stamp of their personality. They are original in ideas and in shaping things and events. They achieve what they will because they are self-dependent, resolute, single minded and self-controlled. They know well their strength and weakness and so use their energies and resources in such a way as never to expose their weakness. And when they achieve their victories, their ambitions and goals, then their joy is an unalloyed bliss for the glory is not to be shared by others. Self-reliance is the best support the best tool and the shortest way to success. Lord Budha said "You are both friend and enemy of yourself. The heaven and hell lies within you. It is upto you what you choose. You are your own lamp, guide and staff. Never depend on others. Be the maker of your destiny. Help yourself and the world will help you". It reminds us as the famous saying "God helps those who help themselves". All successful men and women have been self-reliant. They achieved what they desired because they did not depend on others. They ran fast and in time on the roads of self-reliance. A man walking with the crutches of others help cannot think of running a the cannot compete, he is sure to end with the crutches.

Q. 1 On the basis of reading the above passage, make notes on the contents of the passage in points only, using the abbreviations wherever necessary. Supply a suitable title to the passage.

Ans. Title. Self-Reliance a Key to Success.

NOTES

(i) Qualities:

(a) A self-reliant man

(b) Calm and confident

(c) Relying on one's power

(ii) Other characteristics

(a) Decision making and master of destiny

(b) Original in ideas

(c) Self-dependent and controlled

(iii) Knowledge about weakness and power

(a) a best tool for success

(b) dependence—on others useless

(c) self-reliance—a road of progress

Q. 2. Make a summary of the passage in about 50 'words.

Ans. **SUMMARY**

Self-reliance is a sure key to success and happiness. A self-reliant man is a master of himself. He is calm, composed, confident and self-possessed. He relies on his powers so he is most happy and satisfied. Self-reliant men never suffer from indecision or delay. They have strong will-power and their resolutions are unfailing. They are original in ideas and never blame fate. They are self dependent and controlled. Self reliance is the best tool for success. It is the shortest way to success. A man walking with the crutches of others cannot think of running a race. We must remember, 'God helps those who help themselves'.

PASSAGE-23

Read the passage given below and answer the questions that follow:

POLITENESS HELPS YOU TO COMPETE

What is the first thing foreign tourists notice in India?

Nobody appears to be smiling, friendly or helpful. From the senior immigration official to the lowly baggage handler, everyone is indifferent, surly or rude.

Economy-wide, Indians have what the Americans would call an "attitude," and it shows in a abysmally poor quality of both costomer-service and services in general. Bank tellers chat idly while customers fret in a mile-long queue, the post office refuses to sell stamps unless one gives exact change, and telephone faults cannot be registered since the local exchange does not answer its own phones. Services in India are largely government monopolies, and their quality is most pathetic.

The private sector is not much better. Most companies take up to six months to do simple things like process share transfers, switchboard operators often put callers on hold indefinitely, product warranties are never honoured without repeated threats, and the average shopkeeper will continue to gaze into space as customers enter.

Improving customer-service and services in general should be at the top of the national agenda. The sector-comprising tourism, finance, transport and the like-is the largest and fastest growing part of the Indian economy (whereas both manufacturing and agriculture are shrinking). Services already account for 42 per cent of GDP.

Almost 40 per cent of India's foreign-currency earnings come either from tourism, software and engineering consultancy, or exports (such as garments, handicrafts and gems) which require plenty of customer service savvy. In these areas attributes such as trust, responsiveness to complaints, delivery schedules and quick adaptability to changing needs will become increasingly important.

Good service is a bundle of factors such as politeness, responsiveness, and caring, all of which make transactions smooth, hassle-free and satisfying. Good service does not result from offering the best product or best price, but from being sensitive to customer needs, gracious in behaviour and sincere in honouring commitments. American research shows customers are five times more likely to leave over poor service than poor product quality or high cost. Improving service quality often costs much less than improving product quality, a lesson of particular relevance to poor countries such as India.

If one follows newspapers and the speeches of top executives, one might be excused for thinking India already has lots of world-class companies. Management buzz-words such as Vision 2000 and Total Quality Management abound. Seminars are held all over the place on fancy topics such as "Innovation for Corporate Renaissance" and "Total Employee Involvement", etc. My favourite is "Spiritual concepts for Successful Management".

All this is so much hype and nonsense. What Indian industry needs to learn first and foremost is polite behaviour, how to respond to enquiries, how to process customer complaints, how to treat both employees and customers with dignity, etc. Just ask Indian Airlines passengers.

Indian business people need to go back to basics, not move up to more esoteric stuff. They are kindergarten kids pretending to be in high school (the Global Competitiveness Report ranks the quality of Indian management 43rd out of a total 50 countries). The pretence has worked for so long because India has been a protected market. India must induce competition and invite in those multinationals who are in service-oriented sectors.

Q. 1. On the basis of your reading of the above passage, make notes on it, using recognizable abbreviations wherever necessary. Suggest a suitable title to the passage.

Ans. Title. Need for Polite Behaviour

NOTES

(a) Indifferent attitude

(i) poor customer service.

(ii) pathetic services and govt. monopolies.

(iii) condition in private sector.

(b) Need for improving customer service

(i) service need top priority.

(ii) areas contributing our economy.

(iii) need for trust and adaptability.

(c) Other factors

(i) politeness

(ii) improving service quality.

(iii) treating all with dignity.

(iv) inducing competition.

Q. 2. Write a summary of the above passage in 80 words.

Ans. **SUMMARY**

Foreign tourists are of the opinion that Indians have indifferent attitudes and it shows both poor quality of customer service and service in general. Services in India are government monopolies and these are very pathetic and the private sectors do not give good results. There is great need for improving customer service. It should be given top priority. There are several areas which contributes towards our foreign currency earnings. These require best type of customer service. Politeness in behaviour, creating trust and adaptability should be on the forefront. We should treat all with dignity and improve our service quality. Competition in service behaviour should be induced.

PASSAGE-24

Read the given passage carefully:

PURSUING HIGHER EDUCATION

If you wish to pursue higher studies without taxing your parents with educational debts, it's time to act now. As education costs escalate every year, it is not feasible for parents to spend the lion's share of their savings on your higher education. However, with a number of scholarship programmes available these days, you can fund your own studies, at least in part. All that you need is a sound academic record and the ability to compete with other candidates. If you are not meritorious, look out for loans, which can be repaid once you have finished your degree.

Scholarships

One of the first avenues that students must explore is the National Science Talent Search (NSTS), which is available to students of class V to XII. If you have an interest in Science and can make a good science project, apply to the NSTS. "After school, fellowships are available for different levels of study that include Science, Arts, and Social Science. There are also scholarships available for research abroad, the information for which is posted to colleges and university departments directly."

For scholarships in the US, enquire at the office of the United States Educational Foundation in India (USEFI) which has an office in New Delhi, Mumbai, Chennai and Kolkata. Similarly, if you wish to pursue higher studies in the UK, drop in at The British Council, which has branches all over the country. The

British Scholarship is awarded to gifted studies in various disciplines in the UK. Similarly, Fulbright is a distinguished US fellowship programme for research scholars.

There are also a number of exchange programmes with different countries, provided by the Government of India. The German Academic Exchange fellowship invites PG students in bio-engineering, bio-pharmacology, metallurgy, environment science, agronomy, veterinary science, horticulture and animal husbandry, with two years of teaching or research experience.

Loans

Alternately, you can look for loans, which can be repaid once you start earning. In India, such loans are available from commercial banks and the Life Insurance Corporation (LIC), but both require security. "In banks, some security in the form of immovable property or jewellery may have to be mortgaged, while in the case of LIC, you should have a life insurance policy with premium having been paid for a certain number of years."

If you seek loans to study abroad, such as in the US, you must have a US citizen co-signer and you should have already taken admission in the US university. The whole process requires a lot of hard work, merit and self-motivation, but once you complete your degree, self-funding can be extremely rewarding.

Q. 1. On the basis of your reading of the above passage, make notes on it using headings and sub-headings. Use recognizable abbreviations wherever necessary.

Ans. Title. Education No Longer a Burden

NOTES

1. Availability of scholarships.

1.1. sound academic record

1.2. ability to compete

1.3. some loans repayable after degree

2. Kinds of Scholarships

2.1. N.S.T.S.

2.2. available from class V to XII students

2.3. Fellowship for research abroad

3. Scholarship abroad

3.1. U S E F I

3.2. B.C. & Fulbright

3.3. Commonwealth and Paul Foundation

4. Exchange programmes

4.1. For exchange Bio.-eng.

4.2. Bio pharm.

4.3. Met.

4.4. Loans through L.I.C. and Banks

Q. 2. Write a summary of the above passage in about 80 words. Also suggest a title.

Ans. **SUMMARY**

Education is no longer a burden and we need not tax our parents with educational debts. We have to act because a number of scholarship programmes are available these days. All we need is a sound academic record, ability to compete and some repayable loans. The first avenue is national science talent search which is available to students from class V to XII. Fellowships are available for Science, Art and Social Sciences. Scholarships are available in the U.S., Fulbright and the U.K. for research scholars. There are number of exchange programmes with different countries. We can get loans from Life Insurance Corporation and banks which require some security in the form of immovable property or jewellery to be mortgaged. But the whole process requires a lot of hard work, merit and self-motivation.

PASSAGE-25

Read the passage given below and answer the questions that follow:

NATIONAL SECURITY

Due to external and internal challenges, there is a great need for national security. Our own experience of the armed militancy and transnational terrorism in Punjab earlier, and Jammu and Kashmir more recently, clearly demonstrates the complexities involved in the management of national security. We have had to deal with not only the internal security aspects of the situation involving various dimensions but concurrently cope with diplomatic challenges of internationalisation of the situation by a determined adversary which received support in the process from many quarters. During the same period we had to cope with economic challenges in the shape of the effects of the fourth oil shock, a substantive deterioration in the balance of payment situation, and collapse of the rupee trade with the "former" Soviet Union.

Geo-politically, the international order underwent fundamental changes with the end of the Cold War. The task of assessment for national security in the increasingly complex dimension is not easy. After all, even countries like the United States, which have had far more sophisticated and well-oiled national security machines had totally failed to forecast the collapse of their primary adversary, and they have yet to reconcile to the altered scenario.

While judgment on our success or otherwise in dealing with the challenges of recent periods will vary, the dominant view within the executive establishment seems to be that we have successfully managed, our affairs and the existing system has worked well. The need for change, therefore, is underplayed or outright resisted. On the other hand, many people have argued for such management structures with an eye on the turf, or to manage nuclear policies. The setting up of such structures or creation of posts like that of Chief of Defence Staff (for "single point advice") in many countries occurred when they acquired nuclear weapons or became part of the nuclear strategy implementation of weapon states. But our concept of national security management must transcend these limited objectives. The government had set up a National Security Council in 1990 which did not grow roots. Another National Security Council was set up by the previous government. But these steps did not bring about a change in the method or process of managing national security policy. In any case, in a parliamentary democracy like ours, a "national security council" has to be a committee of the council of ministers chaired by the Prime Minister. The Prime Minister will always have (and is likely to exercise) discretion in the composition of such a committee although ministers of defence, home, external affairs and finance are obvious, almost inevitable members. The crux of the issue, therefore, is not the council, but the supporting system and processes for it to take appropriate decisions. This is apparently the basis for the recommendation of the Standing Committee on Defence (1995-96) in its Sixth Report that the "Government should urgently come up with formal institutional mechanism with adequate support structures to monitor the state of our defence preparedness...."

A centralised staff structure to serve the Cabinet committee would be necessary. Logically and procedurally, this will need to be placed under the Cabinet secretary. It may be recalled that the defence committee of the cabinet used to be serviced by the military wing of the Cabinet secretariat. But for proper co-ordination and integration, much more would be required. This is why there is little advantage in nominating a secretary (like the chairman, Joint Intelligence Committee) to the national security council without an adequate support base even where the functions of the Joint Intelligence Committee appear to be co-terminus with the staff structure required.

To start with, a culture of shared information and evaluation of alternatives has to be strengthened. Similarly, greater emphasis will be needed in scenario-building and crisis management techniques and processes. A future oriented assessment and policy evolving process is required. If we are really serious about the end product which offers to the council of ministers choices of policies and their implications in a final condensed form, we will have to make sure that all possible alternatives and their collateral implications have been appropriately analysed and assessed. The national security staff must not get involved in day-to-day current policy making or other functional executive tasks which appropriately belong to the domain of the existing structures. If these structures require modification, this should be reviewed on its own merits. The greater the complexities and non-linear nature of national security management, the greater will be the task of the staff structures.

Q. 1. On the basis of your reading of the above passage, make notes on it, using recognizable abbreviations wherever necessary. Supply a suitable title.

Ans. Title. Need for National Security.

NOTES

(a) External and internal challenges

(i) terrorism in Punjab and Kashmir

(ii) diplomatic and eco challenges

(iii) fundamental changes in internal order

(iv) India's existing system working well.

(b) Setting a National Security Council

(i) composition

(ii) taking appropriate decisions

(iii) need for coordination

(iv) joint intelligence committee.

(c) Management Crisis

(i) evaluation

(ii) need for future oriented processes

(iii) analysing implications

(iv) suggesting possible alternatives.

Q. 2. Write a summary of the above passage in about 80 words.

Ans. **SUMMARY**

Due to posing of external and internal challenges, there is a great need for national security. There is terrorism and militancy in Punjab and Kashmir. We are faced with diplomatic and economic challenges. There has occured fundamental changes in international order. Even then India is working well with the existing system. She has set up National Security Council. It has to be a committee and other comprising of P.M., ministers to take appropriate decisions about defence preparedness. There is great need for coordination with joint intelligence committee. Everything should be evaluated alternatively, suggesting future oriented processes and analysing implications likely to involve.

PASSAGE-26

Read the given passage carefully:

CYCLING

Cycling survives as a popular pastime because it yields pleasure and benefits. First of all, cycling provides exercise, the need of which is felt by most people. The development of machinery tends to deprive us of adequate opportunities of expending energy while earning a livelihood. Other opportunities should be created through the medium of sport. Of cycling, many people hastily say that it is "hard work", but a fit and practised rider does not agree with this verdict. The art of easy cycling must be cultivated, as will be shown later, but once it has been acquired, a long day's run should not unduly tire any rider endowed with a normal measure of health. Nobody has better described the exercise of cycling than the late Twells Brex, who said enthusiastically, speaking from experience: "You move along by your own glad effort." Many of us wish to use our legs and our lungs, as well as our eyes. An active, healthy person ought not to be content to travel always as a mere passenger—"like an image pushed from behind", as Stevenson says. That is not life. Those who would turn all active cyclists into sedentary motor-drivers, or into idle passengers, would serve the nation better if they restricted their attentions to the aged and infirm, for whom petrol-generated propulsion is doubtless a blessing, and may be a necessity.

It is often said that the cyclist cannot travel as fast or as far as the motorist. Admitting this, the cyclist may be permitted to ask if it is always desirable that travel should involve modern motoring speeds (or accidents). Is the enjoyment of a traveller in search of pleasure to be measured merely in miles, or, what is worse in miles-per-hour, or what is worse still, in miles-per-gallon? Surely the cyclist, pedalling calmly along at a modest twelve miles an hour is able to assimilate scenery more easily, more completely, and with more enjoyment, than the hurrying occupant of a car. Cyclists believe that their method of travel is a sensible and convenient compromise between walking and driving. If bicycles were unobtainable, most keen cyclists would become trampers rather than motorists.

There are at least two distinct types of cyclists. The exercise of pedalling provides an all sufficient satisfaction for one type. This is the purely athletic rider who revels in long, fast rides, in time trials, and other forms of strenious competition, and sometimes attacks records. This type of cyclist goes into strict training, develops leg-thrust, and perfect ankle action and thinks nothing of pedalling at twenty miles an hour. The other distinct type is the tourist, who takes no interest in racing but a deep interest in the countryside and the pageant unfolded by the open road.

Comparatively, few cyclists are interested deeply in both racing and touring. (Around 470 words)

Q. 1. On the basis of your reading of the above passage, make notes on it in points only, using headings and sub-headings. Also use recognisable abbreviations, wherever necessary (minimum 4). Supply a suitable title to it.

Ans. Title. Cycling—An Easy Mode of Exercise

NOTES

1.1. Cycling—a popular pastime.

(a) provides pleasure, benefit & exercise.

(b) hard work but cultivate easy cycl'g

(c) different views of people.

1.2. Travelling as a passenger-no life.

(a) cyclist can serve the nation better

(b) assimilating pleasurable scenery by cyclist.

(c) a sensible and convenient compromise

1.3. Kinds of cyclists

(a) pedalling cyclists—a strenuous competit'n

(b) as tourist cyclists—deep interest in countryside

(c) few have interest in both types.

Q. 2. Write a summary of the above passage in about 80 words.

Ans. **SUMMARY**

Cycling is a popular pastime because it yields pleasure, benefit and exercise. It is a hard work but we must cultivate an art of easy cycling. People have different views about it and say that a cyclist cannot move fast as well as far like the motorist. Even then a cyclist can serve the nation better and he enjoys scenery more easily and more completely. It is a sensible and convenient compromise between walking and driving. There are two types of cyclists—pedalling and tourist. The former is used for competition and the later for enjoyment.

PASSAGE-27

Read the given passage carefully:

TOURISM AS AN INDUSTRY

Tourism has emerged as the world's largest industry. Growing rapidly in the last two decades, today it accounts for 6% of world output and employs some 100 million people around the globe. Since the end of the Second World War, it has developed immense revenue and development potential and stands today as a unique natural renewable resource industry.

Tourism—the travel-based recreation—provides people with a change of place and a break from the monotony of daily life. It brings peoples of different nations together, allowing them to come into close contact with each other's customs and other aspects of life. It reveals the scenic beauty and past heritage of a country to people belonging to other nations. The knowledge and experience gained in the process can lead to greater understanding and tolerance, and can even foster world peace.

The contribution of tourism can be nowhere seen more clearly than on the economic front. A study conducted by the United Nations has shown that developing countries, in particular, can reap handsome benefits out of tourism which greatly boosts national income.

Tourism generates employment, and adds to the entrepreneurial wealth of a nation. While tourism's advantages are many, its undesirable side-effects have raised fresh problems.

Tourism can cause social, cultural or environmental disruption. Of the greatest concern is its damage to the environment. In order to attract more tourists, sprawling resorts are built which take neither the local architectural styles nor the ecology into consideration. Natural systems come to be destroyed as a result of indiscriminate construction to provide water and waste disposal facilities and recreational arrangements to tourists. Overuse of environmental wealth disturbs the ecological balance.

Damage is most in wildlife parks which remain the foremost sites of tourist attraction. Tourist vans and the visitors' feet destroy the ground vegetation, thus affecting the feeding habits of the animals and the landscape as well. Overcrowding brings about congestion, leading to environmental and health hazards.

The Taj Mahal, one of the seven wonders of the world, has suffered a lot of wear and tear from trampling feet of tourists.

Some socio-cultural effects of tourism have been damaging. Tourism often ushers in new life styles; arrangements as desired by tourists are provided in order to make them feel at home. The emergence of this 'other' culture in various places has caused dissatisfaction among the local people. The concern is that the local people tend to imitate the foreign values, breaking away from their own traditions.

To promote safe tourism while ensuring that it remains a profitable industry, it is imperative to understand the factors that hamper the growth of tourism and check them effectively.

General instability of the nation is damaging to tourism prospects. Political disturbances, in particular, pose a serious problem. The growing violence in the international scene and increasing threat of terrorism affects the flow of tourists. Countries like Sri Lanka have been a victim to terrorist threats for long and have therefore suffered setbacks in tourism.

Whatever the problems, India must work hard to reap the benefits from this industry, for the country has everything to attract visitors from far and near. (497 Words)

Q. 1. On the basis of your reading of the above passage, make notes on it in points only using headings. and sub-headings. Also use recognisable abbreviations wherever necessary (minimum 4). Supply a suitable title to it.

Ans. Title. Advantages and Disadvantages of Tourism.

NOTES

1. **Tourism-World's Largest Industry.**

   1.1. means of employm't

   1.2. renewable source industry

   1.3. recreation & bringing people together

   1.4. fostering world peace

2. **Contribution of Tourism**

   2.1. generating employm't

   2.2. adding wealth to nation

   2.3. boosting national income

3. **Undesirable Effects of Tourism**

   3.1. social, cultural & environment'l disruption

   3.2. disturbing ecological balance

   3.3. indiscriminate construct'n

   3.4. damage to wild life.

4. **Effect on Socio-culture**

   4.1. breaking away the tradition

   4.2. political disturbance

   4.3. growing violence in international scene

Q. 2. Write a summary of the above passage in about 80 words.

Ans. SUMMARY

Tourism is the world's largest industry. It is a means of employment and recreation. It fosters peace and brings people together. Tourism is helpful in boosting national income but there are some undesirable effects. It causes social, cultural and environmental disruption. People start indiscriminate construction and disturb ecological balance. The wild life is damaged and there is a break away of the old tradition. Political disturbance too hampers tourism. The growing violence has affected tourism but let us reap the benefits from this industrism but let us reap the benefits from this industry.

PASSAGE-28

Read the given passage carefully:

ESSENTIALS OF A LEADER

Leadership does not exist without followership. A leader has to be accepted by the group which the former is supposed to lead. To gain acceptability, the leader should cause an emotive impact on the group members.

The characters exhibited by leaders make them dear to their followers. A leader is one who effectively inspires employees to achieve worthwhile things. What character of the leader motivates the followers? It is not pomp and show nor flattery nor sanctioning more incentives. Pomp and show creates a sense of awe and the leader is deified rather than emulated. Flattery is unrealistic and cannot serve as a long-term motivational tool. A leader's style should be one that can be emulated by all irrespective of cadre, class and calibre. Simplicity in one's day-to-day conduct is the only thing that can be adopted by all. When the leader is simple, he is counted as one belonging to the group of which he is the leader. That's enough to motivate the people. Motivation is the innate quality that enables an individual or group, to contribute unlimitedly with limited means. It is the proud prerogative of enlightened human beings.

A leader needs to assume the role of a guide; quintessential to fulfilling the role is knowledge ability. Technical and administrative knowledge of the guide in balance quantity and of right kind are essential. The technical knowledge is too vast to acquire by a leader. At best he is either 'Jack of all' or 'Master of few'. But he has to master the human relations aspect of administration in all detail. And when the leader is good at this, his guidance is sought and accepted, then he fulfills the role of a guide. The leader is a negotiator within and outside the organisation.

The leader shapes people and moulds character. To achieve this, the leader should maintain equanimity.

Equanimity is keeping oneself poised and balanced at all times. A leader is simply great, if he can mould his followers with this frame of mind. He does this by his own example.

Q. 1. Read the above passage and make notes in points only using abbreviations wherever necessary (minimum 4 abbreviations).

Ans. Title. Leadership

NOTES

(a) Leadership v/s. followership

(i) a leader and group accept'ce

(ii) need for an emotive impact

(iii) inspiring employees to get results.

(b) Factors motivating the follower

(i) avoiding pomp and show, flattery etc.

(ii) an emulative style

(iii) simplicity

(iv) motivation

(c) Qualities of a leader

(i) assuming the role of a guide

(ii) technical and administrat'e knowledge

(iii) a negotiator in and outside the organsat'n

(iv) maintaining equanimity.

Q. 2. Make a summary of the above passage in 80 words. Also suggest a suitable title.

Ans. Title. Qualities and Activities of a Leader.

SUMMARY

Leadership can exist with followership. For a leader, group acceptance and an emotive impact is a must. He inspires the employees to get good results. A leader motivates his followers not by pomp and show and flattery but by his emulative style. He is simple and motivates his group to contribute regularly with limited means. A leader is a guide with complete technical and administrative knowledge. He is a negotiator in and outside the organisation. He has the quality of equanimity to shape and mould the character of the people.

PASSAGE-29

Read the given passage carefully:

PHILOSOPHY OF GANDHIJI

The work which Gandhiji had taken up was not only the achievement of political freedom but also the establishment of a social order based on truth and non-violence, unity and peace, equality and universal brotherhood and maximum freedom for all. This unfinished part of his experiment was perhaps even more difficult to achieve than the achievement of political freedom. In the political struggle, the fight was against foreign power and all one could do, was either join it or wish it success and give it their moral support. In establishing the social order of his pattern there was a likely possibility of a conflict arising between groups and classes of our own people. Experience shows that man values his possessions even more than his life because in the former he sees the means for perpetuaticn and survival of his descendants even after his body is reduced to ashes. A new order cannot be established without radically changing the mind and attitude of men towards property and at some stage or the other, the 'haves', have to yield place to the have-nots'. We have seen in our time, attempts to achieve a kind of egalitarian society and the picture of it after it was achieved. But this was done by and large, through the use of physical force.

The root cause of class conflict is possessiveness or the acquisitive instinct. So long as the ideal that is to be achieved is one of securing maximum material satisfaction, possessiveness is neither suppressed nor eliminated but grows on what it feeds. Nor does it cease to be such—it is possessiveness, still, whether it is confined to only a few or is shared by many. If egalitarianism is to endure it has to be based not on the possession of the maximum material goods by few or by all but on voluntary, enlightened renunciation of those goods, which cannot be shared by others or can be enjoyed only at the expense of others. This calls for substitution of spiritual values for purely material ones. The paradise of material satisfaction, that is sometimes equated with progress these days neither spells peace nor progress. Mahatma Gandhi has shown us how the acquisitive instinct inherent in man could be transmuted by the adoption of the ideal of trusteeship by those who 'have' for the benefit of all those who 'have not' so that, instead of leading to exploitation and conflict, it would become a means and incentive for the amelioration and progress of society respectively.

Q. 1. On the basis of your reading of the above passage make notes on it, using recognizable abbreviations wherever necessary. Use a format you consider suitable. Supply a suitable title.

Ans. Title. Principles of Gandhiji

NOTES

(a) Political Freedom & Social order

(i) truth and non-violence

(ii) unity and peace

(iii) equality and universal brotherhood

(iv) freedom for all.

(b) Conflcit between groups and classes

(i) valuing the possessions

(ii) survival of descendants

(iii) haves and have-nots

(iv) an egalitarian society.

(c) Causes of class conflict

(i) acquisitive instinet

(ii) substitution of spiritual values

(iii) adopting the ideal of trusteeship.

Q. 2. Write a summary of the above passage in about 80 words.

Ans. SUMMARY/ABSTRACTION

Gandhiji wanted to achieve social order and political freedom for all based on truth, non-violence, equality and universal brotherhood. For establishing a social order there is a possibility of conflcit between groups and classes. Bynature a man always values his possessions and fights for the survival of his descendants. Though, attempts are on for an egalitarian society but it needs to be based on spiritual values. Material satisfaction, does not entail peace or progress. For this Gandhiji advocated the idea of truth by trusteeship for the progress of society as he wanted to avoid conflict and exploitation.

PASSAGE-30

Read the given passage and answer the questions that follow:

THE MAGIC OF BOOKS

The Magic of books has never ceased to charm humanity, "Through the ages, the books have helped man knit his dreams and thoughts, his hopes and aspirations. Secured within its covers, these books bring alive the ancient wisdom, current perspective which help us build the edifice of the future. Books not only enable us to understand things in the correct perspective but also equip us to fight against economic exploitation. However, today with the advent of television boom, the book seems to be lagging behind but most national and international publishers are confident that books will soon regain their position.

To create more awareness about books, the Government of India declared 2001-2002 as the Year of Books with the slogan "Books for all and All for Books". A Book Fair is regularly organised every year at Pragati Maidan. A vast range of books including fiction, non-fiction, academic text books, dictionaries, encyclopaedia, classics, children literature, religious and technical books will be on display and safe at the fair.

In this year of books, the National Book Trust (NBT) has taken up the task of monitoring, supporting all the activities undertaken by education institutions, libraries, publishers and booksellers, the media and the reading public in general. Alongwith this, NBT also proposes to set up a national book gallery-cum-museum that will display rare books, first editions and manuscripts, construct a writer's home; launch a 'Book on Wheels' movement; publish a special series of books for visually impaired; create and print specially designed book marks, calendars and time tables with the logo of the year of Books; organise atleast one book fair in each State during the year; launch a compaign to popularise the concept of Book Club; organise seminars, workshops etc. on reading habit in different parts of the country.

Currently, India ranks third after the U.S.A. and the U.K. in the production of English titles and is the only country in the world which is self-sufficient in book production. There are more than 13,000 publishers bringing out over 60,000 new titles and 13,000 journals and magazines every year. The 10th Delhi Book Fair presents the best of Indian books in a large number of languages and on a wide range of subjects. The air simultaneously offers enormous scope for transacting business with publishers from India and abroad, building new contacts entering into co-publishing arrangements, documentation, preservation and reprinting of old and rare books as well as major international works.

At the fair, there will be enough sitting space for visitors to browse through the books. The main purpose is to reach the maximum number of people and this fair will serve as a miniature showcase of the Indian book publishing industry.

Q. 1. On the basis of your reading of the above passage, make notes on it using headings and sub-headings. Use recognizable abbreviations (wherever necessary) and a format you consider suitable. Also supply an appropriate title to it.

Ans. Title. Books are our Edifice of the Future

NOTES

1.1 Books - Charm for Humanity

(i) Books knit our thoughts and dreams

(ii) Enliven wisdom

(iii) Help against economic exploitation

(iv) Effect of television boom.

2.1 Steps by Government

(i) Celebration of book year

(ii) Organisation of book fair

(iii) Display of books.

3.1 Role of National Book Trust.

(i) Monitoring tasks for books

(ii) Books on wheels movement

(iii) Publishing printing material.

(iv) Creating books habits.

4.1 Contribution of India

(i) 3rd in production of English titles

(ii) Enormous printing every year

(iii) Scope for business.

Q. 2. Write a summary of the above passage in about 80 words

Ans. SUMMARY

Books always offer charm for humanity. These enliven our wisdom, thought, dreams and help against economic exploitation. With the advent of television boom, books seem to be lagging behind. In this effect, the Government of India has taken steps. It organises book fairs regularly where a vast range of books are displayed. It offers a good scope for business even. The National Book Trust has taken up the task of monitoring the works pertaining to books and printing etc. It has started a compaign to popularise reading habits. India is a third country in the production of English titles.

PASSAGE-31

Read carefully the following passage and answer the questions that follow it:

POSSESSIONS

People tend to amass possessions, sometimes without being aware of doing so. Indeed they can have a delightful surprise when they find something useful which they did not know they owned. Those who never have to change house become indiscriminate collectors of what can only be described as clutter. They leave unwanted objects in drawers, cupboards and attics for years, in the belief that they may one day need just those very things. As they grow old, people also accumulate belongings for two other reasons, lack of physical and mental energy, both of which are essential in turning out and throwing away, and sentiment. Things owned for a long time are full of associations with the past, perhaps with the relatives who are dead, and so they gradually acquire a value beyond their true worth.

Some things are collected deliberately in the home in an attempt to avoid waste. Among these I would list string and brown paper, kept by thrifty people when a parcel has been opened, to save buying these two requisites. Collecting small items can easily become a mania. I know someone who always cuts out from newspapers sketches of model clothes that she would like to buy, if she had the money. As she is not rich, the chances that she will ever be able to afford such purchases are remote. But she is never sufficiently strong-minded to be able to stop the practice. It is a harmless habit, but it litters up her desk to such an extent that every time she opens it, loose bits of paper fall out in every direction.

Collecting as a serious hobby is quite different and has many advantages. It provides relaxation for leisure hours, as just looking at one's treasures is always a joy. One does not have to go out for amusement, since the collection is housed at home. Whatever it consists of stamps, records, first editions of books, china glass, antique furniture, pictures, model cars, stuffed birds, toy animals—there is always something to do in connection with it, from finding the right place for the latest edition to verifying facts in reference books. This hobby educates one not only in the chosen subject, but also in general matters which have some bearing on it. There are also other benefits. One wants to meet like-minded collectors, to get advice, compare notes, to exchange articles, to show off the latest find. So one's circle of friends grows. Soon the hobby leads to travel, perhaps to a meeting in another town, possibly a trip abroad in search of a rare specimen, for collectors are not confined to anyone country. Over the years one may well become an authority on one's hobby and will very probably be asked to give informal talks to little gatherings and then, if successful, to larger audiences. In this way self-confidence grows, first from mastering a subject, then from being able to talk about it. Collecting, by occupying spare time so constructively, makes a person contented, with no time for boredom.

Q. 1. On the basis of your reading of the above passage make notes on it, using recognizable abbreviations wherever necessary. Use a format you consider appropriate. Supply a suitable title.

Ans. Title. The Art of Collection.

NOTES

(1) Amassing the possessions.

(i) indiscriminate collection of things

(ii) unwanted objects in attics etc.

(iii) show long associat'ns

(iv) sentimental love.

(2) A harmless habit

(i) avoiding wastage

(ii) collection of small items

(iii) cutting from newspapers

(iv) a useful practice.

(3) Collecting as a hobby

(i) relaxation and amusem'nt

(ii) means of education

(iii) enhancing-friendship

(iv) growth of self-confidence.

Q. 2. Write a summary of the above passage in about 80 words.

Ans. **SUMMARY**

Mostly people are in the habit of amassing possessions without any indiscrimination. They keep unwanted objects in their drawers etc. This shows their sentimental love and attachment towards the belongings. They represent value based long associations with the articles. It is in reality a harmless habit that avoids wastage of things. With the thrifty people it becomes a mania and they cut out sketches etc. from the newspapers. It is a useful practice to adopt collecting as a hobby. We can relax and amuse. It is one of the means of education. It even enchances friendship with others. It encourages self-confidence, contentment and leaves no scope for boredom.

❐